SKISPOTS
ANDO

Francis Johnston

Original concept by **Francis Johnston**
Original photography by the author, unless otherwise credited
Front cover photography courtesy of Neilson Active Holidays

Produced by the Bridgewater Book Company
Project Editor: Emily Casey Bailey
Project Designer: Lisa McCormick

Published by Thomas Cook Publishing
PO Box 227, The Thomas Cook Business Park, Unit 15/16, Coningsby Road,
Peterborough PE3 8SB, United Kingdom
email: books@thomascook.com
www.thomascookpublishing.com
+44 (0) 1733 416477

First edition © 2005 Thomas Cook Publishing
Text © 2005 Thomas Cook Publishing
Maps © 2005 Thomas Cook Publishing
ISBN: 1-841575-10-0
Head of Thomas Cook Publishing: Chris Young
Project Editor: Kelly Anne Pipes
Production/DTP: Steven Collins

Snowsports and related activities have an inherent level of danger and carry
a risk of personal injury. They should be attempted only by those with a full
understanding of these risks and with the training/experience to evaluate them,
or under the personal supervision of suitably qualified instructors or mountain
guides. Mountain conditions are highly variable and change quickly – weather
and avalanche risk level conditions must be carefully considered.

ACKNOWLEDGEMENTS

This book is dedicated to Sofia Barbas and all my family. It is the result of many wonderful days and nights in the mountains, aided by and accompanied by some great characters. Specific thanks go to all my friends and resort professionals in Andorra: particularly Rafael Heres, Marta Rotés, Martí Rafel, Àngels Olivares, Eva Soler, Daniel Guillian, Kevin Marshall, Antonia y Ramon Gueimonde y familia, Hugh Garner, Regina Antolin, Sira Puig i Carreró, Ripu Bakshi, Gordon Standeven, Sergio Armet, Jesus Sanchez, Robin Baker, Pat Cantwell, Dimitri Carcassonne, Bérangère Gouy, Marcel Urigüen, Marc Crichton and the Ministeri de Turisme i Cultura del Govern d'Andorra.

CONTENTS

SYMBOLS KEY

The following is a key to the symbols used throughout this book:

bucket lift	cross-country ski circuit	ATM
cable car	base station	telephone
gondola lift	equipment rental	post office
chair lift	tool point	church
declutchable chair lift	ski pass sales point	supermarket
button lift	elevator	restaurant
magic carpet	information office	café
rope tow	car park	bar
funicular railway	bus stop	medical point
warning – difficult lift	WC	pharmacy
two-way lift	●●●● piste difficulty rating	

- ❶ telephone   ❶ fax   ❸ email   ❿ website address
- ❷ address   ❹ opening times   ❶ important   ➔ page reference
- € budget price   €€ mid-range price   €€€ most expensive

---

ski lift name   journey duration   technical data

TSD6 FONT

6	7 mins ▲ ▼	• 482 m (1581 ft) vertical rise • 1708 m (1869 yd) long • 3000 passengers/hour

ski lift type symbol   two-way lift symbol

number of passengers

INTRODUCTION TO SKISPOTS

Welcome to SkiSpots, an innovative series of specialist guidebooks to Europe's top ski regions, designed and compiled by some of Europe's most experienced snowsports professionals. Whether you ski, board, blade or Langlauf, are a piste virgin or a seasoned powder hound, SkiSpots are as indispensable as your ski pass.

With a snowsports-centric layout and a snowsports-specific information flow, these guides are focused on the major linked ski domains and the resorts that access them: with historical snowfall charts and analysis as a guide to the best dates to visit for optimum snow conditions; base station layouts and resort street plans; detailed information and critiques on all principal ski lifts and pistes; ideas for alternative activities and après ski; and complemented by the history, culture, gastronomy, language and attractions of the surrounding region.

Action-packed and filled with insider intelligence and technical expertise, with a wealth of general information to keep non-skiers interested too, SkiSpots are the next best thing to having your very own private mountain guide.

On a piste map, the sun is always shining, the snow is always powder perfect, the visibility is always excellent and the links are always open. SkiSpots provide an invaluable extension to your piste map, describing the ski area in three dimensions, clarifying ambiguous and complicated routes, directing you away from the links that don't work and towards the areas that will deliver the most satisfying descents.

The author has visited every corner of the resorts and ski domains, taken and timed every lift, skied every piste and most of the powder fields in between and visited every recommended bar and restaurant – it's a dirty job, but someone's got to do it!

Snow excites a childlike fascination in us all; who hasn't felt the urge to rush out and throw a snowball after even the slightest frosting of this magical powder on a crisp winter morning? The first priority of this guidebook is to stimulate your excitement about the mountains, striving to inform and nourish your enjoyment of this wonderful environment and direct you to the best that the resorts and ski areas have to offer.

The first part of the book gives you a flavour of the region you are visiting, detailing the history of the area and the pioneering beginnings of the extensive snowsports infrastructure that you enjoy today, with an overview on the regional food and drink and a basic snowsports-centric vocabulary in the local language to help you engage more readily with your hosts and speed up assistance if and when you require it.

The second part of the guide begins with an all-important briefing on the dangers of the mountains in winter, and the tried and tested ways of minimizing the risks you expose yourself to when participating in adventure sports in this environment, together with the rules and regulations that all slope users are bound to follow. Next comes the introduction to each major resort and ski area and how to access them; with street plans, piste maps and ski area data; ski pass information, resort transport, equipment hire, ski schools, childcare, resort and ski area services; plus snowfall history charts. Each sector of the ski area is then broken down by base station layout, first access points and onward links, with a detailed lift-by-lift description and piste-by-piste critique; every mountain bar and restaurant is covered in depth and suggested point-to-point itineraries are illustrated to assist with route planning to help you squeeze the maximum potential out of your day.

When the après-ski begins, SkiSpots continue with you by suggesting alternative activities and listing the cafés, restaurants, bars and clubs in which to round off your day. The book finishes with some ideas for days away from the pistes, together with an insight into the attractions of the region in summer.

www.ski-ride.com

Due to the ephemeral nature of snow, and the dynamic nature of the mountain environment and the snowsports industry, resort facilities and ski area boundaries can change. For this reason, the SkiSpots series is also supported by an Internet portal, **www.ski-ride.com**, delivering up-to-the-minute news and links to the ski areas: on-site webcams, live snow reports and current weather information, resort fact sheets, events diary, tour operator links and much more – enhancing both this guidebook and your trip.

HOW TO USE THIS BOOK

SkiSpots travel guides give ski lift and piste information in a unique graphical format. Detailed information is given on the type of ski lift, journey duration, capacity, directions to follow on arrival and onward links. All principal pistes are covered: colour-coded by level of difficulty and detailing access routes, descriptions of terrain, best lines of descent and onward links, accompanied by regular piste map illustrations to help you in real-time itinerary planning and route-finding on the move.

Point-to-point route-finder information is not necessarily the quickest option, but rather the best on-piste direction to deliver the most enjoyable route between the specified points. The route-finders are detailed for both competent novices and good intermediates.

ABOUT THE AUTHOR

Francis (Gary) Johnston was born in County Down, Northern Ireland. He was previously employed at a senior level with two of the UK's leading ski, lakes & mountains tour operators, having lived and worked in Andorra, Spain and Portugal. He has also worked in or visited most of the leading French, Austrian and Italian ski resorts, having personally accompanied and guided well over 4000 visitors and travel industry professionals during that time.

Francis now divides his time between Andorra, France and Brighton in England, travelling up to six months each year in the Alps and Pyrenees.

❶ The Alpine environment can be harsh and dangerous, but it is also very fragile – please respect it and leave nothing but your tracks in the snow.

WELCOME TO ANDORRA – BENVINGUTS

Andorra's ski areas are some of the most extensive, best equipped and most modern in Europe. The country now attracts more UK and Irish snowsports visitors than Switzerland, the USA and Canada combined. Yet ask most northern Europeans where Andorra is and nine times out of ten you'll be met with blank looks. The country may be a tiny dot on the map of Europe – so small that its own name doesn't fit inside its borders on most standard maps – but far from being a poor forgotten backwater, the country is a wealthy, modern, independent state, with its capital Andorra la Vella often described as a high-altitude Monte Carlo. Welcome to The Pyrenean Country – *el país dels Pirineus*.

THE PYRENEAN COUNTRY

Andorra, official name Principat d'Andorra, is situated high in the eastern Pyrenees between France and Spain. Although small, the country is still bigger than all the other European micro-states: Liechtenstein is 157 sq km (60 sq miles), San Marino 61 sq km (23.5 sq miles) and the Principality of Monaco 1.5 sq km (0.58 sq miles). With an area of just 468 sq km (180.6 sq miles), Andorra is still tiny (more than 300 times smaller than Wales) yet it attracts over 11 million visitors every year.

True Andorrans are actually outnumbered in their own country by residents of other nationalities: most inhabitants are of Spanish or French origin, with a sizeable Portuguese community and quite a few UK expats, too. At the last census, over 130 different nationalities were recorded amongst Andorra's inhabitants. Catalan is the state's official language, but locals also speak Spanish and French and frequently switch between all these languages mid-sentence.

SHANGRI-LA?

Andorra's inhabitants pay no income tax; the state has no currency of its own; no airports; no trains; no army; no navy and no airforce – it's no wonder that Andorrans have one of the world's longest life expectancies.

The country also has a unique sovereign status as a 'parliamentary co-principality'. It has a head of government but no president; it has two heads of state, yet neither are Andorrans themselves. This odd state of affairs has its roots in the medieval feudal system and has survived largely unchanged since the 15th century, thanks in part to the country's isolated surroundings, encircled by a natural fortress of mountains, with 95 per cent of its border over 2000 m (6560 ft) above sea level.

Despite this insular high altitude position, Andorra is only a three-hour drive from the Mediterranean coast and the buzzing cosmopolitan cities of Toulouse and Barcelona. Andorra's fortuitous position in a major mountain chain which is subject to an Atlantic influence means that precipitation is high – ensuring snow-sure conditions for its ski resorts – yet the proximity to the Mediterranean blesses the area with paradoxically mild temperatures and over 300 full days of sunshine per year.

STATISTICS
- Population: 72,320
- Maximum altitude: 2942 m (9653 ft)
- Minimum altitude: 840 m (2756 ft)
- Area: 468 sq km (181 sq miles)
- Further information: Ⓦ www.andorra.ad

EVOLUTION

Andorra has suffered from a serious image problem in the past: many experienced snowsports enthusiasts stayed away, believing it to be the haunt of booze-fuelled beginners staying in basic accommodation and playing about on limited cruising pistes. Many of these early negative preconceptions had some basis in fact, but massive investment has resulted in a rapid evolution away from these rudimentary beginnings and seen Andorra's profile soar to join the world's snowsports superleague.

The capacity per hour of the country's modern ski lifts is now almost twice the entire population of the country, ensuring queues are kept to a minimum and skiing time is maximized. The excellent facilities, consistently reliable snowfalls and world class ski schools are the major attractions, added to the bargain duty-free prices, this is definitely a destination that's got the lot.

◉ *High capacity cable car connecting Arinsal and Pal*

● *The official crest of the Principat d'Andorra*

REGIONAL IDENTITY

Andorra's history and culture owes much to that of its larger neighbours. The Mediterranean coast around Barcelona was colonized by the Romans in 125BC, marking the birth of the Catalan language from its roots in Latin. The next important era was the arrival of the Moors in AD711. Their invasion thrust as far north as Poitiers in France and their Islamic influence, particularly on Spanish architecture and language, was considerable; but the Catalans looked to the Christian Franks (the French) for protection, ceding Barcelona to them in return for liberating the city from Moorish rule. As a result, the region came under the rule of the Holy Roman Emperor Charlemagne and was known as the Marca Hispanica (the Spanish Mark). Charlemagne respected the rights of the Catalans to administer themselves and is believed to have granted independent rights to the Homes des Valls d'Andorra (Men of the Valleys of Andorra), as a reward for their assistance in his military campaigns. The Spanish Mark remained as a distant province of the Empire, eventually becoming detached as the power of the Catalan aristocracy increased.

Count Ramon Berenguer III of Barcelona (1096–1131) married Dolça, heiress to Provence, thus gaining her French territories. The expansion of the region led to a rapid increase in foreign trade and witnessed the cultural awakening of Catalunya during the next three hundred years.

BIRTH OF A PRINCIPALITY

As part of the diocese of La Seu d'Urgell in Spain, all Andorran monasteries and parishes were owned or controlled by the Bishop of Urgell; however, a local viscount held feudal rights. In 1250, the viscount's only daughter married the French Count of Foix, who declared rights by marriage over Andorra when his father-in-law died. This led to nearly thirty years of feuding over control of Andorra between the house of Foix and the bishopric of Urgell. The Andorrans, caught in the middle, persuaded the two sides to meet and thrash out an agreement. In 1288 the Pariatges Treaty was signed, formally creating the Principality of Andorra. The basis of the agreement was that if one neighbouring lord couldn't control Andorra, then neither could the other. Effectively, the treaty established the first ever recorded declaration of a demilitarized zone, explaining why there are no castles or fortifications to be found in Andorra today. The treaty gave the Lords dual rights, conferring on them both the equal title of Co-Prince of Andorra.

There is still a Bishop of Urgell, who is referred to by Andorrans as the Episcopal Co-Prince. The Count of Foix was known as the French Co-Prince. However, the house of Foix eventually became part of the house of Navarra, which produced Henry IV, King of France, who passed the Co-Prince of Andorra title to his royal descendants. In 1789, when Louis XVI of France was guillotined during the French Revolution, the Co-Prince title passed to the President of the French Republic and the citizens of Andorra were left more or less to look after their own affairs. The country's borders have therefore remained unchanged for centuries.

Having been marginalized on the world stage and, thus, surviving by default, also explains why the country has so much medieval and feudal history still shaping present-day institutions.

TOWARDS THE PRESENT DAY

The Principality was originally divided into six parishes, each essentially having sovereign rights until very recently. In the 1960s, the capital Andorra la Vella grew so rapidly that it was split into two parishes: Andorra la Vella and the newer parish of Escaldes-Engordany, so now there are seven parishes, each with a local government called the Comu (commune).

Four representatives from each Comu, elected to a four-year term, make up the Consell General (general council). The Consell then elect an executive Cap d'Govern as head of government and a Syndic who performs a role similar to the Speaker of the House of Commons in the UK. The Cap d'Govern then elects the ministers. The seat of government is the attractive Casa de la Vall in the old heart of Andorra la Vella.

On 14 March 1993, a modern constitution was ratified and Andorra became a fully independent state and the 184th member of the UN. The Co-Princes now only 'advise, consult and protect' as official joint Heads of State.

The state is now a member of the Council of Europe, but not of the European Union and so is free to maintain its unusual fiscal and duty-free status. It is the only country in the world to have Catalan as its official language, a language which is experiencing a renaissance driven by the continued economic and cultural strength of Spain's Catalan capital, Barcelona.

Andorra benefits greatly from its geographical and constitutional position in this historic and powerful region, absorbing the greater part of regional influence from Catalunya in Spain, while still having the French president as a ceremonial joint Head of State. It is in the centre of a political and economic power base, yet at a uniquely advantageous remove from it.

SKI PIONEERS

The first documented appearance of skis in Andorra was in 1924: Soldeu's postman Miquel Farré was on a routine cross-border trip and noticed that his French counterparts had swapped their snowshoes for long wooden skis. Observing that they were able to move about a lot more quickly and easily, he promptly got a pair. The postman's newfangled mode of transport caused quite a stir back in Andorra and quickly caught on as a way of moving around during the winter months.

The leisure and sporting possibilities of this new mode of transport were also quickly realized. In 1931 the first ski slope was prepared in the Vall d'Incles near Soldeu and in 1932 the Ski Club of Andorra was founded.

The first rudimentary ski lifts didn't appear until 1952; just simple tow ropes powered by lorry motors. Five years later the first mechanical ski lift was in operation: the Coll Blanc button lift in Pas de la Casa, marking the foundation of Andorra's first official ski station. The demand for facilities grew and Andorra's second ski station was founded in 1964 at Soldeu; followed by Arinsal in 1972. All three ski stations were private enterprises, established by local enthusiasts who enjoyed their skiing just as much as they desired to run a business.

The growing popularity of skiing had not gone unnoticed by the Andorran Government and in 1982 the first publically owned station was opened at Pal. Ordino parish followed suit a year later with the development of Arcalís. In 1999 construction began on the cable car connecting Pal and Arinsal. Pas de la Casa stretched out further into Grau Roig, and Soldeu added the huge El Tarter snowbowl to its domain. This brought their ski areas steadily closer, eventually to the extent that the pistes overlapped; but the two enterprises stayed resolutely divided. Each area belonged to a different parish and a long-running feud over communal grazing pastures got in the way of a union, with the ludicrous situation that visitors skied together on some pistes but couldn't use each other's lifts.

Andorra was now competing with the world's top ski countries and needed to distinguish itself from its previous budget-cost image. Therefore, the communes of Encamp and Canillo swallowed their pride in late 2004 and created a joint company to administer and market their two ski areas, Pas de la Casa and Soldeu, as a single domain, capable of competing with Europe's largest ski areas and firmly placing Andorra on the snowsports map.

Ever since Miquel Farré swapped his snowshoes for skis in 1924, snowsports in Andorra have benefited from constant expansion and investment. Today the country has the Pyrenees' most extensive and most modern resorts, with almost 200 pistes extending to over 300 km (186 miles) and with snowmaking facilities guaranteeing around 35 per cent of the skiable terrain. It's a long time since the first field was pisted in 1931 and it's now possible to ski on-piste over 10 per cent of the entire country.

THE FUTURE

Continued investment and improvement of existing facilities are the current focus, but an interesting proposal has been the topic of après-ski conversations among station personnel and regular visitors for years now: the undeveloped slopes on the French mountains immediately above Pas de la Casa are only one beautiful valley away from the small French station of Porté-Pumoyens. Could this become the Pyrenees' first cross-border ski domain?

TRADITIONAL MOUNTAIN FARE

Regional gastronomy has too often been regarded as of secondary importance in the snowsports holiday experience. Now, however, more travellers are seeking to complement their time in the mountains with great meals, too. The rich diversity of European regional cuisine is nowhere more enjoyable than in the actual regions that created it, surrounded by the harvest of fresh natural ingredients that go into making this particular cuisine so distinctive and delicious.

With just two per cent of Andorra's land area suitable for farming, surviving the harsh high-altitude winters has always required a rustic, hearty diet which made full use of the limited range of local foodstuffs. So it's fair to say that regional cuisine was born out of necessity, relying heavily on meat, game, a few hardy fruit and vegetable crops, together with cured and dried foodstuffs harvested and preserved during the summer and autumn. Pork, cured sausages, lamb, poultry, eggs, snails, wild boar, venison, rabbit, duck, trout, wild mushrooms, beans, nuts, berries, cheese, honey, olive oil, cabbage, spinach, onions and garlic all feature as staples in the region's traditional cuisine.

🔺 *Wholesome basics underpin Andorra's gastronomy*

This noble culinary heritage was in danger of being lost with the development and dominance of 'international' hotels and snack restaurants in the resorts. 'Bland but filling' seems to be their maxim. But, away from the standard resort fare, a renaissance of true Andorran cuisine has blossomed – a refinement of traditional, wholesome, seasonal basics has been further enhanced with techniques and ingredients assimilated from the neighbouring regions and their former colonies. After all, Andorra's neighbours aren't exactly lacking in gastronomic pedigree: France, consistently living up to its reputation as the world's foremost provider of gourmet food and fine wine, and Spain, a country of vibrant, spicy Arabic influence and introducer of tomatoes, potatoes and peppers from the Americas into Europe. Something must have rubbed off!

BORDA RESTAURANTS

Tongue-twisting, tastebud-teasing local dishes, redolent of the rigours and pleasures of high-altitude life, have survived and thrived best in Andorra's renowned Borda restaurants. A *Borda* is a traditional stone-built barn, found attached to farmhouses, standing solitarily on the outskirts of villages or huddled together in the remote high pastures. The building has two floors. The ground level is used to house livestock and to store agricultural implements, and the airy, high-ceilinged upper floor is used for drying the tobacco harvest and for storing animal feed.

With the rapid change from agrarian to urban lifestyle in Andorra, lots of these barns fell into disuse. Many have since been converted into attractive, desirable chalets and, most notably, into atmospheric restaurants.

Borda restaurants have become emblematic living museums for the preservation and evolution of the Principality's signature dishes. A visit to a Borda restaurant should feature on your 'must do' list – virtually every resort has, or is close to, at least one.
◐ Generally open 12.30–15.30 hours and 17.30–23.30 hours.

🔺 *Refugi dels Llacs de Pessons, Grau Roig (see page 26)*

RECOMMENDED BORDA RESTAURANTS

La Borda Raubert €€ The most authentically Andorran restaurant in the Principality. ⓐ Carretera d'Arinsal, km 1.3 La Massana
ⓣ +376 835 420 ⓕ +376 866 165
➔ *See feature on page 27.*

Borda de l'Avi €€€ Grilled meats, *escudella* stew, game done on the embers of an open wood fire. Neighbouring cocktail bar and late night venue. ⓐ Carretera d'Arinsal, km 1 La Massana
ⓣ +376 835 154

La Borda del Gran Duc €€+ Tucked down a tiny pedestrian-only alley just off the main street in La Massana town centre. Grills, fish, raclette and fondue. ⓐ Cami Ral, La Massana ⓣ +376 837 968

La Borda d'Erts €€ Two hundred-year-old building. Specialities: slate-grilled meat, *cassoulet* and fish. ⓐ Carretera General d'Erts, Erts (near Arinsal) ☎ +376 836 782

Cal Moixó €€ Rustic mountain cuisine, roasts, game and fresh trout. One of the most authentic country hamlet Bordas. ⓐ Ansalonga Vall d'Ordino ☎ +376 850 884 / 322 593

Borda Estevet €€€ Elegant Borda offering classic grills and local specialities including slate-grilled meats and Andorran trout. Extensive, well-selected cellar. ⓐ Carretera de la Comella, 2 Andorra la Vella ☎ +376 864 026 ☎ +376 864 026

Can Benet €€€ Snails *a la llauna*, meats cooked on an open wood fire, *caldereta de langosta* (spiny lobster stew) and game dishes in season. ⓐ Antic Carrer Major, Andorra la Vella ☎ +376 828 922

La Borda Pairal 1630 €€€ Beautifully converted historic building dating from 1630, with exposed log beams and distinctive water wheel. Wide range of gastronomic, refined dishes. Complete with its own fine wine boutique and over 400 wines on an excellent cellar list. ⓐ Carrer Doctor Vilanova, 7 Andorra la Vella ☎ +376 869 999 ☎ +376 866 661

Borda La Guingueta €€€ Very stylish restaurant just outside Sant Julià de Lòria in the south of the Principality. Intimate venue holding only three dozen diners; featuring a refined menu of internationally influenced dishes and an extensive wine list. ⓐ Carretera de la Rabassa, Sant Julià de Lòria ☎ +376 842 941

Borda de l'Hortó €€ 18th-century inn. Specialities include suckling pig, kid, charcoal-grilled meats, local river trout and French-influenced high-altitude rustic dishes. ⓐ Carretera General, Presa de Ransol, Canillo ⓣ +376 851 622 ⓕ +376 851 971 ⓛ Closed on Mondays

Cort de Popaire €€ Located in the middle of Soldeu village, under the same management as Soldeu's Hort de Popaire hotel. Cosy, atmospheric old Borda with low ceiling, exposed beams, animal feed troughs set in the walls and an open wood-fire grill. As the restaurant is located in a major resort, the menu displays a more international influence. ⓐ Plaça del Poble Soldeu ⓣ +376 851 211 ⓕ +376 853 854 ⓦ www.hortdepopaire.com

La Llar de l'Artesa €+ Popular with seasonal tourists and regular visitors, who refer to it affectionately as the 'Snails & Quails'. Atmospheric old Borda just north of Soldeu on the main road towards Grau Roig. Offers a free pick-up and return taxi service for clients in Soldeu, El Tarter and Canillo. Lively bar downstairs. ⓐ Bordes d'Envalira, km 22 Soldeu ⓣ +376 851 078

Refugi dels Llacs de Pessons €€ High-altitude (2350 m / 7708 ft) piste-side mountain restaurant. Although not strictly a Borda, this old, atmospheric, quality restaurant has the same soul and is the closest thing to one in the Pas de la Casa area. The restaurant is reached via the Cami de Pessons red piste on Cubil Mountain. ⓐ Cami de Pessons, Grau Roig ⓣ +376 759 015 ⓛ Open daytime only

⊙ *See pages 29–34 for descriptions of local specialities.*

LA BORDA RAUBERT

Established for over thirty years, the Borda Raubert restaurant is virtually unknown to tourists, but is renowned locally as the 'archive of Andorran cuisine' for offering regional specialities at their most authentic, as well as for fresh, contemporary adaptations of traditional, almost-forgotten recipes.

Housed in an old farmstead, tucked away by the banks of the Arinsal River on the main road between La Massana and Erts, it is run by Josep Maria Troguet Ribes, who is also the chef. He picks many of the ingredients and flavourings in the woodlands around Pal. Sr Troguet's family has also made an invaluable contribution to the preservation of Andorra's heritage in two books: *Costumari i receptari de la gastronomia andorrana* (Customs and recipes of Andorran gastronomy) and *La nostra cuina* (Our Cuisine), featuring ancient recipes and age-old customs gleaned from senior local inhabitants.

Sample menu

To whet your appetite, Sr Troguet recommends:

Chicory salad with ham or cream of nettle soup

•

*Farmhouse chicken with prunes and pine kernels
or Andorran-style river trout*

•

Elderflower ice cream, accompanied by wild cherry liqueur

La Borda Raubert ⓐ Carretera d'Arinsal, km 1.3 La Massana
ⓣ +376 835 420 ⓕ +376 866 165

COOKING TECHNIQUES

Andorran recipes are heavily influenced by Catalunya, with strong hints of southern France. The following are a selection of the most popular and representative styles:

à la ariégeoise: cooked in a style typical of the neighbouring Ariége region of France; normally a stew generally consisting of cabbage, pork or mutton and beans

a la brasa: roasted on a wood fire; most traditional restaurants feature an open fire grill attended by the chef, the choice of wood being as important as the cooking method in imparting a distinctive flavour

a la catalana: cooked to a typically Catalan recipe, generally applied to all local recipes and dishes, and most usually referring to roasted and grilled meats, but with no real set ingredients other than seasonal produce

a la graella (or **a la parrilla**): barbecued on a cast iron grill over, or vertically next to, an open wood fire

a la llauna: usually reserved for a most popular Catalan snail recipe – the snails are cooked over an open wood fire on a special tin plate (*llauna* = tin); the llauna resembles a cake tier server, round and flat, but with individual indentations to hold each snail open-end uppermost, with a vertical handle in the middle

a la llosa: cooked on a hot slate (the *llosa*); usually a DIY task at your table (same as French-style *pierrade*)

d'olla: cooked in a short-handled Catalan stewing pot (the *olla*); usually associated with stews (*escudella*, see page 34) and other meat dishes – *carn d'olla*

a la planxa: grilled, usually on a hot-plate; the most common cooking method used in snack bars

WELL DONE

Andorrans prefer to eat their meat quite rare, so if your taste is for it more 'well done' (*bien echo*) try asking for it to be 'very well done' (*muy bien echo*) when cooked, otherwise it is likely to arrive closer to 'medium'.

REGIONAL SPECIALITIES

all (*ail* in French): garlic; almost two-thirds of all French garlic is grown in the Midi-Pyrénées; the Garonne Valley, around Toulouse, is one of France's most prolific market garden regions, producing over half a million tonnes of superior quality vegetables and fruit a year

anxova: anchovies; the best are from Collioure on the French Mediterranean coast, and from Escala in Gerona province on the Costa Brava; anchovy paste tapenade (called *anchoïade*), made with olive oil, garlic and basil, is spread on bread as an hors d'œuvre

confit d'oie: preserved cooked joints of goose (usually thighs and drumsticks) set in goose fat and packed in jars

foie gras: infamous luxury goose/duck liver product originating from the Midi-Pyrénées and Gascony; *foie gras d'oie entier* is regarded as the finest

haricots tarbais: fine beans from the French town of Tarbes; considered to be the best variety for cooking

oli d'avellanes: Catalan hazelnut oil, for dressing salads

oli d'oliva: olive oil; the *Denominación de Origen* organic extra virgin oil, from the ancient groves in Lleida province, should be top of your list

mel: honey; of particular note are the rosemary, rhododendron and heather scented varieties from the Pyrenean foothills

FLAVOURINGS & SAUCES

Despite the strong influence of French cuisine on Andorran gastronomy, many of the basic flavourings and sauces are Spanish in origin.

aliño: Spanish version of vinaigrette; olive oil, garlic, parsley, lemon juice or vinegar

allioli (*aïoli* in French): olive oil and garlic emulsified like mayonnaise, but traditionally made without egg yolks; generally served as a very strong, thick dip

bolets: general Catalan term for wild mushrooms (*setas* in Spanish) which feature heavily in Andorran cooking, seasonally fresh or dried; groups of friends and family can be seen scouring woodlands collecting them in spring and autumn

fruita seca: nuts and dried fruit; nuts are found in many Pyrenean recipes, the most popular are *avellanes* (hazelnuts), *ametlles* (almonds), *castanyas* (sweet chestnuts) and *pinyons* (pine nuts)

picada: finely ground hazelnuts, garlic, breadcrumbs, saffron, wine, olive oil and sometimes even a little chocolate; mixed into meatballs (*albóndigas*) as a flavouring, or used in meat and poultry dishes as a base for gravy

salsa romesco: the classic Catalan sauce. Tomatoes, garlic, paprika, parsley, olive oil, ground hazelnuts and almonds, breadcrumbs, salt and vinegar are reduced to use as a flavouring ingredient in cooking, or served thick and creamy as a dip

◆ *Allioli, the classic Catalan garlic dip*

CHEESES

The Ariège département of France, just north of Andorra, offers a wide range of strong *fromages des Pyrénées*. Goat's and sheep cheeses predominate in these high altitude regions, the terrain being too barren to support large dairy herds. The Cadi co-operative based in La Seu d'Urgell, just south of the Andorran border, is a notable local dairy producer.

Bethmale and **Bamalou**: made near Foix in the Ariège, these are the best-known cow's milk cheeses

Cabrioulet and **Cabécou**: goat's cheeses from the same area

Montsec: from Lleida province, this is made from goat's milk and is similar to Camembert

Palomières: from the spa/ski town of Bagnères further west, this is also recommended

Pic de la Calabasse, **Moulis** and **Rogalais**: also good, these are from further afield in the Midi-Pyrénées

Roquefort: the most famous regional speciality cheese, from the village of Roquefort-sur-Soulzon, north-east of Toulouse; it is a full-fat, unpasteurized and unhomogenized ewe's milk soft blue cheese, matured in ancient underground cellars in Roquefort for at least three months; it features in Andorran menus as sauce for steaks and, most usually, crumbled over chicory salads

Tupi: definitely the most distinctive Catalan cheese; sold in jars, it is basically a Vall d'Aran-type cheese, but is matured in a wooden container along with garlic and *aiguardent* (see page 43); delicious, but somewhat of an acquired taste

Urgellet and **Serrat**: two other local Catalan offerings, the latter being a ewe's milk variety

Vall d'Aran: on the Spanish side, this smoky cow's milk cheese is the best known

CURED MEATS

Ham (*pernil* in Catalan) and cured sausages are staples of the Pyrenean diet because they are an excellent way to preserve meat for the long winters. Many Andorran homes have an airy natural cold store in the basement for hanging hams and cured meats.

The most popular ham is the famous Spanish **jamón serrano**, a cured mountain ham, similar to Parma ham; salted, dry-cured, and served in wafer-thin slices as a *tapa*, or topping the almost ubiquitous appetizer *pa amb tomàquet* (see facing page).

There appear to be as many varieties of cured sausages throughout Catalunya as there are choices of cheese in France. They're eaten cold as *tapas* and in salads, added to reinforce stews or simply grilled. The most popular include:

botifarra: an almost generic name for Bratwürst-like large pork sausages; usually 'white' pork, simply flavoured with salt and pepper

botifarra de cérvol: venison sausage; not to be confused with *botifarra de cervell*, which is made from pig's brains

botifarra negra: similar to 'black pudding'

bull de llengua: boiled tongue sausage

chorizo: ubiquitous, spicy Spanish salami flavoured with garlic, chilli and other spices

llonganissa: a long, firm, fine-textured variety from the Catalan mountain town of Vic is considered best and has been awarded a *Denominación de Calidad* quality guarantee

salchichón: salami of very lean pork flavoured with paprika, salt and pepper and hung to cure for over four months

saucisse de Toulouse: famous sausage which bears a 'Red Label' guarantee similar to an *Appellation d'Origine Contrôlée* awarded to the most important regional products

LOCAL DISHES

STARTERS AND LIGHT DISHES

amanida catalana: mixed salad Catalan-style, with slices of cured sausage

calçots: a type of spring onion (similar to Welsh onions), roasted or grilled and served with *allioli* and/or *salsa romesco* dip (see page 30)

cargols a la llauna: a Catalan recipe, originating from Lleida province; snails are cooked over an open wood fire on a special tin plate (the *llauna*); salt, pepper and olive oil are liberally added and the dish is served straight from the llauna

escalivada: red pepper, aubergine and onion, cooked and soaked in olive oil then usually – and best – served cold

pa amb tomàquet (*pan con tomate* in Spanish): toasted bread rubbed with garlic and tomato and then drizzled with olive oil; often a DIY task

trinxats: cabbage and potato hash with garlic; like 'bubble & squeak'

trumfes: potatoes, simply baked in a wood fire

xató: salad with strips of salt cod (*bacallà*), tuna and anchovies

🔵 *Try a Borda restaurant (see pages 23–27) for authentic Andorran dishes*

MAIN COURSES

cassoulet: originating from around Toulouse, Carcassonne and Castelnaudry in France; a stew of haricot beans, sausage, pork, and/or confit of goose and vegetables. In the *ariégeois* style (see page 28), it is made as a ragout of mutton and cabbage

costelles de xai: roast lamb ribs, usually served with *allioli* (see page 30)

escudella: thick soup, more like a stew, of meat, *botifarra* (sausage; see page 32) and mixed vegetables

faves a la catalana: broad beans and *botifarra negra* (see page 32) stew, similar to the famous *fabada asturiana* from the Asturias region of Spain

paella: saffron-flavoured rice, meat and/or fish dish originally from Valencia; usually found in resorts at festivals and high-season weekends, served from giant paella pans cooked out in the open

peus de porc amb bolets: pig's trotters with wild mushrooms

truites a l'andorrana: Andorran river trout, simply grilled or roasted and garnished with seasonal vegetables

DESSERTS

crema catalana: Catalunya's star dessert, similar to *crème brûlée* – rich, sweet custard, flavoured with cinnamon, orange, lemon or aniseed, topped with caramelized sugar

mel i mató: cream cheese drizzled with honey and sprinkled with flaked almonds

music: simply a selection of nuts and dried fruit served on their own or drizzled with honey; useful to pick at while you finish off that extra bottle of wine you ordered!

orejones: dried, sliced peaches and apricots, often presented as a confection or tart

🔺 *Calculate your bill by adding up the cocktail sticks speared in each tapa*

TAPAS

These are small portions of food, usually served to accompany a drink. A traditional Spanish custom, now elevated into a distinct meal event in its own right, similar to the Greek mezedes. Not widely encountered in Andorra to the same level of sophistication as found in Spanish cities, although there are a couple of very notable exceptions, which are listed below:

Don Denis €€ An Andorran institution and one of the captial's most popular lunchtime venues. Dine *a la carta* in the main dining room or – for a more authentic experience – stay in the main bar area with its ceiling hung with dozens of cured hams; take a seat up by the bar and choose from the huge range of excellent fresh tapas served direct from the long, bar-level display.
ⓐ Carrer Isabel Sandy, 3 Escaldes-Engordany ❶ +376 820 692
❶ +376 863 130 ⓦ www.restaurantedondenis.com

Lizarran € Basque-influenced local tapas bar. Packed at lunchtime; just politely reach past the customers sat at the bar to serve yourself from the delicious tapas in, and on top of, display cabinets on the bar. When something new comes out of the kitchen the staff call out and pass the dish around – don't be shy!
ⓐ Avinguda Meritxell, 86 Andorra la Vella ❶ +376 863 994
❶ +376 867 984

VEGETARIAN DISHES

It has to be said, vegetarians will have a hard time when eating out in Andorra, and vegans even more so. The concept of being vegetarian isn't fully understood, or acceptably accommodated, even in the largest hotels. You may have to resign yourself to picking through salads and pizzas to remove anchovies, prawns and ham.

Most of the vegetarian options offered depend heavily on eggs and cheese, with the omelette being king. Buffets and self-service restaurants are easiest, but they still rely on meat and fish dishes for main courses; the only vegetarian option again usually being an omelette – charged at the same price as the meat dish.

Crêpes, pasta and pizzas are all reliable options, as are tapas, many of which are vegetable-only dishes.

The Swiss- and Savoy-style dishes **fondue** and **raclette** are also popular in the more French-influenced Pas de la Casa area. In Andorra, fondue is usually the meat-dipped-in-oil version, so if you are vegetarian, make sure first that the restaurant actually offers the cheese version. This is a blend of two or more cheeses and a little white wine, gently brought to near boiling to liquify, then served at your table in a pot with a flame burner to keep it hot. You are provided with chunks of bread and little spears with which to dip the bread into the bubbling cheese mixture; usually served with potatoes and/or salad.

A half-wheel of the smooth, firm raclette cheese is served mounted on a special heater; this melts the cheese, which you then scrape off hot on to your plate or bread. Raclette is usually served with potatoes and pickles, but in many cases also comes with ham and/or salami.

MENU

To see the menu, ask for *la carta* (*la carte* in French) as 'the menu' in Andorra is taken to mean just the daily set menu.

MENU DEL DÍA (or MENU DU JOUR)

An economical set menu, usually consisting of two or three courses with at least two choices, often with dessert, bread and sometimes even water and/or table wine included.

➔ *See page 51 for phrases and menu translator.*

MOUNTAiN SPORTS NUTRITION

Don't make the mistake of regarding eating on snowsports holidays as merely pit stops for refuelling; a couple of beers and a hamburger won't help you nail that three-sixty or give you the legs to progress into that fresh powder after lunch! Nutritious, warming meals with quality fresh ingredients and frequent non-alcoholic fluid intake are what your body craves at altitude and are essential for peak performance.

Remember that you're in an Arctic environment, participating in a demanding physical activity. This requires a more athletic-minded approach to diet. Rather than treating meals and snack breaks as just a chance to quickly 'put away some grub', it's much better to ensure that you supply your body with optimum nutrition while, since you are still on holiday after all, treating yourself to a more gourmet event. If you had a racehorse worth millions, you wouldn't feed it beer and hamburgers. So why treat yourself as any less worthy? You'll be able to do more runs and, thus, get more out of your holiday if you're properly nourished and rested.

SUGGESTED SNOWSPORTS DIET

Breakfast: a 'continental' breakfast of coffee, a croissant and a cigarette just isn't adequate to support a morning in the mountains. You need slow-release, energy-rich foods such as muesli, bread with cheese or ham, honey and yogurt. The occasional fry-up is fine too as even moderately active snowsports burn around 400 calories per hour.

Lunch: light, warm dishes based on pasta, rice or vegetables with meat or fish to supply plenty of complex carbohydrate energy, protein and fibre.

Dinner: salad, soup or vegetables, followed by fish, fowl or light meat. Don't make it too hearty as a heavy meal will interfere with your sleep.

Snacks: fruit or yogurt; a sandwich; or dried fruits/nuts.

Drinks: fruit juice, tea (herbal is best), hot chocolate, *caldo* (hot consommé), water and more water.

WINE

Again, Andorra is blessed by having France and Spain as her immediate neighbours: giants in the oenological world. The two countries supply 99 per cent of Andorra's bottled nectars, all available at bargain duty-free prices.

Catalan wines are some of Spain's finest; the region's bubbly cava outsells even champagne. Traditionally, Spanish wines are naturally fermented and aged in wood, then bottled slightly oxidized. Increasingly, however, modern French and Californian production methods and tastes are being introduced, resulting in the region's development as one of Europe's best.

Cabernet, Sauvignon, Merlot, Pinot Noir and Chardonnay grapes are now frequently cultivated alongside the most commonly grown indigenous vines such as Ull de Lliebre (more frequently encountered in Spanish as Tempranillo), Xarello, Parellada, Monastrell, Garnacha and Macabeo (known as Viura in Rioja).

Cava is sparkling wine, produced in the same way as champagne, although with different grape varieties. Cava was once also labelled as champagne too, but this is no longer allowed as it contravenes French AOC. Still wine is elaborated as normal, then, as it is bottled, yeast is added to cause a secondary fermentation; CO_2 is a natural byproduct of the yeast's activity, hence the bubbles. The principal grape varieties used in cava are Parellada, Xarello, Macabeo and Monastrell. Cava production began under the Codorníu label in the second half of the 19th century. The firm still makes excellent bubbly and jockeys with rivals Freixenet for the title of world's largest maker of sparkling wine. The smaller family firm, Juvés y Camps, produces a quality cava labelled as *Reserva de la Familia* which is also worth searching out. The price difference between champagne and cava reflects the difference in production and labour costs rather than quality, as well as being a result of established marketing and perceived pedigree.

RIOJA

Arguably Spain's most famous wine-producing region, Rioja is much further west, near the Basque Country. It's a bit too far from Andorra to be considered a 'local' wine, but is readily encountered in Andorra, along with other quality world wines.

SPANISH WINE TERMS

blanco: white wine; **rosado**: rosé wine; **tinto**: red wine

cosecha: followed by the year of vintage; literally 'harvest'

crianza: wine aged at least one year in barrels, then for some months in the bottle until at least two years old before sale

Denominación de Origen (DO): the Spanish version of the French *Appellation d'Origine Contrôlée* (AOC; see page 43)

gran reserva: exceptional vintages aged for two years in barrels and three years in the bottle before sale

reserva: wine selected for long ageing; at least one year in barrels and at least three years old before sale

CATALAN WINE REGIONS

Penedès: west and south of Barcelona. This is Catalunya's most important region and one of Europe's most sophisticated, forward-looking wine-producing areas. Although other areas also produce cava, Sant Sadurní d'Anoia in Penedès is the largest centre of production, accounting for nearly three-quarters of the world market in sparkling wines. Penedès is also the home of the world-famous Torres firm, which has vineyards in North and South America; their white Viña Sol, made with native Catalan Parellada grapes, is Spain's staple quality *blanco*. Other notable Torres wines are Fransola (white), Sangre de Toro and Coronas (reds)

Alella: small DO north of Barcelona, noteworthy for its Marfil and dessert wines

Costers del Segre: in Lleida province, this is home to the excellent Raïmat estate, which produces high quality reds

Empordà (Ampurdan–Costa Brava): Gerona province. The most northerly demarcation and also the most ancient, established by the Greeks and Romans when 'Empúries', as it was then known, was the centre of Catalan maritime trade. Castillo de Perelada is a notable Empordà estate, producing excellent cava and very quaffable *rosado*

Priorat: south of Barcelona; produces very respectable, robust reds. Home of *l'Ermita*, one of the most expensive, limited production, Spanish wines

Tarragona, **Terra Alta** and **Conca de Barberá**: the remaining three Catalan DOs, all located to the south of Barcelona; these regions export the majority of their grape harvest to Penedès for the production of cava

◀ *World-class wines from the regions surrounding Andorra*

FRENCH WINE REGIONS

The **Languedoc–Roussillon** region has been producing wine since pre-Roman times. Grape varieties grown in the region include Grenache, Merlot, Maccabeu, Carignan, Gamay, Cinsault, Malvoisie, Cabernet and Syrah.The fertile river valleys just an hour or so north of Andorra boast a number of world-class, yet relatively little-known, sub-regions:

Corbières: large, important Languedoc sub-region containing a number of quality sub-area AOCs. Produces balanced reds, fruity rosés and dry whites. Of particular note is the Château de Pech-Latt at Lagrasse, near Carcassonne. The monks at Lagrasse Abbey, founded by Charlemagne around the same time as he is believed to have granted Andorra its independent status, planted the first vines here in AD784. The Château ranks among the pioneers of organic vineyard agriculture (*l'agriculture biologique*) and produces excellent reds

Côtes du Roussillon: produces robust, earthy wines redolent of the warm south

Fitou: produces strong, full-bodied reds only from a specific sub-area within Corbiéres, with controlled limits on yield per hectare and a minimum ageing in cellars of nine months. The product is always over 12 per cent alcohol by volume

Gaillac: north-east of Toulouse, in the Tarn département; one of France's oldest wine regions, notable for its fragrant white wines

Limoux: Blanquette de Limoux is a local sparkler of fine quality, produced using the *méthode champenoise*, but using Clairette, Chenin and Chardonnay grapes

Minervois: on the slopes of the Montagne Noire above the Aude Valley. Produces rich reds

FRENCH WINE TERMS

blanc: white wine; **rosé**: rosé wine; **rouge**: red wine

Appellation d'Origine Contrôlée (AOC): the premier quality control, protected by law, awarded to the highest quality wines in specifically demarcated areas

Vin Délimité de Qualité Supérieure (VDQS): quality award just below full AOC

Vin de Pays: followed by the name of the département it comes from; local table wine

Vin Doux Naturel (VDN): naturally sweet wine (dessert wine). Produced in this area from a base of Muscat and Malvoisie grapes. Notable examples are: Muscat de Rivesaltes, one of Europe's oldest pedigree sweet wines; Muscat de Saint Jean de Minervois; Banyuls and Maury

sec: dry; **moëlleux**: sweet; **perlé**: slightly sparkling; **mousseux**: sparkling

APERITIFS, DIGESTIFS & BEER

acqua d'or: the DO name for Catalan brandy. Spanish brandy is now mostly made in the south of the country, in the sherry-producing region, Jerez de la Frontera, but Catalunya has a longer history of production. Catalan brandy is aged in individual casks (not by the solera blending system used in Jerez) and is usually transferred to older casks for longer maturing, resulting in a quality spirit more similar to armagnac and cognac

aiguardent: the colloquial term for any distilled spirit

anis: clear, aniseed-flavoured liqueur; available sweet or dry and sold in faux cut-glass bottles

Armagnac: high-quality brandy from Gascony (with a pedigree predating that of cognac by some two hundred years), long-aged in oak casks

Byrrh: a wine-based aperitif blended with medicinal plants, cocoa and orange peel; made in Thuir, near Perpignan

cerveza: beer. Most beer is sold in bottles or as draught in small beer glasses (cañas). The majority of the beers available at Andorra's bars are standard international brews sold from the tap, particularly with regard to the French offerings. However, two of the most popular Spanish brands have stronger local connections: Damm is the name of a Catalan brewing firm which was established in Barcelona during the late 19th century. Their Estrella Pilsener is one of Spain's most popular lagers and is a real thirst-quencher. Their Edel all-malt beer is a richer, more mellow brew. San Miquel is regarded as the most quintessentially Spanish beer, yet it is in fact only a recent import into Spain. It actually originated in Manila in the Philippines (once a Spanish colony), where it was brewed by Spanish monks. Production was then brought to Spain in the mid-1950s and begun in Lleida province, using water from an aquifer of the River Segre (into which Andorra's Valira River flows)

Hypocras Ariègeois: ancient tonic of wine, medicinal plants, rose petals, ginger and spices; made in Tarascon-sur-Ariège and named after Hippocrates

licor de naranja: Spanish orange-flavoured liqueur; some of the best are produced by Catalan firms Torres and Mascaró

liqueur de violette: subtle violet-flavoured digestif from the Toulouse area

sidra: cider; common in the Pyrenees, although the most readily available are bottled Spanish brands from Asturias

LIGHTER DRINKS

aigua: water. The Pyrenees have a plethora of natural springs and many brands of bottled water: Font Vella, Vichy Catalan and Luchon are the most frequently served in Andorra.

The Principality once had its own bottled Aigua d'Andorra called Font d'Arinsal from the ski resort of Arinsal, although stocks are dwindling fast because the bottling plant has now closed.

Many villages have public drinking fountains and tap water quality is generally excellent, however, following a contamination incident in Soldeu a few years ago, visitors are now advised to drink only bottled water when in the region. Bars and cafés are happy to serve a bottle of water on its own to customers

café: coffee. With breakfast, or even just as breakfast, as a mid-morning and afternoon pick-me-up, after dinner and at just about any other social encounter, a coffee is as much of a national institution in the Franco-Hispanic world as 'a nice cup of tea' is in the UK. The variations in preference are wide-ranging: **descafeinado** is decaf; **café solo** is a small, very strong black coffee; **cortado** is basically a café solo but with a little milk; **café con leche** is a more familiar standard-sized coffee with more milk (same as the French-style café au lait); **carajillo** is a cafè solo with a nip of spirit added, usually brandy – or you can also ask for a carajillo de... and name your poison

horchata: this is the name for various non-alcoholic, energy boosting, nutritionally rich drinks made with tiger nut milk (*chufa*) or barley milk (*ordi*)

sangría: a punch-like blend of wine, spirit, fruit juice and fresh fruit in any number of local recipe variations; more of a refreshing summer drink from the Spanish coast, but readily available throughout Andorra

DELICATESSENS AND GOURMET SHOPS

La Casa Marquet Gourmet delicatessen, serving oysters at the front door and with half-a-dozen dining tables inside in case you get immediate munchies. Also has a branch at Carrer de Bearn, Pas de la Casa. ⓐ Avinguda Carlemany, 44 Escaldes-Engordany

La Casa del Formatge Speciality cheese emporium. Also houses a restaurant called 'Cheese's Art', featuring fondues served in scooped-out loaves. ⓐ Avinguda Carlemany, Escaldes-Engordany

Cava Benito Liquor store specializing in fine and rare wines, whiskies, armagnacs and cognacs. ⓐ Avinguda Carlemany, 82 Escaldes-Engordany

Vives Established since 1895 and specializing in fine chocolates and pastries. Their premises at Carrer Josep Viladomat have an open workshop for observing the team of confectioners at work. ⓐ Avinguda Meritxell, 84 Andorra la Vella; also at Plaça Coprínceps, 1 Escaldes-Engordany and Carrer Josep Viladomat, 38 Escaldes-Engordany

Caves Manacor Huge duty-free supermarket located just 400 m (438 yd) down the main road from El Tarter (bus stops outside). Stocks a massive range of whole hams, cured meats and salamis, spirits and liqueurs. Offers free sample-tasting on selected products. ⓐ Presa de Ransol, km 16 El Tarter

ⓘ Remember, Andorra is not in the EU. Please check our website **www.ski-ride.com** for current customs allowances.

LANGUAGE
Phrasebook

PARLES CATALÀ? DO YOU SPEAK CATALAN?

Having even a basic insight into the language of the country you're visiting will help enormously in getting the maximum enjoyment from your stay. It will help you engage more readily with your hosts and speed up assistance when you require help.

Andorra is the only country in the world to have Catalan as its official language. The language is the regional language of Catalunya, spoken all along this border region from Valencia in Spain to Perpignan in France, as well as in the Balearic Islands. Most of the tourism service personnel you will encounter will speak Spanish (Castellano), but around the Pas de la Casa area, many of the bar and restaurant staff also speak French; most speak or understand some English.

The following is a selection of words and phrases most needed on a snowsports holiday, including a few basics in Catalan:

ENGLISH	SPANISH	FRENCH	CATALAN
Hello	*Hola*	Bonjour	*Hola*
Good morning	*Buenos días*	Bonjour	*Bon dia*
Good afternoon	*Buenas tardes*	Bon après midi	*Bona tarda*
Good evening	*Buenas tardes*	Bonsoir	*Bona tarda*
Goodbye	*Adios*	Au revoir	*Adéu*
Please	*Por favor*	S'il vous plaît	*Si us plau*
Thank you	*Gracias*	Merci	*Gràcies*
Sorry	*Perdón*	Pardon	*Perdoni*
How are you?	*Cómo estás?*	Comment allez-vous?	*Com estàs?*
I don't understand	*No lo entiendo*	Je ne comprends pas	*No ho entenc*
How much?	*Cuánto vale?*	C'est combien?	*Quant val?*
Where is...?	*Dónde está...?*	Où est...?	*On es...?*
Yes	*Si*	Oui	*Si*
No	*No*	Non	*No*

ENGLISH	SPANISH	FRENCH	CATALAN
Monday	Lunes	Lundi	Dilluns
Tuesday	Martes	Mardi	Dimarts
Wednesday	Miércoles	Mercredi	Demecres
Thursday	Jueves	Jeudi	Dijous
Friday	Viernes	Vendredi	Divendres
Saturday	Sábado	Samedi	Dissabte
Sunday	Domingo	Dimanche	Diumenge
Winter	Invierno	Hiver	Hivern
Summer	Verano	Eté	Estiu
One	Uno	Un	Un
Two	Dos	Deux	Dos
Three	Tres	Trois	Tres
Four	Cuatro	Quatre	Quatre
Five	Cinco	Cinq	Cinc
Six	Seis	Six	Sis
Seven	Siete	Sept	Set
Eight	Ocho	Huit	Vuit
Nine	Nueve	Neuf	Nou
Ten	Diez	Dix	Deu
Eleven	Once	Onze	Onze
Twelve	Doce	Douze	Dotze
Thirteen	Trece	Treize	Tretze
Fourteen	Catorce	Quatorze	Catorze
Fifteen	Quince	Quinze	Quinze
Sixteen	Dieciséis	Seize	Setze
Seventeen	Diecisiete	Dix-sept	Disset
Eighteen	Dieciocho	Dix-huit	Divuit
Nineteen	Diecinueve	Dix-neuf	Dinou
Twenty	Veinte	Vingt	Vint
Thirty	Treinta	Trente	Trenta
Forty	Cuarenta	Quarante	Quaranta
Fifty	Cincuenta	Cinquante	Cinquanta
Sixty	Sesenta	Soixante	Seixanta
Seventy	Setenta	Soixante-dix	Setanta
Eighty	Ochenta	Quatre-vingts	Vuitanta
Ninety	Noventa	Quatre-vingt-dix	Noranta
Hundred	Cien	Cent	Cent
First	Primero	Premier	Primer
Second	Segundo	Deuxième	Segon
Third	Tercero	Troisième	Tercer

ENGLISH	SPANISH	FRENCH
PHRASES		
Do you speak English?	*Hablas inglés?*	Parlez-vous anglais?
I would like...	*Quisiera...*	Je voudrais...
Could you help me?	*Me podria ayudarme?*	Pouvez-vous m'aider?
Could you show me?	*Me podria indicar?*	Pouvez-vous me l'indiquer?
Where are the toilets?	*Dónde están los servicios?*	Où sont les toilettes?
I've lost...	*Se me ha perdido...*	J'ai perdu...
What time is it?	*Qué hora es?*	Quelle heure est-il?

ACCIDENTS / SICKNESS / EMERGENCIES		
I don't feel well	*No me siento bien*	Je ne me sens pas bien
Doctor	*Médico*	Médecin
I've had a fall	*Me ha caido*	Je suis tombé
I'm dizzy	*Tengo mareos*	J'ai des vertiges
It hurts here	*Me duele aqui*	J'ai mal ici
There's been an accident	*Ha habido un accidente*	Il y a eu un accident
Dentist	*Dentista*	Dentiste
I've got...	*Tengo molestias de...*	Je souffre de...
Constipation	*Estreñimiento*	Constipation
Diarrhoea	*Diarrhea*	Diarrhée
Earache	*Dolor de oido*	Mal d'oreille
Headache	*Dolor de cabeza*	Mal de tête
Stomach ache	*Dolor de estomago*	Mal d'estomac
Sunstroke	*Insolación*	Coup de soleil
Ankle	*Tobillo*	Cheville
Arm	*Brazo*	Bras
Ear	*Oreja*	Oreille
Eye	*Ojo*	Oeil
Hand	*Mano*	Main
Head	*Cabeza*	Tête
Foot	*Pie*	Pied
Leg	*Pierna*	Jambe
Wrist	*Muñeca*	Poignet
Condom	*Condón*	Préservatif
Tampons	*Tampones*	Les tampons

DIRECTIONS / PLACES / GENERAL		
Left	*A la izquierda*	À gauche
Right	*A la derecha*	À droite
Straight ahead	*Todo recto*	Tout droit

I've lost my way	Me he perdido	Je me suis égaré
Phonebox	Cabina teléfonica	Cabine téléphonique
Postage stamp	Sello	Timbre
Post box	Buzón	Boîte aux lettres
Post office	Oficina de correos	La poste
Supermarket	Supermercado	Supermarché
Tourist information	Oficina de turismo	Office de tourisme

AT THE RESTAURANT

Do you have a menu in English?	Tienen la carta en inglés?	Vous avez la carte en anglais?
Wine list	Carta de vinos	Carte des vins
Dish of the day	Menú del día	Plat du jour
Bill	La cuenta	L'addition
Bottle	Botella	Bouteille
Corkscrew	Sacacorchos	Tire-bouchon
Toothpick	Palillio	Cure-dent
Tumbler	Vaso	Verre
Wine glass	Copa	Verre
Beer	Cerveza	Bière
Draught beer	Caña	Bière pression
Red wine	Tinto	Vin rouge
Rosé	Rosado	Vin rosé
White wine	Blanco	Vin blanc
Water	Agua	Eau
White coffee	Café con leche	Café au lait
Beef	Carne de vaca	Boeuf
Bread	Pan	Pain
Butter	Mantequilla	Beurre
Cheese	Queso	Fromage
Chicken	Pollo	Poulet
Dessert	Postre	Déssert
Egg	Huevo	Oeuf
Fish	Pescado	Poisson
Ice cream	Helado	Glace
Lamb	Cordero	Agneau
Meat	Carne	Viande
Poultry	Aves	Volaille
Roast	Asado	Rôti
Salad	Ensalada	Salade
Soup	Sopa	Potage
Vegetables	Verduras	Légumes

ENGLISH	SPANISH	FRENCH
SKI TERMS		
I'd like a ski pass	*Quisiera un skipass*	Je voudrais un forfait de ski
...to ice skate	*Patinar*	Patiner
...to rent	*Alquilar*	Louer
Avalanche	*Avalancha*	Avalanche
Bindings	*Fixacions*	Fixations
Button lift	*Remonte*	Téléski
Cable car	*Teleférico*	Téléphérique
Chair lift	*Telesilla*	Télésiège
Gloves	*Guantes*	Gants
Gondola	*Telecabina*	Télécabine
Goggles	*Gafas de esqui*	Lunettes de ski
Cross-country skiing	*Esqui de fondo*	Ski de fond
Mountain	*Montaña*	Montagne
Passport photo	*Foto*	Photo d'identité
Ski boots	*Botas de esqui*	Chaussures de ski
Ski lessons	*Clases de esqui*	Leçons de ski
Ski poles	*Bastóns de ski*	Bâtons de ski
Skis	*Esquis*	Skis
Ski wax	*Cera para esqui*	Fart à ski
Socks	*Calcetines*	Chaussettes
Snowchains	*Cadenas de nieve*	Chaînes de neige
Suncream	*Crema solar*	Crème solaire

TEMP:	°C	-25	-20	-15	-10	-5	0	5	10	15	20	25	30
	°F	-13	-4	5	14	23	32	41	50	59	68	77	86

PREPARATION FOR SNOWSPORTS

It's all too easy in these times of low-cost travel and rapid communications to forget that you're travelling from a relatively benign temperate climate straight into Arctic conditions. Furthermore, you're going to be careering around this wild and inhospitable environment standing on two planks or a tray, moving at the speed of a car with not much more than a knitted beanie and a pair of padded gloves to protect you! The only way to ensure your safety and get maximum enjoyment out of your trip is to have respect for the seriousness of the situation you're putting yourself in and prepare accordingly.

Preparation begins at home: join a gym, ride a bike or just walk further and more often. The best and safest skiers and snowboarders are fit ones.

Once in your resort, warm-up at the start of each day and after rest breaks. A few minutes' stretching and/or jogging on the spot will pay dividends in your ability to sustain activity and avoid injury.

Weather conditions in the high mountains change rapidly and dramatically, so dress for all eventualities – it's easier to cool down than it is to warm up. Most heat loss occurs through your head, so always wear a hat. In the tricks parks and when freeriding, wear a helmet – all the best riders do.

ESSENTIAL ITEMS

Carry the following items with you on the mountain:

- water
- sunblock for skin and lips
- a piste map
- spare clothing
- high-energy snacks
- basic first-aid kit

PROTECTING YOURSELF FROM THE EFFECTS OF ALTITUDE

Temperature is inversely proportional to altitude: the higher you go, the lower the temperature drops.

Every 100 m (328 ft) rise in altitude above sea level equates to a shift north of around 161 km (100 miles). By the time you get up to 2500 m (8203 ft) that's equivalent to going from London to the Arctic Circle.

Conversely, the sun's radiation increases with altitude. For every 100 metres you go up, solar UV intensifies by about 2 per cent; so at 2500 metres you're being fried twice as quickly as you would be on a Mediterranean beach.

On overcast and snowy days, the clouds only disperse the UV-rays but don't stop them. Sunscreens absorb a set percentage of the UV reaching you; only a total sunblock and technical eyewear will provide maximum protection. Don't forget that snow reflects the sunlight and UV-rays – make sure you protect under your chin, below and behind your ears, under your nose and your eyelids. Goggles provide all-round protection and enhanced visibility; sunglasses are fine for wearing on the terraces or strolling around a resort, but they're not for riding in. Wearing a hat not only keeps you warm, but protects you from sunstroke too.

Dehydration is a problem in all active sports. When you add an increase in altitude to the equation, the problem becomes compounded and potentially fatal. Dehydration leads to fatigue, and tiredness is the primary cause of most accidents, injury and hypothermia. The best way to ensure that you're well hydrated is to start that way and maintain a good fluid balance throughout the day. The trick is to sip water or isotonic fluids little and often. Invest in a hydration backpack or carry a couple of bottles of water with you.

GEAR SAFETY

Ski boots weren't designed for walking on the piste. On steep slopes it's always safer to keep your skis or snowboard on. If you take them off and there's ice underfoot you'll have even less control than you had with your gear on.

When you do take your gear off, make sure that it is secured. If your skis or board slide away they can severely injure or kill someone in just the few seconds it takes them to pick up velocity. Legally you are responsible: this is not an accident but an avoidable lack of care.

Put your gear in a rack if there is one available. If not, make sure you set your board down upside-down so that your bindings dig into the snow. Skis should be set down with their brake legs digging into the snow or placed upright and rammed deep into the snow where they can't run away if they fall over. Don't lean gear on the sides of cable car cabins or on flat walls. It will slide off and knock down others and they're just like a guillotine when they come crashing down.

AU DELÀ DE CE PANNEAU VOUS ENTREZ DANS
UN DOMAINE HORS PISTE À VOS RISQUES ET PÉRILS
NI BALISE - NI SÉCURITÉ - NI PATROUILLE

THIS IS WHERE THE SKI SLOPES END
CONTINUE AT YOUR OWN RISK
NO MARKERS - NO BARRIERS - NO PATROLS

AN DIESEM SCHILD ENDEN DIE PISTEN
WEITERFAHRT AUF EIGENE GEFAHR
KEINE MARKIERUNGEN - KEINE ABSICHERUNG - KEINE PATROUILLEN

AVALANCHE RISK WARNINGS

Plain yellow flag = risk levels 1 to 2:
low to moderate probability of avalanche

Chequered yellow and black flag = risk levels 3 to 4:
moderate to high probability of avalanche

Black flag = risk level 5:
absolute risk of large avalanche

❶ Zero risk does not exist! Always be aware and prepared.

OFF-PISTE

❶ Check if your insurance policy covers off-piste skiing then follow these rules for optimum safety:
● Never leave the marked ski area on your own, it's safest to travel in groups of three persons minimum.
● Unless you know the area like the back of your hand, always employ a qualified mountain guide.
● Never blindly follow someone else's tracks, they may lead in the wrong direction or even off a cliff!
● Always carry the essential off-piste kit: avalanche transceiver, shovel, probe, map and compass.

If travelling off-piste in glacial areas you should also carry a climbing rope, harness, ice screws, carabiners and rope ascenders/foot slings. However, these items are only effective if you know what they are for and how to use them properly. Many resorts run avalanche awareness and safety equipment training courses. The golden rule is: get wise or get lost!

◀ *Piste signs and markers have been put there by mountain professionals – respect them! They are there not just to protect you, but to protect others too*

SLOPE RULES & REGULATIONS

The International Ski Federation (FIS) has set rules for slope users. These have established a legal precedent. Failure to abide by these rules may result in your ski pass being annulled and you may be banned from using the installations and the slopes. If you cause injury or death you may also be charged with negligence or manslaughter. The following is a summary:

1. Slope users must not endanger others.
2. You must adapt speed and behaviour to your ability and to current conditions.
3. The slope user in front always has priority.
4. When overtaking, leave room for those in front to manoeuvre.
5. Check uphill and downhill before you enter, start or cross pistes.
6. Only stop at the sides of the piste. If you have fallen, clear the slope quickly.
7. When moving up or down on foot, keep to the side of the piste.
8. Respect all piste signs and station information.
9. In the case of accidents, always give assistance.
10. You must give your identity to the Piste Patrol, Emergency Services and other accident victims when requested.

INSURANCE

Accident insurance is not included in ski pass prices. Make sure you are adequately covered or take the insurance supplement. Never travel without comprehensive winter sports travel insurance and always ensure that you are covered for on-mountain rescue and transport to hospital, on top of medical treatment and hospitalization cover. Some sports, such as paragliding and snowmobiling, are not covered by standard travel insurance and you will need to take out extra cover for these.

RESORTS & SKI AREAS
Ski Andorra

AN INTRODUCTION TO RESORTS & SKI AREAS

For such a tiny country, Andorra punches way above its weight when it comes to snowsports.

Since the first ski lifts were installed in 1957, the country's ski stations have continuously ploughed investment into extending their boundaries and upgrading their facilities, services, lifts and pistes. This consistent drive for improvement culminated in the winter of 2004/05 into two of the most important tourism initiatives in Europe and has boosted Andorran skiing into the snowsports superleague.

The already lift-linked stations of Pal–Arinsal agreed a joint marketing and commercial strategy with the little-known but exciting station of Ordino–Arcalís in the neighbouring parish. Although not linked by lifts, all areas now share one joint ski pass, increasing the value and choice for holiday-makers to this region of Andorra, now collectively marketed as the Vallnord ski domain.

The biggest news of that season though was the long-awaited commercial linking of Andorra's biggest and most internationally renown ski areas: Pas de la Casa–Grau Roig and Soldeu–El Tarter. The two ski areas had been physically linked for a number of years, sharing a couple of pistes in a historically disputed valley on the border between the different parishes in which the ski stations reside. The resulting super-domain, called Grandvalira, is a ski area of world-class proportions which now sits proudly in the club of Europe's top 20 ski areas for extent of pistes, lifts and facilities.

Vallnord and **Grandvalira** now represent the international face of Andorran snowsports and continue to be the most progressive ski stations in the Pyrenees. Continued investment and improvement is ensuring that Andorra remains a major player in the European market.

SKI ANDORRA

Andorra's snowsports stations have their own professional association, called Ski Andorra, which oversees the marketing of Andorra as a snowsports destination and implements initiatives constantly to increase quality and safety standards throughout the principality's ski stations. As part of their remit, Ski Andorra have introduced a consistent age policy across all Andorran resorts in respect of child and senior age groups qualifying for reduced rate and free ski passes, as well as promoting a single ski pass permitting access to all of Andorra's ski stations. This Ski Andorra Pass is available from all of the country's ski stations and entitles you to receive a local sector day pass at any of the resorts.

There are two variations of ski pass available, depending on the season:

1. **Low season**: permitting access on five consecutive days, Monday to Friday inclusive.
2. **High season**: permitting access on five days out of six consecutive days, including weekends.

High season is every weekend, the week leading up to Christmas until the week after New Year, all of February and Easter. Low season is all other periods.

ⓘ A passport-type photograph is required. Ⓦ www.skiandorra.ad

ALTERNATIVE STATIONS

Andorra also has a couple of lesser-known alternatives ideal for those for whom the larger resorts either don't cater or don't appeal: Nordic ski enthusiasts have their own dedicated cross-country ski station at La Rabassa (see page 62) near the Spanish border, while the Hotel Parador Canaro near Soldeu offers what could be described as a nano-resort.

LA RABASSA

This is Andorra's dedicated cross-country ski station, based on a tranquil high plateau straddling the Spanish border. The station is a 17 km (12 mile) drive from the town of Sant Julià de Lòria, south of Andorra la Vella. Equipment hire and instruction are available on-site, along with a range of complementary activities including snowshoeing, dog sleighing, inflatable tubes and skidoos. There is also an authentic mountain refuge with a lovely restaurant and a few rooms available for overnight stays.

The station has two green circuits of around 1.5 km (1 mile) each, a 5.5 km (3 mile) blue circuit and a 6.5 km (4 mile) red circuit. The peace and tranquillity of the area provide an insight into the true spirit of this Pyrenean micro-state and the views over the forests towards the imposing Serra del Cadi chain in Spain are sublime.
Ⓦ www.campdeneudelarabassa.ad

PARADOR CANARO

Situated in the Vall d'Incles, on the main road between Soldeu and El Tarter, Parador Canaro has its own gentle, lift-served snowfields offering absolute beginners and nervous novices a tamer environment in which to learn; ideal for visitors with young children who want to experience the joy of snowsports without the expense or hassle of visiting one of the major ski stations. The Parador is a lovely small hotel in a traditional stone-built building right next to Andorra's arterial road. There is free car parking and a bus stop nearby and the hotel's attractive bar and quality à la carte restaurant have a large sun terrace which overlooks the snowfields. Toboggans and ski equipment hire are available on-site and the operation has its own team of ski instructors.
Ⓦ www.paradorcanaro.com

INTRODUCTION

PAL·ARINSAL
LA MASSANA
ANDORRA

Located in the mid- to north-west of Andorra, in the parish of La Massana, the Pal–Arinsal ski area is formed by two lift-linked ski stations that were originally separate entities.

Andorra's first full-size cable car has linked the two ski areas since the 2000/01 season, although there are still no linking pistes. Further development and investment is under way, with the whole station now equipped with hands-free ski pass readers.

La Massana ranks fourth in Andorra's ancient protocol of parishes and is home to the greatest number of British expat residents. This parish also contains the greatest number of mountain summits including, at 2942 m (9652 ft), Pic de Coma Pedrosa, the highest peak in Andorra. To get an idea of the lie of the land, the Pal–Arinsal piste map provides a bird's-eye view over virtually the whole parish (see page 75).

SEVEN LEAGUE BOOTS
Left foot in Spain, right foot in Andorra: Pal–Arinsal has ski lifts at Pic de Cubil and Port Negre which go right up to the border with Spain so you can stand in two countries at once.

PRONUNCIATION
Pal Pal   **Arinsal** Ar~een~sal

◀ *Pic Alt de la Capa viewed from Arinsal village*

Although not as extensive or challenging as the more established resorts in the Grandvalira ski areas, Pal–Arinsal is still a major force in the snowsports economy of Andorra.

ARINSAL SECTOR

Arinsal village, the area's only true resort, is dominated by the English-speaking tour market as a result of the unbeatable deals offered by UK/Eire tour operators who market Arinsal as their lead-in price ski resort for 'beginners-on-a-budget'. The compact ski area, friendly ski school, Brit-orientated ambiance, cheap prices and rocking nightlife ensure that the resort consistently delivers to satisfied guests fitting this profile. It attracts some wider international clientele too: Spanish, French, Dutch, Belgian and even Israeli and Russian visitors (Pal–Arinsal was the first ski area in the Pyrenees to offer ski instruction in Russian).

The Arinsal sector of the ski area is, on its own, the country's smallest ski station, but combined with Pal it has more than enough to interest and test beginners and early intermediates. Confident beginners should be able to access all sectors by the end of their first week. More advanced visitors will have to be creative to keep themselves entertained, but the ski pass sharing agreement with Arcalís (see page 154) should provide an outlet for midweek blues.

PAL SECTOR

Pal takes its name from the hamlet of the same name tucked away in a quiet, picturesque valley just south-west of Arinsal. The hamlet has no lift links with the ski area and seems content to remain as an authentic and historically noteworthy Andorran rural hideaway, untainted by mass tourism except for a couple of roadside equipment rental outlets and one decent quality restaurant housed in a renovated old village barn.

The ski area of Pal is more extensive than that of Arinsal, with attractive wooded slopes and a more defined variety of pistes and terrain, reminiscent of some North American ski areas: pine-forested, well-groomed runs accessible from roadside parking areas and with a well-thought-out base day-lodge complex, without accommodation on-site.

A gondola lift was constructed in 2004, linking the ski area with La Massana, and has effectively grafted the town on as a ready-made 'resort', although it remains a working town at heart without the ambiance of a true ski resort. However, that is set to change rapidly now that the gondola link connects the town directly with the pistes, kick-starting new developments of hotels and services, initiating plans for traffic flow improvements in the town centre and providing an increasingly resort-minded focus. La Massana now boasts the closest ski area to the capital, Andorra la Vella, and the border with Spain, so it should, therefore, increase its already strong appeal to the Spanish weekend tourist market.

SOMETHING FOR EVERYONE

Pal–Arinsal markets itself as a 'Mountain Park', rather than just a ski area, with a host of alternative activities on offer and a mission to attract guests year-round, particularly families with young children. Although the villages lack any real alternative attractions for children, especially in the evenings, the ski area does provide admirable facilities and services to keep the little ones occupied during the day. As a result, Pal–Arinsal still offers Andorra's best choice for families and those visitors looking for a bit more than just a snowsports holiday.

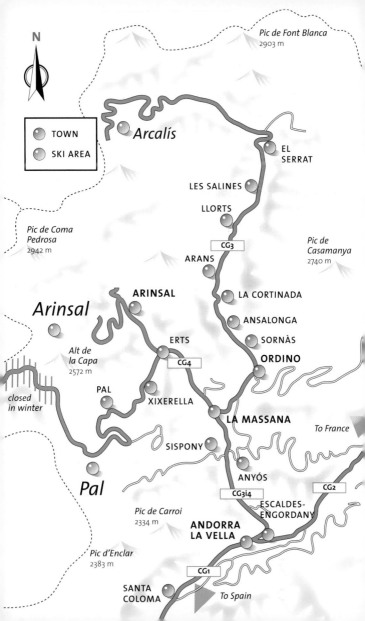

COMING & GOING

There are three main choices for getting to the ski area:

1. Gondola at La Massana.
2. Drive to the roadside lifts or base station at Pal.
3. Gondola at Arinsal.

La Massana, the area's main town and parish capital, is situated at the confluence of the Valira del nord and Arinsal rivers at the widest part of the valley, well below the actual ski areas. Principal access is from Escaldes-Engordany and Andorra la Vella via the tunnels on the CG314 road.

Almost immediately left and right past the tunnels are side roads leading to the hamlets of Sispony and Anyós. The main road continues on into the town centre of La Massana. Pass straight through if you are travelling on to Pal or Arinsal. At the far side of town you come to a mini-roundabout in front of La Massana–Pal gondola base station and covered car parking, for the first lift access point linking to the main base lodge at Pal. Alternatively, continue up the road straight ahead for 2.5 km (1½ miles) to the hamlet of Erts, where you can go straight on to Arinsal or turn left to drive up to Pal base station and the Coll de la Botella area.

DISTANCES
- Toulouse to La Massana   231 km (143½ miles)
- Barcelona to La Massana   226 km (140 miles)
- Andorra la Vella to La Massana   6 km (3¾ miles)
- La Massana to Pal   10.5 km (6½ miles)
- La Massana to Arinsal   4 km (2½ miles)

PAL

6 km (3¾ miles) from Erts, after an attractive, forest-lined drive via the hamlets of Xixerella and Pal, you arrive at a T-junction and the first on-piste access points for Pal ski area. An information cabin with a ski pass sales point is located right by the junction, making it possible simply to park your vehicle and hop on the roadside ski lifts just after the junction. Turn right to get to the lifts serving the most challenging pistes and/or to continue up towards the Setúria sector access point and cable car to Arinsal. Alternatively, turn left at the junction for lifts serving gentler pistes and to continue up to the main Pal sector base station. Spare a thought for the Tour de France cyclists who raced up this steep hillclimb on the famous race's special section in Andorra.

ARINSAL

From Erts, it is only 1.5 km (1 mile) to Arinsal. The village is strung out along the main road and the parallel course of the Arinsal River in three distinct zones, which are all served by a ski bus service:
1. a cluster of residences around the Hotel Sant Gothard, then
2. the residential and tourist resort centre with the main Arinsal gondola and open car parking at its core, before continuing to
3. a satellite accommodation zone and car park at Cota 1550 m.

This upper area has a chair-lift link direct to Arinsal's main 1950 m base station and, when conditions allow (which is rarely), you can ski back down to this 1550 m (5084 ft) level car park. From here the road finally climbs all the way to the 1950 m base station.

● *Bird's-eye view of Arinsal from the gondola*

ARINSAL TOWN PLAN

KEY

i	Information office	⊠	Equipment hire shop
🚠	Gondola	P	Parking
🚌	Bus stop	€	ATM
☎	Public telephone	🏬	Supermarket
⊠	Post box	+	Pharmacy
🎿	Ski pass kiosk	✝	Church

HOTELS & APARTMENTS

1. Hotel Solana
2. St Moritz Apartments
3. Hotel Micolau
4. Hotel Coma Pedrosa
5. Hotel Montane
6. Hostal Poblado
7. Poblado Apartments
8. Hotel Ayma
9. Hotel Arinsal
10. Hotel Princesa Parc

RESTAURANTS (see page 140)

1. Micolau
2. Cisco's
3. El Moli

BARS & CLUBS (see page 142)

1. La Solana
2. El Derbi (Darby O'Gills)
3. Cisco's
4. Surf
5. El Cau
6. Quo Vadis
7. Bogart's

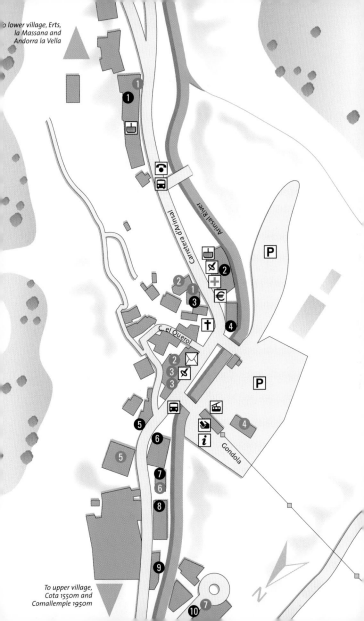

To lower village, Erts,
la Massana and
Andorra la Vella

Carretera d'Arinsal

Arinsal River

el Querol

Gondola

To upper village,
Cota 1550m and
Comallemple 1950m

N

SKI AREA DATA

- Opening time — 08.30 hours
- Last lift up — 17.00 hours
- Skiable area — 707 ha (1747 acres)
- Altitude — 1550–2560 m (5085–8399 ft)
- Vertical drop — 1010 m (3314 ft)
- Access points — 6
- Ski schools — 2

- Ski lifts — 30

Cable cars	1	*Gondolas*	2
Chair lifts	12	*Button lifts*	10
Mini-buttons	2	*Rope tows*	2
Conveyor belts	1		

- Capacity — 31,700 passengers/hour

- Pistes — 41 (= 63 km/39 miles)

Green	4	*Slalom*	1
Red	16	*Mogul*	1
Blue	17	*Children's*	2
Black	4	*Halfpipes*	1
Nordic	0	*FIS*	5
Tricks parks	1	*Carving*	1
FreeRide	2		

- Mountain bars/restaurants — 11
- Hands-free ski pass — Yes + Swatch Snowpass
- Snowmaking — 371 cannons
  19 km (12 miles) (30 per cent of total area)
- Medical centres — 2
- Visitor information — www.palarinsal.com

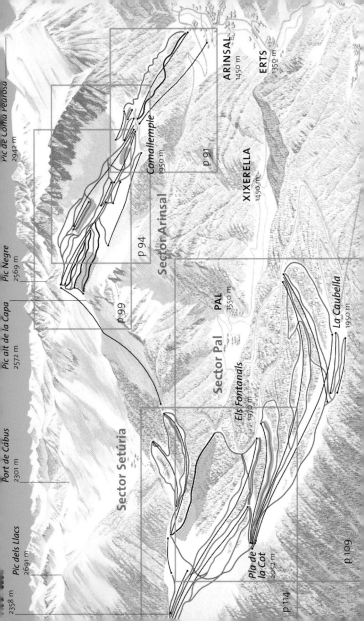

SKI PASSES

All the options available are Vallnord area passes (except local area day passes) covering Pal, Arinsal and Arcalís. A deposit is payable for a hands-free passcard, which can be kept to be recharged in the future or returned to the ski pass kiosk for deposit refund. The passcard should be secured in a left-hand pocket and operates the lift turnstiles by remote control.

High season = every weekend; the week leading up to Christmas until the week after New Year; all February and Easter.

Low season = all other dates (up to 20 per cent cheaper than high season).

All passes are available for adults (12–64 years) and children (6–11 years): half-day (first lift–13.00 hours or 13.00 hours–close); full-day and multiples thereof: the longer the duration, the cheaper the equivalent daily rate. Ski passes are free of charge for all children under the age of 6; for 6–11 year-olds prices are about 25 per cent cheaper than those of adults. To encourage the wearing of helmets, a small discount is also given on children's one-day passes if the child wears a helmet. Ski passes for guests aged 65–70 are available at a much reduced daily rate; passes are free for the over 70s.

A photo is required only for individual passes with more than four days' duration.

❶ Proof of age required for child and senior ski passes.

SKI ANDORRA PASS

See also page 61 for full details of the Ski Andorra ski pass, which permits access to all of Andorra's ski areas. This is particularly useful if you have your own vehicle and want to visit a different resort every day.

SKI PASS SALES POINTS

You can purchase any of the passes offered at any of the sales kiosks which are dotted around the resorts and base stations. The main sales points are at La Massana gondola base station building and at both Pal and Arinsal base lodges. There are also ski pass sales kiosks at the T-junction by the roadside ski lifts on the road from Erts to Pal; at the Coll de la Botella area in the Setúria sector; as well as at the gondola base in Arinsal and at the chair lift base at Arinsal's 1550m area. Vallnord passes can also be purchased at Arcalís ski station (see page 155).

NON-SKIERS

If you're a non-skier, but still wish to travel up to the base lodges at Pal or Arinsal, you can buy a 'pedestrian' pass for each journey on the main La Massana or Arinsal gondolas. There are no other lifts for pedestrians so, to join skiing companions, the only real option on foot is to meet up at Pal or Arinsal base lodge. It is also possible to drive up to both stations and there is an infrequent local bus service from La Massana to Pal base (see page 371). Having a vehicle also allows you to get to the Far West restaurant at the Coll de la Botella in the Setúria sector.

🛈 Accident insurance is not included in ski pass prices. Make sure you are adequately covered (see page 58).

> **PRICES**
> For current prices for all resort services, go to our website:
> **www.ski-ride.com**

SKI BUS

There are two lines operated by the ski bus service:

⊕ **Line 1**   La Massana ›› Arinsal
          Arinsal ›› La Massana

⊕ **Line 2**   Erts ›› Arinsal
          Arinsal ›› Erts

Timetables are posted by the bus stops and are available from the ski pass kiosks, most hotels and the tourist board. Note that times are subject to road conditions and passenger numbers.

A ski bus pass is required to use the service, costing a few euros for the duration of your stay; this can be added to and printed on to your ski pass if purchased at the same time. Ski bus passes are also available from the ski pass sales kiosks, some hotels and the Tourist Board office in La Massana. Naturally, the ski bus can be used by non-skiers too. All equipment should be stowed in the luggage racks under the vehicle.

The ski bus serves the main La Massana–Erts–Arinsal through-road only. However, most accommodation is within easy walking distance of the bus stops and you won't need the ski bus if you're staying in Arinsal centre.

Monday mornings are always hectic with newly arrived groups, so it may be best to walk at this busy period, particularly if you're within a few minutes of the lift station.

Arcalís is only accessible using the scheduled local bus service, by taxi, or on tour operator excursions – unless you've brought your own vehicle.

⊕ *See also pages 370–1 for details of regular local bus services.*

EQUIPMENT

Nearly every sports shop in Andorra has a snowsports equipment hire operation and, since virtually every other shop in Andorra is a sports shop, there is plenty of choice and competition. The largest rental operations in the area are Esports Pic Negre, Esports Rossell and Esports Amadeu.

Most visitors travelling with a tour operator tend to leave the organization of equipment hire to their reps. Newly arrived guests will then usually be taken en masse as a group early on their first morning on the mountain (normally Monday).

There are a number of hire shops in La Massana, Erts and Arinsal villages, as well as larger operations up at the Pal and Arinsal base lodges. Therefore, it is possible to travel up on the gondola in normal footwear before being fitted for your boots and equipment on-site. All of the largest hire operators offer equipment servicing, waxing, edge and base preparation and repair services for your own gear – at a cost.

➔ *See also page 207 for tips on identifying your gear.*

STORAGE

There are equipment locker rooms at the Pal and Arinsal base lodges, so you don't have to lug your gear up and down on the lifts each day. Two locker sizes are available:

1. Those holding up to four pairs of skis or four boards.
2. Larger ones holding up to 10 pairs of skis or 10 boards.

Both Pal and Arinsal base lodges have smaller coin-operated lockers for personal belongings, too. Most of the equipment rental outlets on the mountain will let you leave footwear in the shop, but it is not secured.

Boot storage is available at Arinsal base lodge only.

TUITION

The ski school employs over 160 instructors, many of whom are of British or Commonwealth nationality. Mother-tongue English and a similar sense of humour means there is no language barrier and an emphasis on fun, resulting in enjoyable and rapid progress. There are offices at both Pal and Arinsal base lodge areas, both with Slope School zones, beginners' slopes, children's Snow Parks and crèches (see page opposite).

Public group classes are grouped by language, ability level, age, ski and snowboard. Children aged 4–8 years old have their own separate Snow Park facility; from 6 years old they can join the regular classes out on the pistes, although every effort is made to ensure that they are grouped in similar ages. All package holiday guests join the 15-hour public group classes, which provide 3 hours' tuition daily over 5 days, Monday to Friday; 2- and 4-hour public group classes are also available at an additional cost on Saturdays and Sundays.

Reduced rate prices apply for children aged 6–11 years old. Private lessons are available for Alpine skiing, snowboarding and carving skiing, and must be arranged direct with the ski school. Prices charged for private instruction are per hour and are the same for adults and children. Prices also depend on the season and on how many of you there are.

➔ See page 209 for details of instructor qualifications.

CONTACTS
☏ Pal +376 737 008; Arinsal +376 737 029
✉ palarinsal@palarinsal.com

CHILDCARE

Gentle Snow Parks are fenced-off and equipped with Magic Carpet conveyors and mini-button lifts, colourful obstacles and cartoon statues, where specialist ski school nursery instructors introduce children aged 4–8 years old to the world of snowsports. This service is bookable for 2 hours, 3 hours, or 3 hours for 5 days. Ski hire is not included.

A crèche service, called Baby Club, for walking children aged 1–4 years is also available. Playrooms are bright, warm and well-equipped, with quiet zones for sleepyheads. Some outdoor activities, such as igloo- and snowman-building, are arranged depending on how cold it is, but mostly the children remain safely indoors participating in games and activities or watching cartoons. Staff mainly speak English, Spanish and Catalan. The service is offered on a 2-hour, half-day, full-day, and 5 x half-day basis. Snow Parks and Baby Clubs are tucked safely away to the side of the lower pistes, and parents may rest assured that they are all within easy reach and sight of the base lodges.

🔺 *Being little is a BIG thing*

SERVICES

Medical centres: well-equipped trauma and X-ray suites are located at Pal and Arinsal base lodges. They are accessible from the pistes, so that patients strapped into rescue-sleds can be skied to the door. They are also close to the roads and helipads should emergency transport to hospital be required.

The medical staff will contact your insurance company, but you will have to pay any initial costs, excluded by any excess clauses, on-site. Make sure your insurance covers heli-rescue, on-piste rescue and ambulance transport as well as medical and hospital expenses. Andorra is not in the EU and has no public health service; hospitals are very modern, but are all private.

ⓘ Always carry ID and your insurance details. It is also advisable to carry a small first-aid kit for dealing with minor cuts and bruises (see Health & Safety, pages 53–8).

WCs: located at the base lodges and free of charge. All mountain restaurants in Pal–Arinsal also have public toilets.

ATMs: cash machines are located at Pal base lodge (on the corner of the ski pass office) and Arinsal base lodge (in front of the gondola 1950 m arrival point).

ⓘ Please note that bank cards/credit cards are only accepted at the larger restaurants at the base station lodges. Smaller on-mountain venues accept cash only.

Telephones: phonecard-operated public telephone booths are sited at both base lodges and at Arinsal's 1550 m lift base. Phonecards are available from the base lodge shops. GSM mobile phone coverage is virtually 100 per cent.

Shops: as well as the equipment hire shops, both base lodges also house small 'boutiques' which stock a range of last-minute accessories including camera film, disposable cameras, sunblock, sweets, magazines, phonecards and souvenirs. They also offer an on-piste photograph service. Arinsal and La Massana are the most convenient bases for access to food shops.

Mountain restaurants: there are over a dozen watering holes dotted around the Pal–Arinsal pistes. Almost all are snack-menu orientated, with more extensive self-service buffet and à la carte options on offer at the base lodges. You're never far away from food and drink anywhere in the ski area and the choice on offer is fairly standard, although each on-piste restaurant also has a world culinary theme – Mexican, Chinese, American or Italian. Other than a couple of private enterprises located at the base lodge area at Arinsal, all the on-mountain bars and restaurants are managed by the ski station. Prices are consistent and are cheaper than in similar standard venues in the Alps. All offer a bar service and snack menu all day; more extensive lunch menus are served from 12.30–15.00 hours.

➔ *See pages 125–9 for specific reviews.*

Picnic areas: indoor picnic rooms are located at both base lodges, but it has to be said that they are very uninspiring. There is a reasonably nice outdoor picnic area nestled amongst the trees between La Caubella and La Serra chair lifts at Pal base lodge area; otherwise anywhere safe on the mountain is fine. The best view-point is at the Pla de la Cot area in the Pal sector. It is forbidden to picnic on any of the restaurant terraces. Please take all your rubbish plus any that you find to a bin.

SNOWFALL HISTORY & ANALYSIS

Although precipitation is unpredictable at very long range, patterns do emerge that are observable over a number of seasons. Using this data, you can tell if your preferred period of travel has historically seen good snow cover. The magic figure is 100 cm (39 in) – once snow depth exceeds this mark, conditions are generally good throughout the ski area and will remain so for a more extended period.

Snow cover during Christmas and New Year has generally secured the launch straight into high season, with the February school holiday period also having good cover. The charts also confirm the sound predictability of late spring snowfalls, often resulting in the best conditions of the season. The 2002/03 season was exceptionally good and the 2003/04 season superbly consistent. The seasonal pattern is fairly robust. Mid- to late-March is a good bet, with the bonus of cheaper holiday packages.

The chart below details combined averages recorded over three seasons immediately prior to the publication of this guide. Visit **www.ski-ride.com** for live snow reports.

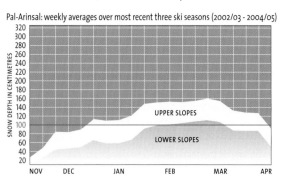

Pal-Arinsal: weekly averages over most recent three ski seasons (2002/03 - 2004/05)

PREVIOUS SEASONS' SNOWFALL BREAKDOWN BY YEAR

The following charts detail the snowfall history for the three most recent seasons. Data from these was used to compile the combined averages chart on the preceding page.

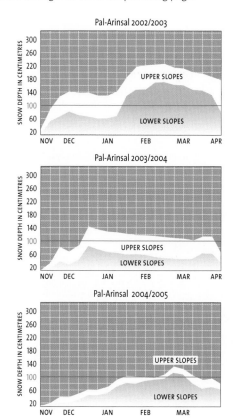

ARINSAL SKI SECTOR

When conditions allow, with good snow coverage down to the village, Arinsal can claim the greatest vertical in Andorra: 1010 m from Pic Alt de la Capa, all the way down to the lowest chair lift base at the Cota 1550 m area – that's over 3300 ft of non-stop descent! Arinsal's true on-piste starting point begins at the 1950 m base lodge at the top station of the gondola. This main area can also be reached by the chair lift at Cota 1550 m or by car, with no need to return to the village until the end of the day.

ELS ORRIOLS GONDOLA 28

4½ mins

- 500 m (1640 ft) vertical rise
- 1500 passengers/hour
- 08.30–17.30 hours

This is the main Arinsal ski lift departing from the centre of the resort. It gives the principal access to/from the Arinsal base lodge at 1950 m (6398 ft). Approach is via a metal bridge over the river from the main road running through the village. A ski bus stop is right in front of the bridge and a ski pass/information kiosk is just to the right of the get-on point.

As this is the main access point, queues can quickly build up, but usually aren't a major problem except on Monday mornings, when newly arrived groups are being guided en masse for their ski school induction. Skis/boards must be placed in the outside holders (assistance given), and poles should be taken inside the gondola. The arrival point is immediately in front of the Edifici Arinsal base lodge; the ski school, ski lifts and the pistes are located up the steps ahead right.

◀ *Arinsal gondola, with views to northern Andorra*

ARINSAL CHAIR LIFT 29

9½ mins

- 400 m (1312 ft) vertical rise
- 08.30–17.30 hours

Slow old chair which was the principal access point before the gondola was built. Skis must be placed in the holders behind your chair (assistance given), boards must be hand-carried. Departs from the Cota 1550 m car park area, at the base of Les Marrades blue piste, and arrives on the base lodge roof terrace.

FIRST DAY & FIRST ACCESS

If you're with a tour operator, then Monday morning will usually be your first day on the slopes. You will be taken for your equipment fitting early on Monday morning, up at the 1950 m base lodge, before ski school begins at 10.00 hours. There are lockers available in the base lodge for your shoes.

1950 m BASE STATION

The snowline at Arinsal really begins at the Comallemple 1950 m base station area. This is the highest altitude reachable by road, with ample car parking, and is at the same level as the arrival point of the main gondola up from Arinsal village. The chair lift from the Cota 1550 m area arrives here too, on the rooftop terrace of the main base lodge services building. This four-floor base lodge (called the Edifici Arinsal) is the main services focus at this level: enter by the stairs from the car park; from the mezzanine area up the steps ahead of the gondola, or directly from the roof terrace.

BASE LODGE

Ground floor: souvenir shop and photo service; ski pass sales and information; ATM cash machine; lockers

First floor: equipment hire and accessories sales shops; snack bar; medical centre; interior stairwell and exterior stairs to upper floors; access to La Tossa II button lift

Second floor: meeting point; Internet café and chillout zone; WCs; self-service restaurant; picnic room (accessed from external stairs to rear of building)

Third floor: Panoramix cafeteria; rooftop terrace and Snow Bar; arrival/departure point of chair lift from/to Cota 1550 m area; access from/to pistes and ski lifts

The base lodge is plain and functional, but the panoramic views over northern Andorra from the rooftop terrace are superb. From the ground floor, steps lead up to the pistes, via a mezzanine access for the base station. The ski school office is on the left at the top of these steps, on the same level as the base lodge roof terrace, and to the right are the two main chair lifts.

Beginners are inducted into the ski school down on the flat wide area just to the side of the gondola. From here you can also safely walk over to the beginners' zone, the children's Snow Park, Baby Club crèche and the Refugi bar/restaurant.

> **ROAD ACCESS**
> From the centre of Arinsal village, it is approximately 7 minutes' drive up to the 1950 m base station.

LES ESCOLES

This is the name of the main beginners' piste here at the Comallemple 1950 m area at Arinsal base station. A gentle snow-field, serviced by its own short rope tow (lift 25), it is overlooked by the terraces at the front of the Refugi bar/restaurant. As this is the principal beginners' zone, the area is very busy with nervous, erratic skiers – which is a very good incentive to concentrate hard and quickly gain confidence so as to be able to move out on to the other pistes. Easy link to El Cortal chair lift.

EL CORTAL

A longer and steeper second beginners' slope in this main debutants' area. El Cortal 4-passenger chair lift (lift 27) serves the piste, although your instructor will keep you on the lowest, gentlest section of the piste on foot only to start. El Cortal green piste and El Cortal lift both run behind the Refugi bar/restaurant, not in front as indicated by the resort's piste map. The top of the piste is accessed via the chair lift; get off to the right on arrival. The top section has a profile more like a blue run, but gradually becomes gentle green in character, running behind and below the Refugi bar/restaurant to the get-on point for El Cortal chair lift.

SKI SCHOOL INDUCTION
Meet-&-greet instructors are on hand each Monday morning to ascertain whether you have any snowsports experience. Classes are then carefully graded to match your ability.

EL CORTAL CHAIR LIFT 27

4¾ mins

- 437 m (478 yd) long
- 2000 passengers/hour

Situated below and to the rear of the Refugi bar/restaurant, this lift presents most beginners with their first experience of using a moving chair lift. It is a slow-moving and easy-to-get-on lift, specifically geared and sited to serve this main beginners' zone. On arrival at the top, get off and go to the right to enter El Cortal green piste; or go left to enter Les Escoles green piste or to ski over to the main lifts and base lodge via the lowest section of Les Fonts blue.

This chair lift is also useful for exiting the Refugi bar/restaurant area, as otherwise you have to walk back to the main lifts and base lodge.

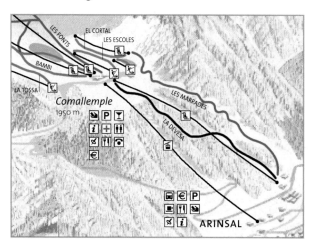

LES MARRADES

The lowest piste in the Arinsal sector is Les Marrades blue. The entrance is at the end of El Cortal green piste, on the far side of the crèche building. The run follows the route of a dirt track road, which winds in horseshoe bends down through quiet wooded slopes to finish at the base of chair lift 29 at the Cota 1550 m level. Unfortunately, due to the low altitude it is rarely open. But, when snow conditions allow, it's worth a go for the novelty of doing the area top-to-bottom. There's a bar at the finish, so toast your good fortune if you visit when this 'home run' is open. Word in Arinsal is that sufficient snow-making equipment will be installed soon to ensure that this route is more accessible.

Forget La Devesa black in this same lower area! Why it's still marked on the piste map is a mystery. It's never open, it's over-grown and unmaintained. Only after huge dumps of snow are first tracks put in by a few brave souls. These seldom-open routes simply allow Arinsal to claim the greatest vertical drop in Andorra.

● *Lower Arinsal slopes, towards the Refugi restaurant and beginners' area*

LA TOSSA II BUTTON LIFT 22

6½ mins

- 250 m (820 ft) vertical rise
- 1800 passengers/hour

A good queue-buster when the main chair lifts are busy. Departing from the bottom of La Tossa red piste and accessible from the rear of the base lodge, it provides a good link to chair lift 18 to access Arinsal's upper slopes and cable car link with Pal. On arrival, exit to the right via the link track to join on to the twin El Serrat red and Port Negre blue pistes to make the onward link to chair lift 18 or to descend to the base station area again.

BAMBI CHAIR LIFT 23

4½ mins

- 130 m (427 ft) vertical rise
- 09.00–17.00 hours

A short but relatively slow ride up to the MexicObelix restaurant at the crest of the hill just where the ski area narrows between the cliffs which tower over this area. This chair lift is often used by ski school groups on their first forays out on the mountain, so beware of frequent fallers as you exit from the chair. Immediately to the right on arrival is the MexicObelix restaurant and there's a gentle link route over to join the lower section of Les Fonts blue piste.

In front of the restaurant is button lift 20, which links with chair lift 18 up to the upper slopes. Immediately to the left is the start of the Bambi red piste, running under the line of the Bambi chair lift and, furthest left, the steep La Tossa red piste. Also to the left is the get-on point for button lift 21 which again links with chair lift 18 for the upper slopes.

LA TOSSA

A short but good red, often used for slalom competitions, and this area's steepest run. Accessed from the narrow, busy confluence area between the MexicObelix restaurant and the get-on point for button lift 21. To enter the piste, keep to the right below the level of the MexicObelix and ride over to the higher ground on the right. After an initial flat area over this crest, the piste then drops steeply and directly towards the base lodge.

This piste gives a good link to button lift 22 and to an entrance on to the first floor walkway of the base lodge, just beside the medical centre, for the quickest route to the car park.

BAMBI

Below the line of the Bambi chair lift, in the middle of the lower slopes area. The higher ground on the left of the piste is usually ungroomed and frequently mogulled: stay focused – everyone at the base lodge is watching!

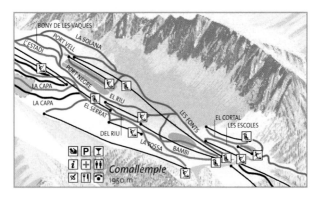

LES FONTS CHAIR LIFT 24

12½ mins

- 376 m (1234 ft) vertical rise
- 1690 m (1849 yd) long
- 2000 passengers/hour

Arinsal's principal chair lift, arriving just behind the Xina Igloo bar/restaurant and giving access to the upper area and the long cruising pistes which make up the bulk of this sector. On arrival, make a U-turn sharp right to enter Les Fonts blue piste. For all other options, leave straight ahead and swing round to the left to join the Port Negre blue piste. A couple of padded benches are positioned at the arrival area for securing bindings.

The entrance for the Xina Igloo restaurant is via a short track at the end of the fence on the left, as is the access to the FreeStyle Area tricks park. This direction also heads towards button lift 17 and chair lift 18, which will take you up to the Port Negre ridge and the cable car link with Pal; stay high on the right-hand side of Port Negre blue piste for the best traverse over to button lift 17.

LES FONTS

This is Arinsal's main arterial piste, running the entire length of the mountain from the Xina Igloo restaurant level all the way down to the base lodge; it provides well over 366 m (1200 ft) of vertical descent. Linked with Les Marrades blue piste, it will take you all the way to the bottom of the mountain.

After a very gentle start, passing under the line of Les Fonts chair lift, the piste becomes a wide motorway cruise with a couple of steeper, narrower sections to keep you on your toes. Beginners will be able to tackle this long, flattering run after their first few days of ski tuition.

PORT NEGRE

This is basically the twin of Les Fonts blue piste, but on the opposite side of the mountain. The top section is a busy confluence zone for several upper area slopes, which join together here and continue as this wide motorway blue. Staying high on the right-hand side at the start gives a fair link over to button lift 17. The upper- and mid-sections are very gentle, running parallel to the line of chair lift 18. A fence runs down the centre of the run, splitting it into two marked pistes. Keep left to stay on the Port Negre; going to the right takes you on to El Serrat red piste. Descending straight down on either piste gives a good link to chair lift 18 or on down to the base lodge via the MexicObelix area.

The route splits into two just above the arrival point of button lift 20. To the left it becomes El Riu blue and crosses over to join the main Les Fonts blue piste, continuing straight down to the right of the button lift it is called Del Riu blue, but this is basically just the continuation of the same main Port Negre.

OFF-PISTE INITIATION

To the left of the Port Negre piste, a hulk of rocky higher ground and a deep ravine separates the two sides of the ski area. Fenced off, but with few dangers for those competent enough, the ravine presents a good introduction to off-piste, when snow cover is good. The best way in is above the arrival point of button lift 20. Steep side walls drop to the narrow ravine floor, providing a gentle exit to the far side of the hill to join Les Fonts blue piste.

❶ See page 57 for safety information when going off-piste.

FREESTYLE AREA

Spread over an area of 40,000 sq m (47,840 sq yd), Arinsal's FreeStyle Area is a well-maintained tricks park, designed and maintained by professional international riders for maximum enjoyment.

The area boasts a halfpipe, rails, kickers, big air jumps, and a permanent Ski/BoarderCross course, plus a chillout zone with padded benches and music system. The park is served by its own button lift (19) and Arinsal has a Pipe Dragon piste groomer exclusively for the daily maintenance of this area. The halfpipe conforms to the official FIS (International Ski Federation) measurements – 110 m (360 ft) long, 15–17 m (49–55 ft) wide, with walls that are 4–5 m (13–16.5 ft) high – and the kickers and rails are well set out to give a decent in-line run. Layout varies depending on snow cover, but is fairly consistent thanks to regular attention from a dedicated maintenance team.

The park hosts frequent events and competitions throughout the season, particularly at weekends, and is one of the star attractions of this sector. Use is unrestricted, but it's not for absolute beginners. The nearest refreshments and food are available at the Xina Igloo bar and restaurant, situated by the arrival area of the park's button lift (19).

🔺 *Aerial view of the FreeStyle Area*

EL COLL BUTTON LIFT 17

| | 3½ mins | ⚠ | • 210 m (689 ft) vertical rise
• 1800 passengers/hour
• Closes 16.30 hours |

A tool point is located by the fence ahead left on arrival. This steep
button lift is the fastest link to the Port Negre area and upper
slopes. Leave straight ahead to link with the Arinsal-Pal cable car;
or turn left along the ridge for the Tubo del Coll black and La Pala
red pistes or to link to button lift 16; or U-turn to the right on
arrival for L'Estadi red piste or to join the link track which swings
left across Pic Negre towards the Port Vell and La Solana blue
pistes, with the Bony de les Vaques blue run accessed by dropping
off the right-hand side of this track. This direction will also take
you towards the Xina Igloo and the FreeStyle Area.

PORT NEGRE CHAIR LIFT 18

| 4 | 10 mins | • 342 m (1122 ft) vertical rise • Closes 16.30 hours
• 2400 passengers/hour
• 1330 m (1455 yd) long |

This is the principal lift to the Port Negre upper area and the link
to the Arinsal–Pal cable car. The lift arrives almost on the border,
Spain lies just ahead, with great views towards the Pal and
Setúria sectors. Exit on the track dropping down to the left
towards the flat, busy Port Negre saddle area. At the bottom of
this arrival track turn right for the short flat link to the cable car,
or veer left out on to the saddle area for all other options to
Arinsal's upper area slopes. For confident beginners, this chair lift
offers true top-to-bottom access for 550 m (1800 ft) of non-stop
vertical descent. Use the Port Vell or La Solana blue pistes to link
with the main Les Fonts blue.

PORT NEGRE AREA

This high pass is saddled between two high peaks, Pic Negre and Pic Alt de la Capa (see page 102), at the top of lifts 17 and 18 and the upper station of the cable car. The area is accessible for competent beginners and the views are fantastic: looking down over the Arinsal sector, with the cable car behind you, the impressive pyramidal bulk of Pic Alt de la Capa towers above right, putting Pic Negre immediately to your left. The summit of Pic Negre marks the international border and the ridges and peaks behind you are all in Spain. Swinging round, to look along the line of the cable car, you are now looking into the Setúria Valley sector and towards the Pal sector pistes.

The cable car is used to reach the Far West bar/restaurant, the snowmobile and dog sleigh circuits and to link towards Pal. The Port Negre area itself gives you access to all of Arinsal's upper area slopes, including Pic Alt de la Capa via lift 16. Pic Negre is used as a launch point for paragliding flights: trips in tandem with a qualified pilot are bookable at the main ski pass offices (activity available subject to weather conditions).

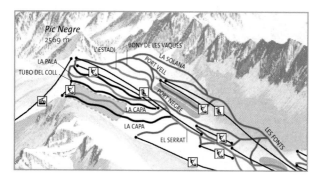

L'ESTADI

This piste is a good red, with a steep, wide, fall-line profile, often with some moguls, starting from the Port Negre area. To begin, follow the link route in the direction of the Port Vell and La Solana blue pistes then, just before the track swings left to go under the line of chair lift 18, drop off on to the face of the hill directly between the two lifts. The top section is a wide red motorway which then swings left under the chair lift into a great natural halfpipe gully. The exit brings you out on to the gentle Port Negre blue piste. Traverse immediately right for a good link with button lift 17, or continue straight down for chair lift 18 and Arinsal's 1950 m base area.

On the same hillside, just to the left of L'Estadi, is the easier Bony de les Vaques blue, which is reached from further along the upper link track. The drop-in at the start can be tricky but the upper section is then gentle. However, the lower section runs through a short gully which should be graded red rather than blue. The whole mountainside is wide and open, offering good freeriding on powder days.

PORT VELL & LA SOLANA

Both pistes are accessed by the busy link track from the Port Negre area. The track runs out into a wide pass: keep high left to enter La Solana blue straight ahead, or swing down to the right for the Port Vell blue. La Solana piste is the easier option, and it eventually joins up with the major Les Fonts blue piste. The Port Vell piste is steeper and descends through a wide but often choppy gully before schussing out to the Xina Igloo and FreeStyle Area located below.

TUBO DEL COLL

Accessed from the Port Negre area, using lift 17 or 18 or the cable car if arriving from Pal. Confusingly, the local piste map shows this run starting on the far side of La Pala red piste, yet it actually begins before it. From the Port Negre saddle, take the blue link ridge track in the direction of button lift 16 towards Pic Alt de la Capa. About 20–25 m (65–82 ft) along, the Tubo del Coll then begins by dropping off the left-hand side of the ridge. The entrance usually has a pronounced lip to drop-in over, straight on to a steep, good black profile descent which is often mogulled. The route then narrows into a steep natural halfpipe gully, before finally mellowing out after the mid-section to a fair red profile schuss joining with the lower section of La Pala red piste.

LA PALA

Along the ridge link track from the Port Negre saddle, La Pala red begins on the left just before the point where you would veer to the right to gain access to lift 16. The entrance, off the ridge, is immediately steep and has a good red gradient.

There are two main options for the descent:

I. Turn immediately right to traverse across the hillside to access a challenging black profile gully (this is the one marked on the piste map as the Tubo del Coll), or to access the open face of the Pic Alt de la Capa slopes and the FreeRide Area if lift 16 is closed; or
2. Take the direct route for a fast good workout on the main red pisted run to link with button lift 17 or to continue towards the lower Arinsal area via El Serrat red piste, which links well with lift 18. The actual route of La Pala, and Tubo del Coll, varies slightly each season depending on snow cover.

PIC ALT DE LA CAPA

This is the imposing pyramidal peak which towers over Arinsal, offering this sector's highest and steepest slopes. The highest lift-accessible point is reached via button lift 16, although this is seldom open because these exposed slopes often suffer from high winds. Fresh snowfalls are frequently blown off the mountainside, leaving the uppermost slopes bare and inaccessible. When the conditions are right, this area offers Arinsal's most thrilling rides and the feeling of having truly conquered the mountain.

Two routes are marked, both called La Capa – one red and one black – but the slopes are never fully pisted and the whole area is designated as a FreeRide Area, allowing users to experience an off-piste buzz within this safer, protected zone. It's a great place to build cheese wedge kickers, to launch off for some seriously big air when powder conditions provide a soft landing zone. Put your best posing head on though, as everyone on the lifts and at the Xina Igloo will be watching – but then you probably know that!

To access the area, use lift 16 from the Port Negre ridge or, if this is closed, follow the directions given for the alternative access from La Pala red run at the lower altitude (see previous page).

Once on the face, the most technical route is achieved by keeping furthest to the right when descending, with a couple of rocky outcrops to negotiate before running out on to El Serrat red piste, to lift 18 or to continue towards the lower Arinsal area. All lift links in this lower area are good.

The far side of the mountain, facing Pal, past the ridge fence which marks the ski area limit, is signed as 'off-piste' and looks inviting. However, please note that this descent is not used for good reason: the slopes face south and are very unstable. Only tackle them accompanied by a qualified mountain guide.

PAL–ARINSAL CABLE CAR 15

  6½ mins ▲▼
- 385 m (1263 ft) vertical rise
- 09.30–16.15 hours

The approach to/from the upper station is via a flat track from/to the Port Negre saddle area – keep to the right!

At the lower station, approach from/to the pisted area is just behind the Far West restaurant. An information kiosk and a helipad are located up on the road level above this area, and there is some roadside parking here, too.

The snowmobile, dog sleigh and snowshoe circuits also start here:
➔ *go to pages 130 and 132.*

For the Setúria sector slopes:
➔ *go to page 119.*

To access the Pal sector after arriving from Arinsal, take chair lift 13 straight ahead, then the Cami Superior blue piste towards Pla de la Cot:
➔ *go to page 118.*

Arriving at the upper station in Arinsal, simply walk out on to the Port Negre saddle to access the whole sector:
➔ *go to page 99.*

The cable car is easily reached even by novices, who can use the lift to go between the two ski sectors and make on-piste links between both base lodges. If you miss the last lift, return to the nearest base lodge and descend to the resort by gondola to take a taxi.

PAL SKI SECTOR

Following the cable car link with Arinsal, and now with a gondola link with La Massana town, Pal's profile on the international market has increased and adds extra interest and value to a snowsports holiday in this region of Andorra. The Pal sector has a very different character from that of its linked twin, Arinsal; gentle wooded slopes and a convivial family ambiance have been cultivated over the years to appeal to the area's main users – self-drive weekenders from Barcelona and its environs. The whole sector is accessible to confident beginners, but Pal's Cubil Mountain also offers the area's most enjoyable red profile cruising pistes, too.

LA MASSANA–PAL GONDOLA 30

5 mins ▲▼	• 2250 m (2462 yd) long • 1600 passengers/hour • 08.30–17.30 hours

Pal–Arinsal's most recent investment has been the construction of this main large gondola lift to connect La Massana town with the lowest slopes at Pal base lodge area, effectively grafting the town on as a ready-made resort and making La Massana a viable option as an accommodation base for this area. La Massana gondola base station is located at the upper end of town, at the start of the road up to Erts, Pal and Arinsal, and has covered car parking and a ski pass office. The arrival point is just beside the extensive base lodge and beginners' zone at Pal ski sector. It is possible to put gear on after arrival and ski away from the upper station towards the lifts and pistes ahead.

◀ Pal–Arinsal cable car, facing towards Cubil

LA CAUBELLA BASE STATION

The snowline and ski area at Pal begins at the La Caubella base station area. Reachable by road, with ample car parking, it is at the same arrival level as the gondola up from La Massana.

If you are arriving via the gondola, simply leave the building out on to the wide flat pisted area in front. Over to your left are the base lodge service buildings and the base of the main El Planell beginners' slopes. The gondola building also houses the station's Baby Club crèche service. The building nearest on your left is the ski school office, with class meeting point marker poles clustered on the pisted area immediately in front. There is a tool point fixed to the far wall of the steps which lead up the side of this building.

If you are arriving by car, there is ample free parking surrounding the base station, fanning out in a linear fashion away from the base lodge; a regular shuttle service runs round the outlying parking zones to ferry you to/from the central services and piste access. From the parking level, simply walk straight into the base lodge, or down the steps to the pistes. There are various alternative activities on offer at La Caubella: a short gentle toboggan piste, bungee trampolines and a children's skidoo circuit, all close to the gondola station.

The main base lodge is also quite extensive and offers good facilities, making it an ideal spot for non-skiing visitors to relax and watch/meet their skiing friends and family.

WCs are located on both levels of the main base lodge and there are also some built into the wall at piste level directly between the two main lodge buildings. If you run short of cash, an ATM is located on the corner of the ski pass office on the upper level of the ski school building.

BASE LODGE

Piste level: El Planell snack bar/café terrace; Esports Rossell rental shop; self-service canteen; arcade machines; WCs. The medical trauma centre is housed under the terrace and is accessed from the pistes over by the trees at the far corner of the building. Equipment and personal belongings lockers are also located under the terrace; entrance beside the medical centre. Stairs lead up to the first floor level from the side of the terrace as well as from the interior lobby in front of the self-service canteen.

First floor: boutique; Esports Caubella rental shop; Internet point; public telephone; Cafeteria La Caubella and bar; WCs; La Borda à la carte restaurant; access from/to car park level.

The base lodge is reasonably bright and attractive. The first floor cafeteria and bar are definitely the best quality in the area, with the sunny piste-side terrace overlooking most of the beginners' slopes. The whole area around La Caubella is sheltered by surrounding pine forest and is without doubt Andorra's most attractive children's/beginners' area. As picnics are forbidden on restaurant terraces, the station has provided interior and exterior areas at the ski school building, closest to the gondola station.

The El Planell green pistes sweep down to the foot of the lodge and the area is served by an easy-to-use ground level magic carpet conveyor belt ski lift. Chair lifts 3 and 4 are just a short walk/skate in front of the lodge, and El Beç blue piste flows gently away down to the right, to chair lifts 5 and 6.

If you're coming via the cable car link from Arinsal, then the whole base station is spread out in front of you as you approach on the El Planell pistes.

❶ Travel with care through this area as it is a novices' zone.

EL PLANELL

This is the name of the beginners' snowfield in front of the base lodge, flowing directly down to the foot of the main terrace and flat wide base station area, fanning out between the base lodge and the gondola building. The slope is gentle, wide and sheltered with woods to either side; lift 2 runs up the left side, serving the lowest slope, and is a simple-to-use conveyor belt, usually referred to as a magic carpet. To the right, chair lift 3 rises gently to the uppermost point on this main green piste and gives access to a couple of blue profile pistes to progress to once you're ready. Likewise, from the base of the El Planell green piste you can progress on to the wide gentle blue El Beç piste, down to take the Carbonera II chair lift (5) back up to the highest beginners' point to complete a full loop of this area.

From here you can then begin to move out into the rest of the sector by taking either La Serra chair lift (4) from the base station area or La Serra II chair lift (6), accessible from the bottom of El Beç blue, via the Pla de la Cot area at the Bella Italia bar/restaurant at 2052 m (6732 ft).

ONWARD LINKS FROM THE BASE STATION
Either take the slow (10½ minute) La Serra chair lift (4) or follow the El Beç blue down to the faster La Serra II (6). The El Beç blue route is the quickest and is a gentle warm up.

❶ For children, the ski school operates a Snow Park in the area immediately beside the start area for El Beç blue, in front of the ski school building.

LA SERRA CHAIR LIFT 4

10½ mins	• 193 m (633 ft) vertical rise
	• 1800 passengers/hour
	• 09.00–16.40 hours

Constant assistance from the lift operators is given on this slow beginners' area chair, which takes a gentle and almost horizontal journey through the treetops to arrive at the Pla de la Cot area beside the Bella Italia bar/restaurant.

Go to the right for the Corpalanca red (accessing chair lift 10 for onward links towards the Cubil area, Setúria sector and Arinsal); or U-turn to the right for the lowest, gentlest section of La Serra blue which flows down into El Planell beginners' area again; or U-turn right around the far side of the other chair lift arriving to the right to begin El Besurt II blue and to access El Besurt red; or simply go straight on for the Bella Italia and to take El Gall blue towards the Cubil area pistes and for all onward links.

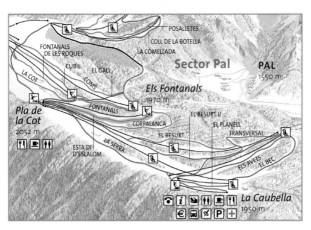

LA SERRA II CHAIR LIFT 6

5 mins

- 272 m (892 ft) vertical rise
- 2400 passengers/hour

This lift is definitely the best route out of the base station areas towards the main Pal sector and for onward links. It is reached by El Beç, Els Avets and El Besurt II blues, Transversal green and El Besurt red pistes; or from the roadside just below for the quickest access to Pal sector by car (parking and ski pass kiosk here too). Looking uphill, this lift is the one on the right (the chair rising from the left is the short La Carbonera lift serving the debutants area). On arrival, U-turn to the left between the two chair lift arrival points to join the lowest gentle section of La Serra blue piste which eventually runs down to the base lodge via El Planell green slope; or U-turn to the right to begin El Besurt II blue and El Besurt red; or go right for the Corpalanca red and onward links; or go straight ahead for the Bella Italia bar/restaurant and to start El Gall blue for all onward links.

🔺 *La Caubella base station at Pal*

PLA DE LA COT AREA

This is a wide plateau on slightly higher ground which interrupts the flow of the pistes travelling from the Cubil area. A rope tow (lift 8) helps with uplift through this flat section, although it's probably best not to use the pistes to pass through this area unless you're a novice, or simply wish to reach the Bella Italia bar/restaurant – the best bypass from the Cubil slopes is to descend all the way down to the base of La Serra button lift (7) and use it to bring you to the far side of the Bella Italia for the onward link, however this still requires a short inclined section past the other lift arrival points before you reach any real gradient.

One little-known feature of the Pla de la Cot area is the viewpoint on the rocky outcrop opposite the restaurant. Go round to the far side of the rope tow line and walk up on the far side of the fence to the highest point for great views over a deep valley and most of central and northern Andorra – a good spot for a picnic. The peaks across the valley are the Pic de Carroi, with the radio mast, and the Pic d'Enclar, highest right, on the Spanish border.

EL BESURT II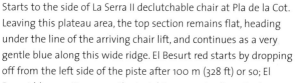

Starts to the side of La Serra II declutchable chair at Pla de la Cot. Leaving this plateau area, the top section remains flat, heading under the line of the arriving chair lift, and continues as a very gentle blue along this wide ridge. El Besurt red starts by dropping off from the left side of the piste after 100 m (328 ft) or so; El Besurt blue continues gently straight on, eventually swinging down to the left, crossing and merging with the Transversal green towards the get-on points for lifts 5 and 6. The lower section of the run is a much better true blue profile, even mild red.

EL BESURT

A variation from the blue piste of the same name, accessed by taking the same shared top section. The El Besurt red begins by dropping off to the left side of the upper blue run, immediately on to a wide, tree-lined decent red piste which is north-facing and so, although at low altitude, holds snow well. The route takes a fairly direct fall-line descent, before swinging out to the right into the trees to become a tricky narrow exit track ending on the Transversal green: check your speed here and beware of piste traffic coming from the right. The Transversal takes you for a further gentle few hundred metres to link with lifts 5 and 6.

Another option is to ride off the right of the piste at the point where it passes under the line of chair lift 6, shortly after the top section. You can then follow the steeper and deeper narrow clearing down the line of the lift's pylons. As before, exercise caution as you approach the Transversal junction point, particularly from this off-piste route, as there is a 2 m (6½ ft) drop-off to finish.

TRANSVERSAL

Although marked on the piste map as a green piste, this long winding contour-hugging route is quite narrow, can be very choppy underfoot from heavy usage and would be a challenge for true novices; it really should be treated as a good blue.

The piste follows the line of a hillside track which winds its way through peaceful, dense woods, crossing over the line of El Besurt blue piste and joined steeply from the left by the El Besurt red before running down to the get-on point for lifts 5 and 6. The gradient is mostly quite gentle, but the lack of turning space creates knots of slow-moving traffic.

CORPALANCA

A short, enjoyable red – the best way for good intermediates to quickly bypass the Pla de la Cot area en route to onward links towards Cubil Mountain, the Setúria sector and cable car to Arinsal. In good conditions, this piste is a fast, forgiving motorway that is an ideal first red for improvers wanting to progress to red standard. The Pista d'Eslàlom competition red course descends parallel to the left, although this is usually closed to the public. There are good links with lifts 6 and 7 at the bottom left.

EL GALL

Wide, gentle link route out of Pla de la Cot, traversing across the lower slopes of Pic de Cubil toward button lift 9 and met by all the best reds from this mountain. Eventually runs out to a very flat junction with the Coms red and La Comellada black exit track to make a poor link for lifts 7 and 10: better to reach these by leaving El Gall to the right and descending by one of the crossing reds.

LA SERRA BUTTON LIFT 7

  3 mins
- 82 m (269 ft) vertical rise
- 900 passengers/hour
- Closes 16.45 hours

A short, very steep button drag which links the roadside Els Fontanals area beside El Cubil chair lift (10) up to the Pla de la Cot. If you fall off, traverse through the trees to the left to join the Pista d'Eslàlom red to return and try again. On arrival, turn right behind the back of the Bella Italia restaurant (steps from here up to the terrace) towards El Gall blue; or turn left for the Corpalanca red, El Besurt II blue, El Besurt red and La Serra blue.

EL CUBIL CHAIR LIFT 10

11½ mins

- 461m (1513 ft) vertical rise
- 1375 m (1504 yd) long
- Closes 16.30 hours

Main link chair to the top of Pic de Cubil and for the onward link to the Setúria sector and Arinsal. Despite being a major link lift, this is a slow non-declutching chair and so plenty of time should be left to return to your home sector towards the end of the day. The Pic de Cubil slopes are Pal sector's best cruising reds and are home to the designated Bumps Area mogul field on the Coms red piste. The summit of Pic de Cubil also offers a fantastic 360° panorama over the whole sector and most of Andorra's peaks and borders beyond.

On arrival at the top, turn left for La Serra red; turn right for Cubil (+ Coms) red or the Tossa blue link towards Setúria/Arinsal.

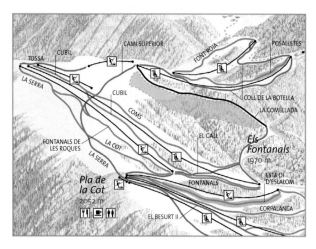

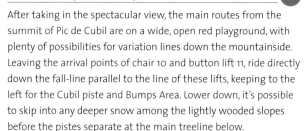

CUBIL / COMS (BUMPS AREA)

After taking in the spectacular view, the main routes from the summit of Pic de Cubil are on a wide, open red playground, with plenty of possibilities for variation lines down the mountainside. Leaving the arrival points of chair 10 and button lift 11, ride directly down the fall-line parallel to the line of these lifts, keeping to the left for the Cubil piste and Bumps Area. Lower down, it's possible to skip into any deeper snow among the lightly wooded slopes before the pistes separate at the main treeline below.

🔺 *Pic de Cubil slopes, Pal sector, viewed from Pla de la Cot*

The main Cubil run is a fast fall-line red, which descends directly to the base of the mountainside via the Fontanals red for good links with the La Serra button lift (7), for Pla de la Cot and onward links towards the base lodge area and El Cubil chair lift (10), to return to the top of Pic de Cubil again. The Coms piste mid section is designated as a Bumps Area mogul field, being left largely unpisted but safely maintained.

FONTANALS DE LES ROQUES / LA COT

These are a couple of fair reds which you can see sculpted into the upper left of Pic de Cubil in the Pal sector. They are accessed to the left on arrival from button lift (9) and chair lift (10). The start section is shared with La Serra red, signposted here as Serra Superior.

Shortly after starting your descent keep to the left of the piste to begin the Fontanals de les Roques red. For La Cot red, follow the upper route of La Serra out to the right but then take the wide sweeping turn to the left just at the point where La Serra begins to take on its blue profile traversing towards the Bella Italia restaurant area at the Pla de la Cot ahead.

Both the Fontanals de les Roques and La Cot pistes emerge on to La Gall blue below, making good links with El Cubil button lift (9) to return to the top of Pic de Cubil, allowing you to descend further via this blue or to cross over it and make the best links with button lift (7) and chair lift (10) via the short, fast Fontanals red.

LA TOSSA BUTTON LIFT 12

2 mins

- 3 m (9.8 ft) vertical rise
- 40 m (44 yd) long
- Closes 16.30 hours

A short, almost horizontal drag providing the link across the flat ridge towards the Setúria sector and Pal–Arinsal cable car. Approached from all Pic de Cubil summit lifts by turning right on arrival to traverse on to the wide Tossa blue – keep your speed up to make the best link. On arrival at the far end, keep straight on for Setúria or go ahead right, towards the fence, for La Comellada black and the FreeRide Area.

COMELLADA / FREERIDE AREA

Pal's only black piste, bordered to the right by lightly wooded glades designated as the FreeRide Area. Both are accessed from the Cami Inferior blue track, in the area by the fence 100 m (109 yd) in front of the arrival point of chair lift 13.

In good snow conditions, the steepest start for La Comellada piste is to drop in from the gap in the fence highest to the left. From the main wide entrance, the piste is immediately steep and is usually mogulled all the way down this top section. The FreeRide Area has exactly the same profile, but is an unpisted area in the woods to the right.

Both routes finish just above the roadside below, traversing out to the right following the line of the road as a very flat, long track towards El Cubil chair lift (10) and La Serra button lift (7). This area is definitely worth a visit, but the long and laborious slog out to the lifts dulls the enjoyment factor.

CAMI SUPERIOR / INFERIOR

Basically these are just the natural, contour-hugging link tracks running away from the top of chair lift 13 to link the Setúria sector to the main Pal sector: the lower, more rideable track, known as the Cami Inferior, also accessing the start of La Comellada black and the FreeRide Area.

Both tracks traverse diagonally across the slopes of Pic de Cubil (take care crossing the pistes and button lift routes). Neither track is too tricky and so can provide beginners with a route to Pal's La Caubella base lodge area all the way from the Arinsal sector. Intermediates can drop off on any of the reds en route for a more challenging descent.

COLL DE LA BOTELLA

The sole link route towards the Setúria sector from the Pal sector, beginning as a very gentle blue ridge track under the line of the arriving chair lift (13). After the flat top section, you emerge out on to the top of the Setúria pistes, with the chair lift (14) arrival point just to your left. Experienced skiers can go up over the high ground straight ahead or go left for the Font Roja and Posalletes reds; novices should keep furthest right for the easiest, but still choppy, descent known as El Colze – which isn't marked on the piste map. The El Colze meander rejoins in from the right and the Coll de la Botella continues as a wide blue straight down towards the Far West restaurant and Pal–Arinsal cable car station ahead.

Veer to the left to make a good link to chair lift 13 or, to continue your descent on this motorway blue, out left to below the Far West for the get-on point for the Setúria chair (14) which serves the two main reds in this sector (including the public Slalom Stadium).

LA BOTELLA CHAIR LIFT 13

- 242 m (794 ft) vertical rise
- 1030 m (1127 yd) long
- Closes 16.15 hours

Link lift from the Coll de la Botella area towards the Pal sector. On the journey up, the Coll de la Botella blue piste is directly below to your left; the Posalletes Slalom Stadium drops parallel to your right. On the uppermost section of the trip you get a great view over the Pal sector spread out ahead, giving you time to get your bearings and see where you're heading. On arrival, go straight ahead for the Cami Superior blue link track.

SETÚRIA CHAIR LIFT 14

4 mins

- 370 m (1214 ft) vertical rise
- Closes 16.15 hours

This is a reasonably short, quick chair with a decent vertical uplift, serving all the Setúria sector slopes above the Coll de la Botella area, but not making a link towards Pal. It departs from the bottom of the Coll de la Botella blue and Font Roja red pistes at the lowest altitude in this sector. The journey up is above the bird-song-filled woods of this peaceful valley, with views over the pistes, the Coll de la Botella area's Far West restaurant and the cable car station to the left and, to the right, over the Setúria Valley and up to the Spanish border.

On arrival dismount to the left, then go straight over to join the Coll de la Botella blue, or U-turn immediately left to begin the Font Roja red and to access the Posalletes red.

FONT ROJA

The Font Roja is a good but short red piste which shares a wide top section with the Posalletes slalom course, before looping out wide to the left to mark the ski area's most southerly limit. This piste is often very quiet and can usually be tackled at full tilt, before mellowing out as a gentle track over to the get-on point for chair lift 14.

If snow conditions are poor, the lower section of the run can be closed. In this case you will be diverted out to the right along the flat dog sleigh circuit traversing the hillside to join the lowest section of the Coll de la Botella blue to continue descending for the link with the same chair below.

POSALLETES SLALOM / CARVING COURSE

A good fast red, specially designated as the station's public access Slalom Stadium and Carving Course, beginning from the wide shared upper section of the Font Roja red at the top of this sector's slopes. Courses are varied every few days, set out either for Slalom, GS or Carving and usually only closed for competitions at weekends. There's a great view of the entire Posalletes route from the terrace at the Far West bar/restaurant, to which you have direct access from the piste by swinging right at the end of the course, past the get-on point for the La Botella chair (13). The fastest route to return to the top of the course is to carry straight on at the finish, veering left to continue down the lower Coll de la Botella blue to link with the quick, declutchable Setúria chair lift (14).

Outside of competition events there is no infrared timing system in place, so you'll have to rely on your buddies to time your run to establish that world-beating record.

> ### RETURN FROM SETÚRIA SECTOR
> Towards the end of the day, you'll need to return to your own resort sector. Link lifts close at 16.15 hours.
> For Pal/La Massana, take the La Botella chair lift (13) and follow onward links as per page 118.
> For Arinsal, take the cable car for onward links as per pages 100–101.

▶ Posalletes Slalom and Carving Course, Setúria sector

POINT-TO-POINT ROUTES: COMPETENT NOVICES

ARINSAL 1950 M BASE LODGE » PAL–ARINSAL CABLE CAR

Les Fonts chair lift (24) → Port Negre → Port Negre chair lift (18)

PAL–ARINSAL CABLE CAR » ARINSAL 1950 M BASE LODGE

Link track → Port Vell → Les Fonts

PAL–ARINSAL CABLE CAR » PAL (LA CAUBELLA) BASE LODGE

La Botella chair lift (13) → Cami Superior → La Serra → El Planell

---

PAL (LA CAUBELLA) BASE LODGE » PAL–ARINSAL CABLE CAR

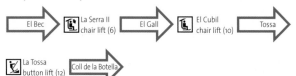

El Bec → La Serra II chair lift (6) → El Gall → El Cubil chair lift (10) → Tossa

La Tossa button lift (12) → Coll de la Botella

POINT-TO-POINT ROUTES: GOOD INTERMEDIATES AND ABOVE

ARINSAL 1950 M BASE LODGE » PAL–ARINSAL CABLE CAR

PAL–ARINSAL CABLE CAR » ARINSAL 1950 M BASE LODGE

PAL–ARINSAL CABLE CAR » PAL (LA CAUBELLA) BASE LODGE

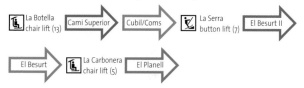

PAL (LA CAUBELLA) BASE LODGE » PAL–ARINSAL CABLE CAR

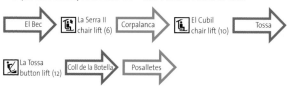

MOUNTAIN BARS & RESTAURANTS

With such a compact ski area, you're never far away from a piste-side bar or restaurant. Most are of the snack bar type, however there are a couple of larger, more serious restaurants, too. Where there is no table service you should pay at the till first, then take your order receipt to the food service counter. Prices are consistent throughout the ski area and are generally fair. All have free WCs. ◐ All offer an all-day bar and snack service. Lunch is served between 12.30–15.30 hours.

ARINSAL SECTOR

The main refreshment and eating zone in this sector is based in and around the Edifici Arinsal base lodge. The main food and drink services are on the second floor and the roof terrace, the latter easily reached from the main pistes.

DonkiNauta Situated on a mezzanine area of the second floor by the main interior stairwell. All-day Internet café and central meeting point: serves crêpes and sandwiches, freshly squeezed orange juice, coffee, canned/bottled drinks and some cocktails.

Self-service/Buffet Located just past the DonkiNauta bar on the second floor. A large bright canteen offering a fair selection of hot dishes, plus *menu del día*.

Panoramix Occupying the entire upper level of the base lodge, this is the main pit stop in this sector: huge roof terrace and Snow Bar, fair-sized interior seating salon and busy fast-food snack bar, offering sandwiches, chips, chicken nuggets, jacket potatoes, etc. The terrace overlooks this sector's lower pistes and has great views towards the peaks of northern Andorra.

◀ *Giant paella at Cafeteria Caubella, Pal base lodge (see page 128)*

El Refugi Overlooking the beginners' zone at the far side of the main lower slopes area. Restaurant, café-bar, sun terraces and WCs. A basic, but cosy, old mountain refuge building, popular with station personnel/instructors and usually packed at lunchtime. Ground floor restaurant offers a snack menu, a *menu del día*, salads, plus fresh meat dishes grilled to order. Rustic café-bar on upper floor offers a full bar service plus snacks and has its own upper roof terrace. The best way to exit this area when you're leaving to go back on the mountain is to take the El Cortal chair lift from the rear of the building, saving a walk across the pistes and giving you enough height to ride over to all other lifts and the base lodge.

MexicObelix At the top of the Bambi lift. Some seating straight off the piste, just by the front door beside the chair lift arrival point (providing a vantage point for a spot of *schadenfreude*, watching people fall off!). Inside there is a full bar and snack bar offering a Tex-Mex-themed menu: nachos, tacos, quesadillas and burritos, as well as chips, hamburgers and paninis. The large terrace to the rear has great views over the lower sector slopes and base station area. WCs are on a lower ground floor accessed from outside at the front: take care, as the steps down can be icy.

Xina Igloo The highest altitude snack bar in the Arinsal sector. At the top of the Les Fonts chair lift and handy for the Freestyle park. Small single-storey building with a bar, WCs, a plain bright interior saloon and a small suntrap terrace with views over the upper Arinsal sector. Chinese-themed snack menu: stir-fry, spring rolls and pork rolls, plus chicken nuggets, chips, paninis, etc. Access to this venue is via a short pisted track at the far end of the fence in front of Les Fonts chair lift arrival point, or via the Freestyle park's button lift (19).

PAL SECTOR

Pal's base lodge serves as the main food, drink and rest stop, offering a wide range of services to suit most tastes and budgets, however there are also two good on-mountain venues.

Far West Situated at the lower Pal–Arinsal cable car station, occupying a lovely position overlooking the Setúria Valley and Spanish border. The building is a large, two-storey wooden cabin, with good-sized wood-decked terraces facing the sun for most of the day. It is possible to ski up to and away from the terraces, although the pisted approach area is quite flat. From the main front terrace you enter into a long snack bar/café service area, with the main interior saloon further in to the right. Stairs lead up from beside the till area to a pleasant first-floor dining space, which is open only in high season and/or on bad weather days as the sun terrace is the main attraction here. The American-style fast-food menu offers hamburgers, chips, sandwiches and salads; hot (*caldo*) broth is also available. Note that cutlery is plastic and there is no table service. WCs are accessed from outside at the front of the building nearest the cable car.

🔺 *Far West bar/restaurant, Coll de la Botella, Setúria sector*

Bella Italia Apart from the Far West bar/restaurant at the Coll de la Botella, Bella Italia is Pal's only other on-mountain restaurant, but you're never further than one piste or one lift away from reaching it from anywhere in the main sector. This bright and colourful chalet is centrally located on the mid-level La Serra blue piste running from Cubil Mountain, at the arrival level for La Serra (4) and La Serra II (6) chair lifts and La Serra (7) button lift. It boasts panoramic views of the Pic de Cubil slopes from a piste-side terrace (note there is no table service) and offers the usual snack menu, but with an Italian theme to some of the dishes: pizzas (ready-made), pasta and paninis. Enter straight from the terrace into the service area; the compact dining room is to the right. WCs are accessed from the outside on the back right.

LA CAUBELLA BASE LODGE

Pal's base station buildings sit overlooking the El Planell beginners' snowfields, with a large ground floor terrace accessed directly from the pistes. There is a piste-side kiosk selling drinks and waffles as well as drinks vending machines dotted around for handy grab-&-go options. Exterior stairs lead up to the first floor services, while a couple of wide doorways lead from the terrace directly into the large ground floor saloon and the heart of the lodge building towards the self-service restaurant and WCs.

El Planell bar/terrace The big terrace has a barbecue grill and salad buffet in high season and at weekends, and is equipped with a powered canopy to cover the whole exterior seating area on poor weather days. The large interior saloon has a café-bar service and a fast-food point offering sandwiches, chips and chicken nuggets as well as soft drinks and lager on tap.

El Planell self service A basic canteen on the ground floor, at the back of the central lobby area, offering a selection of fresh salads, hot dishes, simple desserts and drinks. There's little natural daylight and the venue is very echoey

The central interior stairwell lobby, in front of El Planell self service has a selection of arcade machines and the main ground floor WCs. The stairs lead up to the lodge foyer area on the car park level, accessing the souvenir shop and photo-services, an Internet point, the Cafeteria Caubella and La Borda restaurant.

Cafeteria Caubella Don't be put off by the 'cafeteria' in the name, the first floor of Pal's base lodge provides the station's best choice for meals. An open fire and welcoming stack of wine barrels add to the more traditional Spanish ambiance of this bright and roomy restaurant which is usually buzzing from mid-morning through to late afternoon. A full bar service, plus tapas and cakes, is offered, along with a range of salads, pasta and grills. Table service is available, or you can order snacks at the central till point. WCs are off the corridor through to La Borda restaurant at the far end of the bar.

La Borda The station's most gastronomic lunch venue, with full waiter service, featuring à la carte Catalan classics, plus a three-course *menu del día*. Its airy dining room is a quieter option – it has just a dozen tables, although it could easily hold more. The best tables on a good day are set out on the narrow covered balcony, affording great views down the peaceful Sispony Valley. Since this restaurant is tucked away at the far side of the base lodge, furthest from the slopes, it's probably best to walk around the outside of the building to get there – that way you can bring your gear with you. Reservations are required at weekends and at high season periods. ☏ +376 737 002

ALTERNATIVE ACTIVITIES

As befits Pal–Arinsal's image as a 'mountain park', the station also offers a wide range of alternative activities based throughout the station to complement the main piste-based sports.

❶ Activities may not be covered by travel insurance (see page 58).

DOG SLEIGHS

Mushing (or muixing) is one of the station's most popular alternative activities. Teams of husky dogs pull passengers in Arctic sledges guided by an experienced musher through the woods in the Setúria Valley. Based at the Coll de la Botella area, close to the Far West restaurant and lower Pal–Arinsal cable car station.

SNOWMOBILES

Budding 007s will love the adrenaline buzz of this great motorsport. Each Skidoo can carry two people. Drive the machine yourself or hang on tight as a passenger, tackling the course at your own pace or racing with an experienced guide.

A waymarked circuit winds through the woods in the Setúria Valley from the Coll de la Botella, or, for children, there is a junior circuit at Pal base lodge which is equipped with special scaled-down child-sized machines.

HORSE RIDING

Departing from the Pal base lodge area, with routes and duration depending on your experience and budget. Available only by prior arrangement. Contact the station by email or telephone first.

➔ See page 80 for contact details.

▶ *Children's snowmobile at Pal base lodge*

● *Ski biking at Arinsal*

SKI BIKES

Swap wheels for skis and get on your bike: accompanied by an experienced instructor, you use the lifts to access the pistes, descending seated on these basic bikes. Wearing a pair of mini-skis fixed to your standard ski boots for balance, you steer by simply leaning and turning the handlebars. Find out more from the information cabin located beside Arinsal's base lodge roof terrace.

SLEDGING

No previous experience is needed for this classic snow-based fun activity: simply sit down and hold tight to race down the snow-fields on a glorified tray! Available daily at Pal base lodge area; and at Arinsal base lodge at evening events.

SNOWSHOE WALKS

This is definitely the best way for non-skiers to get out on the snow and into the mountains. Modern snowshoes are made of lightweight materials and are very easy to master. They work by spreading your weight over a wider surface area, allowing you to walk more easily over deep snow, using a pair of ski poles for balance. Waymarked itineraries have been prepared through the Setúria Valley, departing from the Coll de la Botella.
❶ Keep to the sides of the pistes when moving on foot.

BUNGEE TRAMPOLINES

Adults and children alike can experience the thrill of bungee trampolining at Pal base lodge. Strapped into a harness and suspended on elastic ropes above a trampoline, you can safely jump and somersault as high as you dare.

FLIGHTS

The views of the Pyrenees are even more breathtaking when seen from a bird's-eye viewpoint. Helicopter rides can be taken from any of the helipads at Pal, Setúria or Arinsal. When booking, you can also arrange to be picked up by car from your accommodation and driven to the take-off point. As well as sightseeing trips, you can book a helicopter to visit other ski resorts, for heli-skiing or for airport transfers.

Alternatively, launch yourself off the highest slopes harnessed to a steerable paragliding canopy, in tandem with a professional pilot, for an incredible sensation of soaring silently above the slopes, with skiers far below your feet. Then land back on the edge of the piste for a dramatic return to the base lodge.

Hot-air balloon flights can also be organized but are weather-dependent: flights last around $1\frac{1}{2}$ hours, and you are shadowed by a vehicle that whisks you back to your resort at the end of the flight. It is essential to book in advance

➔ See page 80 for contact details.

⬥ *Paragliding for a bird's eye view of the Pyrenees*

TORCHLIT DESCENT

A weekly spectacle held at Arinsal base lodge, whereby instructors from the station's ski school put on a display of synchronized skiing just after sunset, holding flaming torches to light their way. This is usually organized by tour operators, who combine this spectator-only event with sledging races and include *vin chaud* and snacks in the price. Transport is provided to take you back down to the village. See your rep or, if you're travelling independently, enquire at the base lodge ski pass office.

NON-SKIERS

A ski pass is not always necessary to take part in the alternative activities on offer, however, only the main Arinsal and La Massana gondolas are accessible to pedestrians.

Both Arinsal and Pal base lodges are good for meeting up with your skiing friends, but you will need a vehicle to reach the Coll de Botella area where most of the featured activities are based.

OTHER ENTERTAINMENT

Pal–Arinsal employs a 'welcome team' that arranges regular entertainment, especially during high season, which is mainly directed at younger visitors: activities include face-painting, dressing up, live music, etc. Otherwise, just take the time to chill out, relax on a sun-lounger, admire the scenery and enjoy the fresh, clear mountain air.

◗ *Torchlit descent above Arinsal base lodge*

APRÈS-SKI

When the sun goes down, the focus for fun turns away from the pistes and towards the resorts. La Massana town has some shops, but nightlife is fairly low key. In contrast, Arinsal really knows how to party. Most bars stay open until 03.00 hours and there's always some live music or themed event going on. Just remember, if you're too hungover to hit the hill tomorrow that's nearly 20 per cent of your skiing time and ski pass wasted, too!

⬣ Sunset on La Massana's peaks

SHOPPING

La Massana is the largest town in the Pal–Arinsal area, but its range of shops is fairly limited, although it does have a pharmacy, newsagent, a couple of small supermarkets and a butcher/fish-monger as well as a laundrette, a hairdresser and a florist. Arinsal village only has a few sports shops, a small supermarket, a phar-macy, a couple of convenience stores, newsagent/souvenir shop and a laundrette. If you need more extensive retail therapy, the glitzy commercial attractions of Andorra la Vella are just down the valley and easily accessible by bus or taxi.

CASH MACHINES

Both La Massana and Arinsal have centrally located ATMs, as do all the main resorts and towns.

English-language instructions are quick to find and operation will usually be as familiar as at your own bank.

➔ *See Arinsal town plan on page 73 for ATM location.*

BOWLING & GAMES ARCADE

The Princesa Parc Hotel complex also has a four-lane ten-pin bowling alley and arcade games saloon, with pool tables, air hockey, table football, half-a-dozen full-scale arcade games consoles and an Internet station. This games zone is in a huge bright basement area under the hotel, beside the Centre de Relax. It has a full bar service and is open until midnight. The bowling alley is very popular and it is best to book lanes in advance; priority is given to hotel residents.

PAMPERING

Where Arinsal really scores for après-ski is with its plush Centre de Relax; it's part of the Hotel Princesa Parc, but is open to non-residents. The centre boasts a large hydromassage pool, whirlpools, saunas and Hamman steam room plus a range of beauty and massage treatments.

SPECIAL EVENTS

Throughout the season the ski stations arrange events for major national holidays and local festivals. Expect open-air live music and fireworks. See **www.ski-ride.com** for current details.

CAFÉS & RESTAURANTS

Most of the bars in Andorra operate as cafés and offer at least a basic snack menu. The following are some of the most popular café-bars and recommended restaurants in the resorts of La Massana and Arinsal.

🕐 Most venues are open for dinner 19.30–midnight.

➔ *For further authentic Andorran venues, see pages 24–6.*

LA MASSANA

Borda de l'Avi €€€ This is a quality Borda restaurant, specializing in grilled game and meat dishes. Located at the far end of La Massana, on the road to Arinsal, just within walking distance of the town centre. ☎ +376 835 154

Prat del Colat €+ An attractive, friendly local café-bar and restaurant, beside a small park and children's playground, a short stroll out of town on the road to Erts. Run by the welcoming Gueimonde family who used to run Arinsal's Hotel Coma Pedrosa. ☎ +376 837 925

Café Pons €+ A bright coffee house and patisserie right on the main street, close to the gondola station, offering a nice range of cakes, snacks and fresh fruit juices

Versio Original €€+ La Massana's newest, hippest café-bar/restaurant, with a well-thought-out menu and a trendy ambiance. DJ and music till 03.00 hours on Fridays/Saturdays. Just off La Massana main street, up the steps from the little statue of a schoolboy. ☎ +376 839 309

● *Toasted bread rubbed with tomato and garlic, a classic Catalan starter*

La Borda del Gran Duc €€+ Rustic traditional restaurant offering gourmet dishes, grills, fondues and raclettes. It is tucked away down a little path off the main street near the tourist board information cabin. ❶ +376 837 968

ARINSAL

Refugi de la Fondue €€+ Riverside restaurant opposite the Hotel Chalet Verdu, just past the Princesa Parc Hotel. French-influenced quality venue offering a wide range of salads, pasta, fish and meat dishes, plus an excellent selection of fondues, raclettes and vegetarian dishes. ❶ +376 839 599 ⓦ www.fondue-lodge.com

Borda la Callissa €€ Cosy, intimate little bar/restaurant (also known as the Red X Bar) right next door to El Ranxo in Arinsal's Mas de Ribafeta area. Features Indian cuisine. ❶ +376 839 710

El Moli €+ Centrally located small bar/restaurant on the main street, facing the gondola station. Daytime and evening menu: pizzas, pasta, salads, jacket potatoes, curry, chilli con carne, plus a few Chinese dishes; eat-in and take away. Also offers a range of cocktails. Operates a strange system whereby you have to report to the bar first before being allocated a table, even when it's empty! ☎ +376 835281

Cisco's €€ Well-regarded Tex-Mex restaurant in an attractive saloon above the music bar of the same name; just off the main street near the gondola station. Ribs, steaks and chillis, washed down with Margaritas. No telephone, just book earlier in the day.

Micolau €€ Part of the Hotel Micolau, right on the main street just before the church. A lovely traditional stone-built inn with a cosy ambiance and an open fire grill. Good *menu del día* and à la carte menu, especially for grilled meats. ☎ +376 835 052

   EV's Deli and convenience store next door is under the same management, offering daytime takeaway pies and pasties as well as a selection of British canned foods for self-catering visitors.

El Ranxo €+ Pack an appetite because you'll need it at this great Argentinian steak house. Their house speciality is the absolutely enormous Cro-Magnon Ribs, which really are like something out of *The Flintstones*. Meats are grilled on an open fire and the décor is ranch style in an attractive split-level saloon. Located in the Mas de Ribafeta area of Arinsal, a short walk up off the main road from the junction just below the Hotel Solana. ☎ +376 835 439

➔ *See Arinsal town plan on page 73.*

BARS & CLUBS

Most resort hotels have in-house bars, many of which can be fairly animated, depending on the liveliness of each week's clientele. La Massana has a few proper late night spots, but it's Arinsal that really keeps Andorra's party flag flying. The following are some of the best venues in each resort:

LA MASSANA

Porquets Si A small local pub and Internet café located on the Avinguda el Través, which is the road that swings out round the far side of La Massana towards Ordino.

Chic Nightclub Weekends only. A fair-sized club with mostly House and Euro Dance nights. Situated down on the river level behind and below the Comu da la Massana in the middle of town.

Versio Original An upmarket café-bar and restaurant with a wine-bar feel. Designer décor and quality food service. DJ till 03.00 hours on Fridays/Saturdays. Located in a side street, up the steps from the little statue of a schoolboy, off the main street.

Cheers Pub Main-street bar close to the Hotel Marco Polo. Exudes a proper pub feel; pool tables, arcade machines, lively atmosphere and a good mixed crowd.

QTR (VIP Club) A small out-of-town late night club with two distinct zones: House and Underground in one and Commercial Dance and Ragga in the other. Located in Anyós, a short taxi ride to the south of La Massana.

ARINSAL

Rocky Mountain A large venue with a good atmosphere. Live music and comedy nights; plus kebabs and snacks served until around midnight. Based on the ground level of the Amadeus apartments at the Cota 1550 m area at the upper end of Arinsal. The bar sponsors an evening minibus service to/from this upper area – simply flag it down.

Quo Vadis A legend in its own night-time! Undisputedly Arinsal's key pub, with a welcoming international bar team, DJ, plasma screens with daily footage of current visitors on the slopes, plus great snowsports videos and live TV sports showing regularly. Most visitors start off the night in the 'Quo'; many never leave. All-day English breakfasts, snacks and an evening food menu. On the main road, in the centre of the village, on the ground floor of the Poblado apartments. Ⓦ www.quovadis-arinsal.com

Bogart's In-house music pub at the Hotel Princesa Parc. Live music almost every night and a quality feel to the décor and ambience. Accessible to non-residents.

El Cau Facing the Quo Vadis in the middle of the village, this is a two-floor venue, promoting one of Arinsal's biggest weekly events – the 70s Night. The entrance just off the main road leads first to the lower mezzanine level music bar with a small dance floor and nightly DJs. The huge upper floor, accessed via a separate entrance straight off the main road and up the interior ramp, is the setting for the gloriously kitsch 70s Night and other themed events. Pack an Afro wig and a medallion or two.

Surf A large music bar and restaurant, housed in the old stone building beside the Arinsal gondola, on the opposite side of the river from the main road. Varied programme of events, but mostly DJ and commercial dance music.

Cisco's A well-established bar/restaurant in a lovely old converted house, just off the main road in the middle of town. Compact, rocking music bar on first floor; popular with the ski station's Latin American personnel. Good Tex-Mex restaurant on the upper floor above the bar.

El Derbi (Darby O'Gills) Irish bar theme, although proper Guinness is also available in most good bars in the resort. Pleasant venue, with pool table and convivial atmosphere. First bar on the right when approaching the village centre from lower Arinsal.

La Solana Tiny, British-managed music bar/club which punches way above its weight – they've had international DJ Brandon Block here, twice! Good varied events programme and après-ski buzz. Tucked in under the Hotel Solana, at the roadside towards the lower end of Arinsal village.

Red X Bar The bar at the Borda la Callissa Indian restaurant just a 300 m (328 yd) stroll up the side road from the junction below the Hotel Solana. Quite chilled and cosy, attracting a nice after-dinner crowd, but frequently offering live music and entertainment, too.

Sant Gothard An in-house basement disco bar with nightly entertainment, found in the Hotel Sant Gothard at the very lowest part of Arinsal. Open to non-residents.

La Jungla Down in the lower village at the Bordes d'Arinsal area, facing the side road which leads to the Xalet Besoli aparthotel. Music bar, popular with locals, which tries hard and is worth a look in on a good night.

Ambit The area's only true club, located down at the tiny hamlet of Erts, towards La Massana. Really only a weekend venue and promoted mostly to a Catalan clientele. Small, nicely converted old Borda barn, with a decent music policy – mainly House, Trance and Euro Dance.

Hotel bars Arinsal's hotels all have their own in-house bars which, dependent on the ambience created by current guests, can be fun and relaxed. At the very least they're ideal for starting the night off and for a final wee cheeky one before bedtime.

◯ *Pal–Arinsal anniversary concert at Arinsal village*

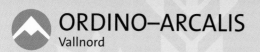

INTRODUCTION

Andorra's most compact and least known station boasts its purest Alpine profile and most gnarled terrain. Its distinct microclimate, combined with a fleet of Pininfarina-designed piste-grooming machines, ensures great conditions from the first to the last run of the day.

In the far north-western corner of Andorra, nestled among the high wild peaks on the French border, Arcalís has always been seen as Andorra's secret ski area. Its name links it to the parish capital Ordino, though the slopes are 14 km (8½ miles) from the town. The ski area has no neighbouring resort village or on-site accommodation, which has contributed to Arcalís being little-known internationally and to its air of mystique. The linking of Ordino—Arcalís and Pal—Arinsal as 'Vallnord' will change this.

The ski area is compact but offers a range: from long cruising blue runs for novices, to over 50-degree gradient true blacks and extensive lift-served off-piste for experts. Arcalís is Andorra's most Alpine ski zone, with pistes tucked in among the classically shaped fold-mountain peaks and savage rocky surroundings. The high valleys have a distinct microclimate, endowing the area with an enviable snowfall record, without extremes of temperature. Arcalís is usually over 90 per cent open and rarely suffers from icy pistes.

PRONUNCIATION
Arcalís Ar~cal~lees

◀ *Arcalís base station, towards the Serra de Tristaina*

With the introduction of the Vallnord ski pass, visitors staying in Arinsal or La Massana can share in the magic of Arcalís on their holiday to Pal–Arinsal. It is also possible to stay closer to Arcalís, in the attractive, French-influenced parish capital of Ordino or in one of the handful of small family-run hotels in a string of tiny hamlets in the peaceful long valley leading up to the ski area. However, the only reliable way to reach Arcalís is still to have your own vehicle; there is an infrequent bus service from La Massana, but the only easier alternative from Arinsal is to join one of the mid-week excursions organized by the main UK tour operators.

There are two distinct zones to the ski area: the rugged cirque immediately above the base station and the wide, gentle, sunny high Coma bowl nearest the French border. Intermediates will love the fast undulating reds that run right down to the base area, and more expert ability visitors will also enjoy this zone's two steep and mogulled black runs high on the flanks of the rocky peaks. Novices have lovely sweeping blues to tackle, while true beginners have a small debutants' area just above the upper base lodge. The higher Coma zone is expansive and open, with beautifully groomed motorway blues and gentle reds, but the main attraction is the lift access to some memorable off-piste routes.

Arcalís also has a couple of unique features: an abandoned road tunnel (Túnel del Rat, see page 177) in the high Coma Valley, which is worth wandering into to see its ice stalactites and stalagmites; and a huge, whimsical, circular metal artwork perched precariously on the edge of the cliffs above the base station (see page 181). Arcalís adds to the value of a snowsports holiday to the Vallnord resorts and you should plan to visit for at least a day.

▶ *Túnel del Rat, Arcalís*

COMING & GOING

With no accommodation at the ski area, you will approach Arcalís along the long valley from La Massana and Ordino on the CG3 road. From La Massana, follow signs to Ordino from the round-about at the upper end of town near the Pal–La Massana cable car base station. It's a 2 km (1¼ mile) drive to Ordino, then swing left, following directions for Arcalís station via the hamlets of Sornàs, Ansalonga, La Cortinada, Arans, Llorts, Les Salines and El Serrat. There are a few quiet hotels dotted along this road.

Nearing the ski station, the road passes through a tunnel to emerge facing the base lodge and main parking area. There are two car parks to the right, or, if road conditions are good, you can continue to climb higher to the parking bays close to the upper base lodge and roadside piste access points.

Ski pass kiosks are on the left at road level at both the lower and upper base lodges. The main chair lifts serving this first Cercle d'Arcalís ski sector, and making the links with the further Coma Valley sector, are just above the roadside by the lower base station. From the upper parking area, button lifts serve this side of the ski area and one chair lift links to the Coma sector, departing from just above the upper base lodge area.

DISTANCES
- Toulouse to Ordino   233 km (145 miles)
- Barcelona to Ordino   228 km (142 miles)
- Andorra la Vella to Ordino   8 km (5 miles)
- La Massana to Ordino   2 km (1¼ miles)
- Ordino to Arcalís   14 km (8½ miles)

SKI AREA DATA

- Opening time — 09.00 hours
- Last lift up — 17.00 hours
- Skiable area — 442 ha (1092 acres)
- Altitude — 1940–2640 m (6365–8661 ft)
- Vertical drop — 700 m (2297 ft)
- Access points — 1
- Ski schools — 1

- Ski lifts — 14

Cable cars	0	Gondolas	0
Chair lifts	5	Button lifts	8
Rope tows	0	Conveyor belts	1

- Capacity — 16,510 passengers/hour

- Pistes — 25

Green	6	Tricks parks	2
Red	11	Freeride	2
Blue	6	Children's	1
Black	2	Halfpipes	1
Nordic	0	FIS	1

- Hands-free ski pass — Yes + Swatch Snowpass
- Snowmaking — 61 cannons
  Covering 28 ha (69 acres)
- Medical centre — 1
- Mountain restaurants — 3 + 1 high-altitude snack bar
- Visitor information — www.vallordino.com

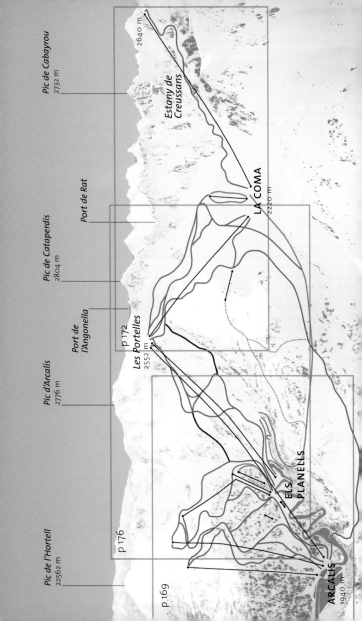

Pic de Cabayrou
2732 m

Pic de Cataperdis
2804 m

Port de Rat

Pic d'Arcalis
2776 m

Port de
l'Angonella

Pic de l'Hortell
2562 m

2640 m

Estany de
Creussans

LA COMA
2220 m

p 172

Les Portelles
2552 m

ELS
PLANELLS

p 176

p 169

ARCALÍS
1940 m

SKI PASSES

All options available are Vallnord passes (except for local area day passes) covering Arcalís, Pal and Arinsal. A deposit is payable for a hands-free passcard, which can be kept to be recharged in the future or returned to the ski pass kiosk for deposit refund. The passcard should be secured in a left-hand pocket and operates the lift turnstiles by remote control.

High season = every weekend; week leading up to Christmas until week after New Year; all February and Easter.

Low season = all other dates (up to 20 per cent cheaper than high season).

All passes are available for adults (12–64 years) and children (6–11 years): half-day (09.00–13.00 or 13.00–close); full-day and multiples thereof: the longer the duration, the cheaper the equivalent daily rate. Ski passes are free of charge for all children under 6; from 6–11 prices are approximately 25 per cent cheaper than those of adults. To encourage the wearing of helmets, a small discount is also given on children's one-day passes if the child wears a helmet. Ski passes for guests aged 65–70 years old are available at a much reduced daily rate; passes are free for the over 70s.

A photo is required only for individual passes with more than four days' duration.

❶ Proof of age is required at the time of purchase for all child and senior ski passes.

PRICES
For current prices for all ski passes, tuition, childcare and other services, please go to our website: **www.ski-ride.com**.

SKI ANDORRA PASS

See also page 61 for full details of the Ski Andorra ski pass which permits access to all of Andorra's ski areas.

SKI PASS SALES POINTS

Vallnord passes can be purchased at any of the Arcalís, La Massana, Pal or Arinsal ski pass kiosks (see also page 77); Arcalís local sector day passes are only available at the station itself. There are two ski pass sales points at Arcalís; one by the roadside at the lower base, encountered when you first arrive at the station, and one by the roadside at the rear of the upper base lodge slightly further up the same road.

NON-SKIERS

To be honest, there's little for non-skiers to do at Arcalís and none of the lifts is accessible for pedestrians. However, since no lifts are required to get here, it is possible for non-skiers to travel up with their skiing companions. The two base lodges offer a couple of bars and restaurants, and the upper lodge overlooks the children's Snow Park, with sunny terraces and views of the pistes and impressive peaks above. One idea to really make the most of your visit, if your fitness level is up to the challenge, is to hike up into the Coma Valley from the end of the road above the base station. This is driveable in summer and is the route of La Bassera green piste during the ski season. Snowshoe hire and guided walks to panoramic viewpoints are also available.

❶ Accident insurance is not included in ski pass prices. Make sure you are adequately covered (see page 58) or purchase the insurance supplement when you buy your ski pass.

SKI BUS

A free shuttle bus runs every 10 minutes between the lower and upper base lodges in Arcalís. A couple of early morning ski buses run from Andorra la Vella to Arcalís, with just one return journey in the afternoon. The local bus runs slightly more regularly between Ordino and Arcalís, but you'll need to wear normal footwear and carry your boots to travel on this service. Timetables are available from any tourist office.

➔ See pages 370–1 for details of regular local bus services.

EQUIPMENT HIRE

Most people bring their own or rented gear from other resorts when visiting Arcalís, although the ski area does have its own small rental operation, based in the same building as the roadside ski pass kiosks beside the lower base lodge. The shop offers waxing and servicing of equipment too, as well as snowshoe hire.

➔ See also page 207 for tips on identifying your gear.

STORAGE

Since all visitors arrive by vehicle the need for equipment storage is not so important and no real provision has been made – unless you hire on-site and leave your gear overnight at the rental shop (no charge if you've hired from them). There are small personal belongings locker rooms in the lower and upper base lodges.

TUITION

Arcalís ski school has a team of around 50 instructors, of whom 15 or so are good English speakers (or indeed English). The ski school office is located just above the upper base lodge, with nearby parking on the upper roadside.

Public group classes are grouped according to language, ability level, age, ski or snowboard, and are available for 3 hours per day over 5 days (Mon–Fri) or for either 2 or 4 hours only at weekends. Children aged 4–8 years old have their own Snow Park; from the age of 6 they can join the regular classes on the pistes, although every effort is made to ensure that they are grouped in similar ages. Reduced rate prices apply for children aged 6–11 years old.

Private lessons are also available and are offered for Alpine skiing, snowboarding, carving skiing, Telemark skiing and off-piste; book direct with the ski school. Prices charged for private instruction are per hour and are the same for adults and children. Prices also depend on the season and on how many of you there are. A specially designated beginners' zone is nestled in a sheltered wooded copse served by a magic carpet conveyor and short button lift, not far from the ski school office

Since most visitors to Arcalís are experienced snowsports enthusiasts, the ski school has geared its services to this market and offers what may be the highest level of technical tuition available in Andorra. There is lots of off-piste potential in the ski area and this is integral to the marketing and principal attraction of Arcalís. The ski school promotes avalanche search and rescue training and off-piste initiation courses as part of its services.

➲ See page 209 for details of instructor qualifications.

CONTACTS
🛈 Arcalís ski station: +376 739 600
🛈 Arcalís ski school: +376 739 622
🄴 secnoa.booking@andorra.ad

CHILDCARE

A children's Snow Garden is situated directly in front of the upper base lodge. It has large, brightly coloured inflatable obstacles for playing on, and during high season there are animation teams in cartoon character costumes. The area has its own short button lift and is part of the services offered by the ski school, which provide specialized children's ski instructors to monitor the little ones. The area is in full view of the base lodge. There is a second small Snow Park area nestled in the wooded slopes to the front of the ski school office which is served by a short magic carpet conveyor. Again, access to this is bookable via the ski school. The Snow Garden and Snow Park facilities are available for children aged 4–8 years old and are bookable via the ski school for 2 hours, 3 hours, or 5 days x 3 hours per day. The cost of ski hire is not included in these prices.

🔵 *Arcalís' Snow Garden, beside the upper base lodge*

A bright, well-equipped crèche is available on the piste-side level of the upper base lodge, for infants aged over 1 year old; advance reservation with the ski school is recommended. This nursery service is provided on a 2-hour, half-day, full-day, and 5 x half-day basis. Staff speak Catalan and Spanish and French, although some English is spoken, too.

SERVICES

Medical centre: on the ground floor of the lower base lodge, close to the pistes so accident victims can be brought in by rescue sled. It is just by the roadside for ambulance access. For more serious emergencies, there is a helicopter pad in the main car park area.

The medical staff will contact your insurance company. However, you will have to pay for any initial costs, excluded by any excess clauses, on-site. Make sure your insurance covers heli-rescue, piste rescue and ambulance transport as well as medical and hospital expenses. Andorra is not in the EU and has no public health service; medical centres are well-equipped and the hospital is very modern, but all are private.

❶ Always carry ID and your insurance details. It is also advisable to carry a small first-aid kit for dealing with minor cuts and bruises (see Health & Safety, pages 53–8).

WCs: located at the base lodges and at the restaurant in the Coma sector; all free of charge.

ATMS: no cash machines here – the nearest are at Ordino.

Telephones: phonecard-operated telephone booths are on the lower levels of base lodge buildings. Phonecards are available from the shop at the rear roadside level of the upper lodge. GSM mobile phone coverage is virtually 100 per cent.

Shops: other than the one equipment rental shop down by the lower base lodge, which sells the usual selection of last-minute accessories, the only retail outlet at Arcalís is a small newsstand and photograph service at the rear of the upper base lodge.

Mountain restaurants: the range of venues is limited. Two large self-service restaurants cover both floors of the base lodges, one at each lodge. There is an on-piste mountain restaurant in the Coma sector and a cosy high-altitude snack bar at the top of the lift arrival points at the upper link area between the two sectors. The self-service restaurants offer a similar selection of snack foods and daily hot dishes with vegetables, although the Coma restaurant also houses a separate, bright à la carte restaurant. Prices are a little lower than in other Andorran stations.

➔ *See pages 185–6 for specific reviews.*

Picnic areas: indoor picnic rooms are provided at both base lodges, but the upper lodge's room is small, plain and echoing. By contrast, the picnic saloon at the lower base lodge is one of the nicest in Andorra. Located on the uppermost level, tucked under the timber-built eaves, with plenty of natural daylight and with wood clad walls, wooden bench seating and tables, this room has a cosy feel and is just above the main bar and restaurant area should you need to augment your packed lunch. There is also a picnic room at La Coma restaurant in the Coma sector, but again this is quite plain and bare.

Out on the mountain, perhaps the most spectacular picnic spot is above the arrival point of the Creussans chair lift (14) at the highest point in the ski area on the French border above the Coma sector. The views over the French and Spanish border areas and over the Coma ski sector and Andorran peaks beyond are breathtaking; on a clear day you can see right over to Soldeu and Pas de la Casa.

▶ *Ski-touring at the Port de Creussans, Arcalís*

SNOWFALL HISTORY & ANALYSIS

Although precipitation is unpredictable at very long range, patterns do emerge that are observable over a number of seasons. Using this data, you can tell if your preferred period of travel has historically seen good snow cover. The magic figure is 100 cm (39 in) – once snow depth exceeds this mark, conditions are generally good throughout the ski area and will remain so for a more extended period.

Arcalis' well-documented microclimate, and the resulting lack of extreme temperature swings, helps to protect and maintain existing snow conditions; the station becomes a magnet for local enthusiasts when the other Andorran ski areas begin to suffer. Lack of snow has never really been a problem. Late February to early March is the most likely time to have snow, with conditions only beginning to deteriorate in late March, but increasingly predictable end-of-season dumps are always worth waiting for.

The chart below details combined averages recorded over three seasons immediately prior to the publication of this guide. Visit **www.ski-ride.com** for live snow reports.

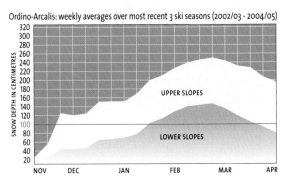

Ordino-Arcalis: weekly averages over most recent 3 ski seasons (2002/03 - 2004/05)

PREVIOUS SEASONS' SNOWFALL BREAKDOWN BY YEAR

The following charts detail the snowfall history for the three most recent seasons. Data from these charts was used to compile the combined averages chart on the preceding page.

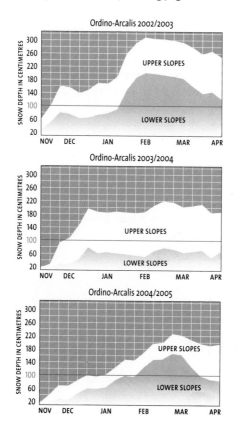

ARCALIS SKI SECTOR

Arcalís is Andorra's smallest ski area, yet it holds an allure among those in the extreme skiing fraternity, positioned as it is in some of the Pyrenees' most gnarled terrain. The profile of the red and black slopes is much steeper than those in the other Andorran stations, but study the lines of descent first if freeriding, as there are many rocky outcrops and sheer cliffs.

Despite its attractions for experts, Arcalís has plenty to offer confident beginners and intermediates too, making it an ideal outing for mixed ability groups. Access to the ski area is simple once you're at the base station, with all major lifts departing from just above the main parking area.

BASE STATION

On arriving at Arcalís you have two choices as to where to begin, either directly from the roadside lifts beside the lower base lodge at 1940 m (6365 ft), or from the roadside-accessible pistes and lifts close to the upper base lodge further on up the area's only approach road. The lower start point allows access to the main Arcalís Cirque towering above you, as well as a direct chair lift link into the distant Coma sector. The upper level gives you the choice of direct access to the beginners' zone, a direct chair lift link into the Coma sector, as well as the option of warming up on the lower section of La Font blue piste (F) down to all of the lower base area's lifts. Both the lower and upper areas of the base station have large day lodges, where all of this sector's services and facilities are located. The only equipment hire shop is by the roadside in the lower area.

◀ *Arcalís Cirque ski sector*

EDIFICI ARCALIS BASE LODGE

This is the lower base lodge building at 1940 m (6365 ft), situated at the tight bend where the road continues to climb towards the upper parking areas. In front of the lodge there is a smaller building by the roadside, on the left under the get-on points for the chair lifts, which houses the ski pass kiosk and the station's rental shop. The main lodge building is plain and functional, but it has good facilities and is easy to reach from the pistes.

Piste level (approached via the steps up from the roadside): WCs; public telephones; medical centre; station administration offices; central stairwell to first floor.

First and second floor: L'Hortell self-service cafeteria and bar; stairs to upper road access and picnic room.

Top floor: mezzanine-level entrance/exit at upper road level; cosy attic space furnished as interior picnic room.

ELS PLANELLS BASE LODGE

The upper level day lodge is similar to the lower Edifici Arcalis, but as it's at a higher altitude it catches the sun for longer in the day. The self-service restaurant and bar (see page 185) has a terrace overlooking and accessible from the pistes. The ski school office is in a chalet above the lodge, with the beginners' zone and children's Snow Garden in front at this same level.

Lower ground floor: crèche; picnic room; WCs; public telephones.

Piste-side ground floor: piste-side terrace with BBQ, snack kiosk and sunloungers; Els Planells self-service restaurant and bar; stairs to upper level.

Second floor: Els Planells cafeteria and bar; stairs up to back of building to roadside entrance/exit.

Upper floor: roadside entrance/exit; exterior ski pass kiosks; shop.

LA PLETA (H)

This is the main beginners' slope, served by two button lifts (Els Vailets TK4 and Els Marrecs TK5), situated above the upper base lodge. The ski school office is in the separate chalet-style building, just above the upper base lodge. The slope is definitely green in profile, wide and gentle, although piste traffic does flow through this area on the parallel shared access routes of the Les Canals (G) blue and La Portella del Mig (J) red – remember to stick furthest away from the road to stay in the quietest zone. There is also a lovely secluded area hidden away in the woods just below this area to the right when descending. It is set out as a children's Snow Park but is open to all beginners, with hoops to slide under, slalom poles to ski round and plenty of crash mats fixed to the trees for safety; it's a real asset for novices visiting the station. This Snow Park zone also has its own short button lift (L'Escola TK8) and a magic carpet conveyor.

L'HORTELL BUTTON LIFT TK1

 5 mins
- Difficult lift – no beginners
- 340 m (1115 ft) vertical rise

A steep button lift for experienced riders only, departing furthest to the left from the lower base station. On arrival at the top, turn to the right to traverse over to the wide confluence area under the line of the nearby chair lift. L'Estadi d'Eslalom red competition course begins at the timer's hut by the lift pylon, dropping down to the right. L'Hortell red is really all of the wide mellow red motorway which flows through this area. It has three variation routes below this point (the main piste plus El Bosc and L'Avetar reds); stick left of the chair lift line for them all.

L'ESTADI D'ESLALOM (A)

A wide, fast, fall-line competition piste running down under the line of the L'Abarsetar chair lift (TS10), with catch netting all down the right-hand side. Entered from a wide confluence area from L'Hortell red or by the traverse route from the L'Hortell button lift (TK1), the course officially begins at the timer's hut beside the chair-lift pylon in the middle of the slopes in this wide shared crossover area. Either tuck for a real downhill racer experience, or use the full width of the piste to carve sweeping GS turns. Keep to the right at the finish to make a good link with L'Hortell button lift (TK1) or curb your speed and veer left for good links to L'Abarsetar (TS10) and La Basera (TSD12) chair lifts just below left.

L'HORTELL (B)

Starting from the huge pistes confluence area beneath the line of the L'Abarsetar chair lift (TS10), this enjoyable cruising red is accessible by the L'Hortell button lift (TK1) but is best approached via the main TS10 chair lift and Les Congestes red piste (C) to provide the longest descent possible. L'Hortell red begins to the left of the L'Estadi d'Eslalom competition piste (A) and starts as a wide, mild red. The spur to the far left is El Bosc (E) variation down through the wooded slopes towards the upper base lodge. Shortly after beginning the L'Hortell there is another wide junction; keep left to continue on L'Hortell or go right to take L'Avetar red (D) variation. All these routes share similar characteristics, as fast standard reds with plenty of opportunity to freeride off into the lightly wooded, deeper snow and rock jumps to the sides and between the pistes, giving almost limitless potential for putting in new tracks in this sector. Good links with all lower station lifts.

L'ABARSETAR CHAIR LIFT TS10

| 7 mins | • 392 m (1286 ft) vertical rise |

The middle lift at the lower base station, accessing the uppermost pistes in the main cirque. The journey up has great views over the whole sector, up to the cols on the upper right, and over the principal reds and competition course which descend underneath the chairline. On arrival, you can leave either left or right, but both pistes U-turn down the line of the arriving lift again and meet up below: leaving to the left takes you on to the start of La Font blue (F) and towards Les Congestes red (C); leaving to the right and then keeping furthest over to the left takes you on to Les Canals blue (G), although you can also keep to the right and link over to La Font blue and Les Congestes red to continue as above.

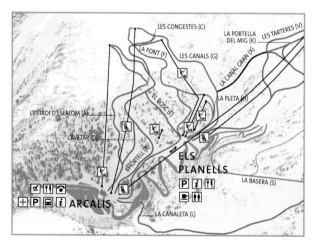

LA FONT (F)

A good blue which will challenge early standard improvers.
Begins at the top of the L'Abarsetar chair lift (TS10), taking a fairly
direct route down through this rugged cirque bowl. The run has
some mellow red pitches and offers intermediates a good
workout, particularly playing off the sides, taking shortcuts
through the rocky inter-piste slopes. You can also branch off to
the left to traverse via pistes G and H to get to Les Portelles chair
lift (TS6) to link with the Coma sector; otherwise stay on the main
fall-line route to link with L'Abarsetar button lift (TK3) to the top
again, or keep going to reach both base lodges.

LES CANALS (G)

Similar profile to La Font blue, but with a mellower gradient and
a wide motorway feel. Links well with Les Portelles chair lift (TS6)
for the Coma sector, as well as flowing past the upper lodge area
before joining the lower section of La Font as above.

L'ABARSETAR BUTTON LIFT TK3

  5 mins

- difficult lift – no beginners
- 230 m (755 ft) vertical rise

A long button lift which runs steeply up the rocky slopes directly
under the Arcalís cirque to give access to all this sector's mid to
lower pistes. Pay attention on the journey up: this lift has a vicious
kick to start, 60° gradient pitches, a dogleg bend to the left at its
mid-point and the line of travel is crossed by piste traffic. On
arrival, go right for Les Canals blue (G), or go left for La Font blue,
Les Congestes red and all other options in the lower sector.

LA BASERA CHAIR LIFT TSD12

7½ mins   • 612 m (2008 ft) vertical rise

The principal access lift, linking directly with the upper Coma sector and giving access to the challenging reds and blacks that flow over the rocky cols back into the main cirque. From the get-on point at the lower base station, the journey up has good views over the entire lower sector plus the serious La Portella d'Arcalís black (K) to the high right. Approaching the top, the chair pylons pass through a cutting in the ridge into the open Coma Valley. On arrival, veer to the right for all pistes: U-turn down to the right to start La Portella d'Mig steep red (J); or go around the rear of the little Les Portelles snack bar to start the wide gentle La Balma red (N) and to access La Portella d'Arcalís black and the patrolled off-piste zone; or keep high and traverse along the flat upper contour track, around the top of La Coma chair lift (TSD7) arrival point, to access the start of El Túnel (U) and Els Terragalls (P) blues.

LES PORTELLES CHAIR LIFT TS6

6 mins   • 475 m (1558 ft) vertical rise

Departing from the roadside area close to the uppermost car parking bays, just above the upper base lodge and ski school, this chair saves running down to the La Basera lift (TSD12) if you want to keep tackling the steepest upper reds and blacks from the Portelles link area, as well as providing a link into the Coma sector. Journey up runs parallel to the right of the La Basera chair but the arrival point is lower – onward routes are more or less the same.

LA PORTELLA DEL MIG (J) / LES TARTERES (V)

The wide upper approach area is an open mild red, but as soon as you funnel through the col the piste immediately steepens to a very good red; keeping furthest left gives the most challenging descent. Keeping to the right gives the option of taking Les Tarteres red (V) variation route, which is a fast schuss motorway running out on the highest line to the right.

If riding off-piste to the high left, be sure to ride out away from the lift lines as there are cliffs between them just below. La Portella del Mig mellows to fair status, sweeping ahead towards a huge confluence zone where you can veer left to continue the enjoyable twisting route towards a good link with chair TS6, or veer ahead right to schuss over to join the lower Les Tarteres (V) variant and the entrance to the gnarled La Canal Gran black (X). The lower Les Tarteres red from this point is the best section of the run, dropping on a steep fall-line down to the right of the cliffs before joining the lower part of La Portella del Mig as above.

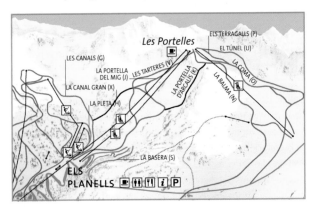

LA CANAL GRAN (X)

Wow! One of the jewels in Arcalís' crown. Less than 800 m (875 yd) long, but with a vertical drop of 340 m (that's over 1100 ft) and up to 60° gradient, this little gem just has to be attempted by all advanced ability visitors. Begun from the wide hairpin bend on Les Tarteres red (V), the entrance is a challenge in its own right; you have to drop in over a 2 m (6½ ft) lip on to wide gully below to start, and once in you're pretty much committed. Turning with the fall-line down to the left you are immediately on a true black, funnelling into a steep couloir that forces short turns, and dealing with constant moguls. Caution to the right as there are protruding rocks; keeping to the left will give the most rugged line anyway – if you're up for it. The adrenaline buzz ends in a wide run-out to join Les Canals blue (G) below, giving you time to catch your breath and make easy links to all lifts below.

LA PORTELLA D'ARCALÍS (K)

Another serious black in the upper Arcalís cirque, this time dropping over a col from the upper Coma sector. Accessed by taking the top section of La Balma red (N) from any of the three chair lifts with rise to the Portelles link area between Arcalís' two sectors (i.e. lifts TSD12, TS6 and TSD7). Follow the upper route of La Balma red towards the huge pyramidal peak dead ahead, then turn right at the base of this rocky bulk to ride over the col into the Arcalís sector beyond. The route straight away takes on a true black status, with a 45° + mogulled slope with a wealth of variant lines into the bowl below. The run is only 640 m (700 yd) long from top to bottom, but is a real thigh-buster. Joins on the La Portella del Mig red (J) for all link options from the main sector.

COMA SKI SECTOR

To reach the Coma sector from the base station, take either the quick declutchable La Basera chair lift (TSD12) from the main first arrival zone next to the lower lodge, or the slower fixed Les Portelles chair lift (TS6) from above the upper base lodge. On arrival at the top the whole Coma sector spreads out below you in a wide, sunny, open bowl. Once in this sector, you can return to this upper link point again by using La Coma chair lift (TSD7), accessing all of this sector's main cruising pistes and allowing you to drop back into the Arcalis cirque via the steep reds and blacks over the col between the two sectors. There's a basic, but cosy, snack bar at the highest point here and another more substantial restaurant at the 2220 m (7283 ft) level near the base of La Coma chair.

The Coma sector is readily accessible to novices too, offering them a real high mountain experience with plenty of flattering cruises and an interesting long green route returning all the way back to Arcalís base station.

🔺 *La Coma chair lift arrival area*

LA BALMA (N)

A long sweeping red with blue characteristics, from the top of the Coma area, which provides a link to the entrance of La Portella d'Arcalís black (K) and to Els Feixans button lift (TK13) serving the snow-patrol protected off-piste zone. As well as for access to these attractions, La Balma can be combined with the enjoyable La Canaleta fast red (L) to provide an almost 3 km (2 mile) leg-burner all the way back to Arcalís base station.

OFF-PISTE INITIATION

Using the short Els Feixans button lift (TK13) Arcalís offers the unique attraction of accessing a specially designated Off-Piste Zone (Zona Fora Pista) with a couple of tried and tested, snow-patrol protected, freeriding routes through unpisted and unmarked terrain. From the top of the TK13 button, simply ride out ahead into the gentle snowfields before choosing your own line down the steadily steepening wilder slopes below. Keep your wits about you to pick a safe route through the rocky and wooded terrain, but there's nothing too extreme in here and the area is graded as a red equivalent. Depending on the route you take, you can emerge to take La Canaleta fast red (L) right down to Arcalís' lower base area, or drop out on to La Basera green (S) for a much more gentle traverse via the upper base lodge.

This area is patrolled, but treat it with the respect all off-piste riding deserves: never ride off-piste alone and never rely on another's track: they may have headed off a cliff!

LA COMA (O)

From the top of the Portelles link area in the upper Coma bowl, La Coma blue sweeps down through the middle of this wide open sector, with lots of freeride fun to be had popping off the piste into little gullies and deeper snow pockets. Two options present themselves at the start section behind Les Portelles snack bar: either drop off under the line of the arriving La Coma chair (TSD7) for a short steep variation on Els Terragalls blue (P), or take the regular La Coma route leading away from the bar down the wide motorway piste, parallel to the chairline. Shortly after this you will be swinging left to meet with Els Terragalls, which joins from above left. La Coma leads the onward descent as a wide, perfectly groomed ribbon of corduroy piste through this gently undulating upper bowl and is a flattering cruise for novices. Nearing the lower section, you again have a couple of variations: either swing over to the left to merge with the route of the lower El Túnel blue (U) towards the Snow Park tricks zone and to make the best link over to La Coma restaurant, or keep right down the fall-line for the short fast red El Mur (T) to schuss out towards La Coma chair lift (TSD7).

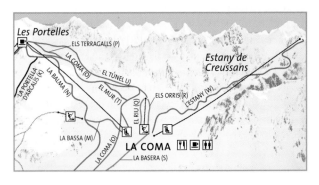

EL TÚNEL (U)

Similar to La Coma blue, starting from the same uppermost Portelles link area, but taking an even more sweeping line wide out to the left around the base of the impressive ring of peaks surrounding the Coma bowl. El Túnel can be used as another perfect cruise for novices or as a flat-out race track with slightly banked turns for the more experienced – with a twist that should appeal to all visitors, an ice cave!

TÚNEL DEL RAT

After the upper section of the El Túnel blue reaches the far side of the Coma bowl, it swings down to the right on a much steeper pitch before the long flat mid-section. Slow up and stop safely off the left-hand side of the piste immediately at the bottom of this steeper

🔺 *The fabulous ice stalagmites in the Túnel del Rat*

section. An abandoned road tunnel project planned between Andorra and France cuts deep into the cliffs; it really is worthwhile to view the forest of ice stalactites and stalagmites which festoons its interior. The icicles are most spectacular when viewed from inside, with the daylight from the tunnel mouth behind them. Take your skis or board off to scramble down carefully over the snowdrift partially blocking the entrance, exercising caution when walking on the tunnel floor as it's often a sheer sheet of ice. Leaving the tunnel, you'll now have to hike or skate along the flat section of El Túnel piste before being able to ride away again.

TRICKS PARK

Over the past couple of seasons Arcalís' Piste Services team have worked hard to develop a permanent halfpipe and park. The park is situated close to La Coma restaurant in the lower Coma sector, corresponding to El Riu green (Q) piste on the piste maps, the area's uplift being provided by L'Orris button lift (TK9). A fair-sized pipe, a couple of rails and big air ramps boost the area's natural stream gullies and windblown kickers to present a diverting tricks zone, covering approximately 15,000 sq m (3.7 acres), within easy reach of the station's facilities. Once you've exhausted the possibilities in the park, you can leave the area by making the easy link over to La Coma chair lift (TSD7) or take La Basera green (S)/ La Canaleta red (L) back to base. The main attraction of Arcalís for good riders though is the more consistent quality of the snow and the access to so many exciting freeride routes.

LA COMA CHAIR LIFT TSD7

5¾ mins	• 332 m (1089 ft) vertical rise

Easy link from all of the Coma sector pistes and from La Coma restaurant. Takes you up to the upper Coma bowl and accesses all routes back through the bowl as well as the best reds and blacks over into the core Arcalís sector. The views on the journey up are great: looking ahead and around to the right to the encircling mass of peaks and over all the pistes in the expansive Coma bowl. On arrival, go right for Els Terragalls (P) and El Túnel (U) blues; go left for La Coma (O) blue, La Balma (N) and La Portella del Mig (J) reds and to access La Portella d'Arcalís (K) black. There is a small snack bar at the top here too but please note that it has no WCs.

CREUSSANS CHAIR LIFT TS14

4

| 7 mins | • No novices
• 420 m (1378 ft) vertical rise
• 09.10–16.00 hours |

Arcalís' most north-westerly lift, leaving from just below La Coma restaurant and rising up almost to the French border. Although the lift is a fixed chair, it runs at a fair speed and has a magic carpet conveyor to ease getting on. The journey up the rocky face of the mountains separating Andorra and France affords bird's-eye views over the seriously steep terrain below, giving you an opportunity to plan the slickest lines down the couloirs; the single piste descending from this area is the narrow red L'Estany (W). At the mid-point, you pass over the route of the descending piste and the lift-line flattens out over a small tarn (L'Estany means 'the lake'), before rising steeply again. As you approach the top, quickly raise the safety bar and then make a swift exit to the right on arrival, as this area is very narrow. U-turning to the right, you are now on the start of L'Estany red. However, the main function of this lift is to bring thrill-seekers to the almost limitless off-piste available in this wild border zone. It's worth stopping to take in the panorama. Left at the top of the piste there's a track leading up the 50 m (164 ft) or so to the col. Here you have a truly breathtaking view over the high Pyrenean wilderness beyond, with the highest summit in Catalunya – Pic d'Estats (3145 m/10,318 ft) – looming straight ahead on the far side of the French valley below, and vistas behind you over Arcalís and much of Andorra on a clear day. The high Tristaina Valley to the left of L'Estany red piste is an enjoyable and popular off-piste excursion from this point.

ⓘ Always employ a qualified local mountain guide whenever venturing off piste.

L'ESTANY (W)

Arcalís' only southerly-facing piste, but high and guaranteed to have snow and providing the only on-piste descent from the highest lift-reachable point in the ski area. The top section is mild and wide enough, with a couple of purposefully positioned gaps in the fence to allow extreme riders to leave for the steep off-piste routes. The piste then narrows into what is a mountain track winding down through this rugged terrain; with tight turns, some short steep sections and a couple of flat schusses, overall delivering a decent red profile. Run out is on to Els Orris green near the tricks park.

LA BASERA (S)

La Basera will be encountered by all visitors at least once; either by dropping in from the off-piste zone, trekking round to see the Big 'O' sculpture, or simply as a gentle route back to Arcalís base station. Shortly after leaving the Coma bowl a junction to the left starts the fast La Canaleta (L) red which drops off steeply before running out towards the lower base station area via a short tunnel. Continuing on the flat La Basera, you can't miss the monument ahead left – a massive steel circle which creates the illusion that it's just about to roll off down the mountainside – a whimsical but impressive sight. Advanced skiers can pick a line down to meet La Canaleta piste from the left-hand side of the sculpture, but exercise extreme caution beyond this point as there are precipitous cliffs dropping to the base station far below, adding an exciting dimension to this otherwise very pedestrian route.

⬤ The Ring of Fontargent, *a sculpture by Mauro Staccioli, Arcalís*

POINT-TO-POINT ROUTES: COMPETENT NOVICES

ARCALÍS BASE » LA COMA RESTAURANT

TSD12 La Basera chair lift | El Túnel (U) | Els Orris (R)

LA COMA RESTAURANT » ARCALÍS BASE

La Basera (S) | La Font (F)

POINT-TO-POINT ROUTES: GOOD INTERMEDIATES AND ABOVE

ARCALÍS BASE » SNOWPARK

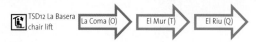

TSD12 La Basera chair lift | La Coma (O) | El Mur (T) | El Riu (Q)

SNOWPARK » ARCALÍS BASE

TSD7 La Coma chair lift | La Portella del Mig (J) | La Font (F)

▶ *Moonrise over the Ordino Valley*

MOUNTAIN BARS & RESTAURANTS

As the Arcalís area is small, and since most visitors are looking for more of a wilderness experience, there is no need for many watering holes on the pistes. However, both sectors have sufficient establishments to cater for daily visitors. Food and drink prices are also some of the cheapest encountered at Andorra's ski areas.
 All main food service is 12.30–16.00 hours; bar service is all day.

ARCALÍS SECTOR

The two base lodges each house self-service cafeterias covering two floors; there's no discernible difference in the quality or range on offer but the upper lodge does have the advantage of a sunny terrace overlooking the children's Snow Park and the pistes. Both venues also provide a full bar service.

L'Hortell bar/cafeteria Self-service restaurant at the lower base lodge, offering a set-course daily menu, grills, pasta dishes and snacks. The first floor saloon is the main bar and snack area; the second floor has the full self-service selection. The atmosphere is canteen-like, buzzing with station personnel who also have their offices in this building. It has a lovely little attic dining area which is set aside for those with picnics; no one will mind if you choose to sit up here if it's quiet, as long as you return your trays and leftovers to the main restaurant level when you've finished.

Els Planells bar/cafeteria This upper base lodge self-service restaurant mirrors that of the lower lodge, both in layout and in selection. It also has a fair-sized sunny terrace, complete with a snack kiosk and high-season BBQ. There are plenty of sunloungers and good views over the nearby pistes and mountains.

 La Coma restaurant

COMA SECTOR

There is one restaurant location here, just above the chair lift get-on points in the lower snowbowl. There is also a cosy bar serving snacks at the Portelles area at the top of the main link chair lifts.

La Coma Boasts a sunny piste-side terrace overlooking the three lift get-on points just below, with views up the entire Coma snowbowl and impressive cirque of mountains enclosing it. The main entrance leads in from just above the piste level on to a mezzanine stairwell, with arcade games and drinks/confectionery vending machines immediately ahead; WCs and a plain, bare picnic room are downstairs; the self-service restaurant is up on the first floor; the top floor houses an à la carte dining room.

The bright, canteen-like **self-service** saloon offers a range of snacks (paninis, pizza slices, hamburgers, etc.) and basic grilled dishes, plus a small salad buffet and a range of pasta, fish or meat dishes which are varied daily. There is a microwave oven near the entrance area for reheating food if it's cooling too quickly out on the terrace. The **à la carte** dining room on the top floor is Arcalís' best on-mountain dining experience and has a bright, open chalet feel, with plenty of natural daylight and good views from the picture windows. The food is a more refined version of the grills and fish dishes offered downstairs.

Les Portelles A snack bar at the point where all three link chair lifts meet at 2552 m (8373 ft). There are sunloungers on the side of the piste to the front, with a cosy café-style bar inside serving drinks and snacks. Old black and white photographs of the Ordino Valley adorn the wood-clad walls and there is a cluster of high tables in this attractive little hut, but note that there are no WCs.

▶ *Touring by snowmobile on the flanks of Pic de Font Blanca, Arcalís*

ALTERNATIVE ACTIVITIES

Arcalís exists almost purely as a ski station, without a supporting resort infrastructure. There are very few alternatives to traditional snowsports on or off the pistes, apart from the following options. ❶ Activities may not be covered by travel insurance (see page 58).

SNOWMOBILES

If you had to pick just one alternative snowsport then surely it has to be skidooing. This exhilarating motorsport is available on-site at Arcalís station, departing from the control cabin in the lower car park. The prepared circuit takes about 15 minutes to complete, looping down along the banks of a mountain stream, with a steep descent to kick start the adrenaline buzz, before blasting up to the Arcalís base station level again along the narrow track of the official High Pyrenean Route along the flanks of Pic de Font Blanca which, at 2904 m (9528 ft), is the second highest peak in Andorra. Along the way, you pass a small stone-built refuge which is frequently used by ski-tourers overnighting prior to making the 3-hour ascent of Pic de Font Blanca.

Group and advanced snowmobile lessons are available, as well as evening excursions into the ski area once the pistes have closed. For further information, ❶ +376 334 187; ❷ passaportdemocions@andorra.ad

SNOWSHOES

Snowshoe hire is available from the ski hire shop at the main base station. There are also snowshoe excursions you can go on accompanied by an instructor/guide. If your fitness level is up to the challenge, you can walk up into the high Coma Valley and visit the ice cave at the Túnel del Rat (see page 177).

APRÈS-SKI

Once the ski station closes all visitors leave for the valley's villages or to return to another resort, the Ordino Valley having no real 'resort' centre other than the parish capital itself. This can of course be viewed as a real asset to the region and many visitors deliberately choose the Ordino Valley for this very reason. Peaceful hotel lounges and welcoming family-run country restaurants where you have to make an effort to converse in the local language may be exactly your idea of après-ski heaven. If so, then Ordino will not disappoint you, being one of the least touristy regions of the Principality.

SPORTS CENTRE

A bright, modern public facility based in the parish capital Ordino. Facilities include an indoor swimming pool and children's pool, spa with whirlpool and Turkish bath, gymnasium, aerobics and spinning classes, a squash court, four-lane ten-pin bowling alley and an exterior climbing wall. ☎ +376 878 110

CAFÉS & RESTAURANTS / BARS & CLUBS

Virtually all of Andorra's bars operate as local cafés too, offering at least a snack menu. There are a handful of local bars in the hamlets dotted along this valley, as well as some more serious restaurants in and around Ordino town. This region offers no organized 'nightlife', a few of Ordino's bars providing the only real focus for any impromptu liveliness. Those listed overleaf are some of the most popular café-bars and recommended restaurants in the Ordino area.

➔ For further authentic Andorran venues, see pages 24–6.

Topic €€ An attractive wine bar and restaurant in the centre of Ordino with a small roadside terrace overlooking the river and town. Offers a quality à la carte menu focused on seasonal produce, with wood-fire grilled meats and fish, plus fondues. Open late at the weekends and can get quite lively.
☎ +376 736 702

Vertical Limits Café-bar in the centre of Ordino which is used as a meeting point for mountain guides and houses a small library of mountain sports literature and guidebooks. It has a decent range of pastries and a very reasonably priced lunch menu, plus snacks and crèpes served until around 23.00 hours. Occasional live music.

Pub Xaloc Tucked under the Vertical Limits café-bar down a little side alley in the centre of Ordino. The area's only real late-night venue but basically just a local music bar. Mostly DJ, but with occasional live music.

Babi €€ Quaint family-run restaurant with a French influence, specializing in seasonal market produce and Catalan classic dishes (see pages 28–9). Located in the centre of Ordino.
☎ +376 835 343

Messina €+ Reasonable quality pizzeria with attractive modern décor, opposite Ordino's tourist board office. ☎ +376 838 900

Cal Moixó €€ Attractive, good quality Andorran *Borda* restaurant in an atmospheric old building. Rustic mountain cuisine, roasts, game and fresh river trout. In the hamlet of Ansalonga on the valley road up towards Arcalís from Ordino. ☎ +376 850 884

INTRODUCTION

SOLDEU EL TARTER
Valls de Canillo

GRAND VALIRA

Soldeu–El Tarter (SET) has long been Andorra's most extensive ski area and it has a high international profile. Many associate it with the Principality, but also with the idea that it is tailored to those on a budget and/or looking for a resort that focuses more on après-ski than on skiing. This was the case in the 1970s and 80s, but things have changed enormously.

In the winter of 2004/05, the ski station agreed a joint ski pass with neighbouring Pas de la Casa–Grau Roig: the merged resorts are now marketed as Grandvalira. The area ranks in Europe's top 20 for extent of pistes and facilities, with Soldeu–El Tarter firmly establishing itself as the most upmarket resort in the Principality and with a ski school rated as one of the world's best.

Located in the north-east of Andorra, in the parish of Canillo, and strung out along the main arterial road which cuts through northern Andorra from the French border at Pas de la Casa, Soldeu and El Tarter are two villages sharing an interconnected ski area, with piste and lift connections with parish capital Canillo. A glance at the piste map gives a good overview of the layout of the villages and of the topography of the region (see page 203).

PRONUNCIATION
Soldeu Sol~day~oh

Canillo Can~ee~yo

El Tarter El~tar~tay

◄ *Home runs and ski bridge at Soldeu base*

SOLDEU SECTOR

Soldeu village is the main resort focus in this region, dominated by the English-speaking tour operators who have helped build the international profile of the resort, albeit originally aimed at the cheap-and-cheerful, young-and-lively demographic. Soldeu has steadily developed into a serious player in European snowsports, with an increasingly cosmopolitan clientele. The village's roots as a youth destination still run deep, with a good selection of lively bars and a focus on nightlife, but it also has five 4-star hotels and a wellness spa to cater for its increasingly sophisticated visitors.

The ski area begins on the opposite side of a deep ravine, running parallel with the main through-road, with two blue and two black pistes making the home run right back to the foot of the village, via a wide skiable bridge over the river. Direct access to the beginners' area and all onward pistes and links is provided by a fast gondola lift departing from a spacious base station at the upper end of the village.

The extent and variety of the ski area is vast, particularly when combined with the full Grandvalira ski pass, with an excellent beginners' zone, plenty of long cruising blues and fast reds, mild blacks and open freeriding terrain. The neighbouring El Tarter sector is well interlaced with the Soldeu pistes and lifts, requiring no more than one lift to make the best connection after arrival at the gondola top station. The links east towards Grau Roig for the Pas de la Casa sectors are also straightforward, needing only two lifts to cross over. Confident novices should be able to venture into all sectors by the end of their first week, while intermediates and more advanced riders will be spoilt for choice. Together with its quality accommodation, lively après-ski scene and reasonable prices, Soldeu reigns as Andorra's best all-round resort choice.

EL TARTER SECTOR

El Tarter, a cluster of accommodation and services, lies 3 km (2 miles) west of Soldeu. A couple of hotels are situated at the base of the lifts and home-run pistes, but most are in a residential zone on the opposite side of the main through-road. There is a sprinkling of bars and shops in the residential area, but most visitors use the local bus or take a taxi to the more substantial resort at Soldeu, a 5-minute drive away. Between Soldeu and El Tarter there is roadside accommodation at Vall d'Incles; guests staying here tend to make the journey to Soldeu for evening entertainment and need to catch the ski bus to reach the lifts and pistes.

A new gondola lift was inaugurated in the 2004/05 season, providing fast uplift directly from the large open car park, up to the beginners' zone and main services at the lower lip of the wide El Tarter snowbowl above. This lovely sheltered bowl provides something for all abilities and is the main focus of this sector, with only one more lift needed to link with either Canillo's El Forn sector or to Soldeu. As with Soldeu, most novices should be able to venture out between all sectors by the end of their first week.

CANILLO SECTOR

Canillo lies 5 km (3 miles) from El Tarter, on the through-route towards Andorra la Vella and Spain. It is an attractive village, quiet and not touristy, but has the country's only Olympic-standard ice rink and a large modern sports centre, as well as a substantial base station with a gondola lift to the compact, family-orientated El Forn ski sector, with onward lift and piste links to El Tarter.

Wherever you choose in the Soldeu–El Tarter–Valls de Canillo area as your holiday base, you can be sure that you will experience Andorran snowsports at their most dynamic.

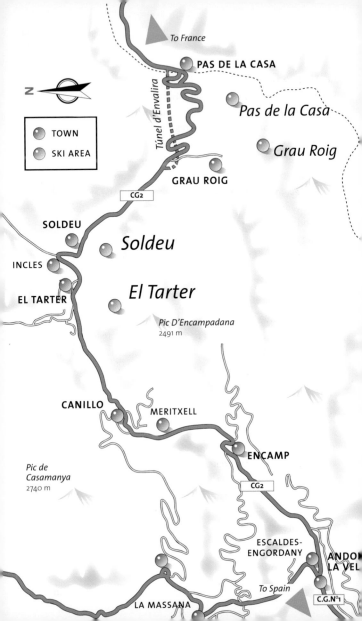

COMING & GOING

From France: after passing through the customs station, which straddles the RN20 road approaching Andorra, you have two choices: turn right at the first roundabout for the quickest route via the Envalira tunnel (toll), or go straight on to the border at Pas de la Casa. The route via Pas de la Casa involves driving over the Envalira Pass (Port d'Envalira) which, at 2408 m (7900 ft), is the highest road pass in the Pyrenees and can be cut off by heavy snows (snowchains obligatory). On the other side, both routes join at a roundabout: keep straight ahead on the CG2, passing through the satellite accommodation zone of Bordes de Envalira before Soldeu comes into view next ahead. (El Tarter and Canillo are a short distance further on the same road, a little closer to the capital Andorra la Vella.)

Soldeu's main multi-storey car park is almost immediately on the left, under the gondola lift base station, which is next on your left. There are also some roadside parking bays, plus an open-air car park down to the left in the village centre. Virtually all of the resort's hotels, bars and restaurants line the main road.

The CG2 goes straight through Soldeu, next passing through a satellite accommodation area at Incles, before approaching El Tarter. There is a side road to the right into the village, otherwise continue on the main road via the tight right-hand bend ahead for the base station on the left or the lower village on the right.

Canillo is just 5 km (3 miles) further on, still on the CG2. Arriving in its small town centre, the ice rink ('Palau de Gel') is on your right and the gondola base station and multi-storey car park is off to the left via a side street. There are also some short-stay parking bays on the main roadside, plus a small car park to the right immediately after the ice rink.

From Spain: the access route is via La Seu d'Urgell, 10 km (6 miles) south of Andorra on the N145. After passing through customs and passport checks on the border, the road becomes the CG1 and continues towards the town of Sant Julià de Lòria. On approaching Sant Julià, veer left at the first roundabout to bypass the town and head towards Andorra la Vella. The rush-hour traffic through Andorra la Vella is no fun, but the government has made efforts to re-route traffic via a still busy bypass from the Santa Coloma district at the southern end of this small but bustling capital. Approaching the first suburbs, follow the signs to the right towards France (signed 'França') and Escaldes–Engordany. Keep straight on up the bypass to exit at a mini-roundabout above the upper end of the capital. Turn right to follow the signs for Encamp and França. Encamp is 3 km (2 miles) from here and is easily bypassed by veering right at the first roundabout, following the signs for Canillo and França and passing under the lines of Grandvalira's Funicamp cable car. Canillo is now only 4 km (2½ miles) ahead, with El Tarter and Soldeu just slightly further on (see page 197 for details).

DISTANCES
- Toulouse to Soldeu   192 km (119 miles)
- Barcelona to Soldeu   186 km (116 miles)
- Andorra la Vella to Canillo 12 km (7½ miles)
- Canillo to El Tarter   5 km (3 miles)
- El Tarter to Soldeu   3 km (2 miles)

❍ *Andorra's main roads are well maintained and quickly cleared of snow*

SOLDEU TOWN PLAN

KEY

i	Information point	⇘	Ski pass kiosk
🚠	Gondola	✗	Equipment hire shop
🚌	Bus stop	P	Parking
€	ATM cash machine	🏪	Supermarket
☎	Public telephone	✚	Pharmacy
✉	Post box	✝	Church

HOTELS & APARTMENTS

1. Hotel Sport
2. Edelweiss Apartments
3. Sport Hotel Village
4. Hotel Himilaia Soldeu
5. Hotel Piolet
6. Hotel Soldeu Maistre
7. Hotel Montaña
8. Hotel Naudi
9. Popaire Apartments
10. Font Apartments
11. Hotel/Apartments Hort de Popaire

RESTAURANTS (see pages 281–2)

1. Sol i Neu
2. Slim Jims
3. Fontanella
4. Cort de Popaire
5. Colorado Tex Mex
6. l'Esquirol

BARS & CLUBS (see pages 284–6)

1. Piccadilly
2. Villager
3. Iceberg
4. Fat Alberts
5. Avalanche
6. T-Bar
7. Capitol
8. Pussycat
9. Aspen

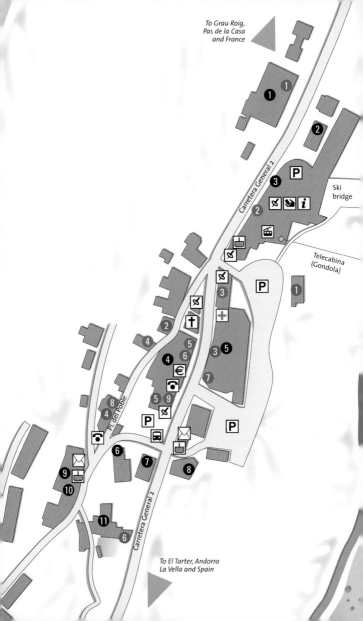

To Grau Roig,
Pas de la Casa
and France

Carretera General 2

Ski
bridge

Telecabina
(Gondola)

Pl. del Poble

Carretera General 2

To El Tarter, Andorra
La Vella and Spain

SKI AREA DATA

- Opening time — 09.00 hours
- Last lift up — 17.00 hours
- Skiable area — 1776 ha (4389 acres)
- Altitude — 1710–2640 m (5609–8660 ft)
- Vertical drop — 930 m (3051 ft)
- Access points — 6
- Ski schools — 2 (450 instructors at 7 different centres)

- Ski lifts — 63

Cable cars	1	Gondolas	3
Chair lifts	28	Button lifts	17
Rope tows	9	Conveyor belts	5

- Capacity — 94,500 passengers/hr

- Pistes 108 (= 193 km/120 miles)

Green	18	Freeride	4
Red	37	Mogul	2
Blue	32	Children's	6
Black	21	Halfpipes	1
Nordic	1	FIS	3
Tricks parks	3		

- Hands-free ski pass — Yes
- Snowmaking — 914 cannons
  64.3 km (40 miles) = 33.3 per cent of ski area
- Medical centres — 5
- Mountain bars/restaurants — 17 sites
  Figures given are for the full Grandvalira domain.
- Visitor information — www.grandvalira.com

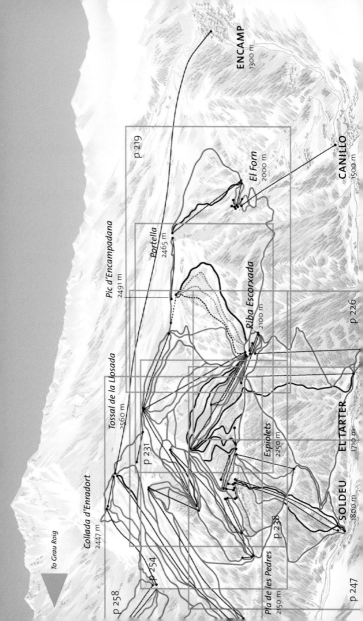

To Grau Roig

Collada d'Enradort
2447 m

Tossal de la Llosada
2560 m

Pic d'Encampadana
2491 m

Portella
2465 m

El Forn
2000 m

ENCAMP
1300 m

CANILLO
1500 m

Riba Escorxada
2100 m

Espiolets
2250 m

Pla de les Pedres
2150 m

SOLDEU
1800 m

EL TARTER
1710 m

p 219

p 226

p 231

p 238

p 247

p 254

p 258

SKI PASSES

For beginners, there is a day pass available giving access to El Forn sector at Canillo; this permits travel on the Canillo gondola and use of the lifts in that small sector only.

Soldeu–El Tarter (SET) local sectors ski passes are available as day passes only; all other options over two days' duration are full Grandvalira area passes covering Soldeu–El Tarter (including Canillo) and Pas de la Casa–Grau Roig. A small supplement applies if accessing Grandvalira via the cable car at Encamp.

All ski passes are hands free; a deposit is payable for the pass-card, which can be kept to be recharged or returned to a ski pass kiosk for deposit refund. The passcard is secured in a left-hand pocket and operates lift turnstiles by remote control.

High season = every weekend; week leading up to Christmas until week after New Year; all February and Easter.

Low season = all other dates (only three per cent cheaper than high season).

All passes are available for adults (12–64 years) and children (6–11 years): half-day (09.00–13.00 hours or 13.00 hours–last lift); full-day and multiples thereof – the longer the duration, the cheaper the daily rate. Ski passes are free for all children under 6; from 6 to 11 prices are approximately 20 per cent cheaper than adults. A small discount is also given on children's day passes if the child wears a helmet. Ski passes for guests aged 65–70 are available at a much reduced daily rate; passes are free for the over 70s.

🛈 Proof of age is required for child and senior ski passes.

SKI ANDORRA SKI PASS

See also page 61 for full details of the Ski Andorra ski pass, which permits access to all of Andorra's ski areas.

SKI PASS SALES POINTS

The main sales points are at Canillo gondola base station; El Tarter gondola base station building and on the approach to the nearby chair lift; and Soldeu gondola base station. Grandvalira ski passes can also be purchased at any of the Encamp, Grau Roig and Pas de la Casa access points (see page 299).

NON-SKIERS

Non-skiers who wish to travel up to the restaurants and service areas at the top of the gondolas at Canillo, El Tarter or Soldeu can buy a 'pedestrian pass' permitting one return journey. There are no other pedestrian lifts to higher areas from the gondolas, but the views from these mid-level stations are superb; facilities are good and your skiing friends and family can access these stations on-piste during the day. Some of the alternative activities on offer in the ski areas are accessible using a pedestrian pass (see page 300).

The Funicamp cable car from Encamp is an excellent option for pedestrians, as it arrives at the high-altitude Collada d'Enradort area at 2447 m (8028 ft) – the restaurant and facilities here are excellent and the views are amazing (see pages 342 and 354).

🛈 Accident insurance is not included in ski pass prices. Make sure you are adequately covered (see page 58).

PRICES

For information on current prices for all ski passes, tuition, childcare and other resort services, please go to our website: **www.ski-ride.com**

SKI BUS

Within the villages of Canillo, El Tarter and Soldeu themselves, there's no real need for a ski bus service as the gondola lift base stations are all within walking distance. However, if you want to move between the resorts or are staying in one of the satellite accommodation areas then you'll need some form of transport. There is a ski bus service provided by the SET stations, called the Gel Ski Bus, which plies between Canillo and Bordes d'Envalira, via El Tarter, Incles and Soldeu; it is free to SET/Grandvalira current ski pass holders and runs roughly once per hour between 08.45 and 23.20 hours, with a break between midday and 15.00 hours. Additionally, there are scheduled local bus services between all the villages and Andorra la Vella, which can be used to make local connections as well. Timetables are available at ski pass kiosks and at tourist board offices (see page 201).

⬥ *Soldeu village centre*

EQUIPMENT

Hire of equipment at Andorran resorts is easy; there's a sports shop on every village street and at every base station, and virtually all have a rental service. The most established companies in the SET area are Esports Bonnell, Pic Negre Sports and, especially, Esports Calbo. As well as boot hire, all offer traditional Alpine skis, carvers, snowboards and snowshoe hire. All also offer equipment servicing and repair, waxing and edges/base preparation for your own gear, as well as technical clothing and accessories.

Most visitors travelling with a tour operator leave the organization of gear hire to their reps, usually being taken for fitting en masse early on their first morning on the mountain. With so much similar-looking rental equipment on the mountain it's very easy to confuse your gear with someone else's and vice versa. All hire gear is marked with a serial number; make a note of this and observe what your gear looks like before leaving it near other similar models. Other than using a lockable rack, a good tip is to mix and match each ski with one of your mates' if you need to leave them unattended; snowboarders should carry a light chain and padlock to secure their gear.

STORAGE

Most hotels have their own equipment storage rooms and sometimes lockers, too. There are also locker rental operations at various convenient points around the main services areas: at the base station of the Canillo gondola lift and at the El Forn area at the top; at El Tarter's base station and Riba Escorxada area at the top of the gondola lift; at Soldeu's gondola lift base station and next to the information kiosk at the top of the gondola lift in the Espiolets area.

TUITION

The ski school has offices at the top of all three gondola lift access points in the area, Soldeu, El Tarter and Canillo, offering a range of instruction for all ability levels for Alpine skiing and snowboarding. Public group classes are grouped by language, ability level, age, ski and snowboard. Children aged 3–6 years old have their own separate Snow Garden; from 6 years old they can join the regular classes out on the pistes, generally grouped with similar ages. Public group lessons are for 15 hours, 3 hours per day over 5 days (Monday–Friday). Reduced rate prices apply for children aged 6–11 years old.

Private lessons for Alpine skiing, Telemark and snowboarding must be arranged directly with the ski school. Prices charged for private instruction are per hour; per half day or per full day, and are the same for adults and children. Prices also depend on season, time of lesson and how many of you there are.

Snowboarders have a dedicated Surf School based at the Soldeu sector; this twin operation also promotes an initiative called Freestyle Camps, which offers a more adventurous programme of instruction for early intermediates and above to introduce you to jumps, rails and halfpipes.

SET SKI SCHOOL

The SET ski school is regarded as one of the best in the world, tailored around the UK and Eire tour operator market, and has won many awards for excellence. The school is the biggest of its type in Europe, employing around 230 instructors, over 100 of whom are English-speaking. The effectiveness of instruction and rate of student progress are excellent; plus there is an easier, more flowing rapport between instructor and client.

The development of the school has been greatly assisted by the unique nature of the political and labour situation in Andorra: the country relies upon immigrant workers because of its small population, and the labour laws have been set up specifically to welcome workers with foreign qualifications.

INSTRUCTOR QUALIFICATIONS

Controls have been tightened in the last few years regarding how many training/teaching hours need to be logged by instructors to achieve entry-level and subsequent qualifications (currently 270 hours minimum) and an Andorran government department was also set up to take responsibility for instructor training courses for native Andorrans. This department investigates each external ski nation's qualifications and has compiled an equivalence matrix to compare with their own standards; as a result the Andorran entry-level qualification is now one of the highest in the world, and foreign instructors with qualifications that are acceptable else-where are now regularly required to complete a 'top-up' course to secure a work permit here. This supplementary qualification is unique to the Andorran situation and continues to push stand-ards even higher. The Andorran education system closely mirrors the neighbouring French model, but has been consistently more advanced as the tiny state strives to assert its independence; the snowsports' training situation now also reflects this and the Principality can boast tuition quality thresholds that are now even higher than those of the world's leading ski nation next door.

Over 20,000 British and Irish guests pass through the Soldeu school every winter, with around 2300 individuals per week in high season, spread out over the area's three stations. On Sundays, at every tour operator's welcome briefing to newly arrived guests, an SET instructor attends to make a short presentation and to explain exactly what happens on the first morning on the mountain, giving information on private lessons and on flexible taster lessons between ski and snowboard disciplines, too.

GROUP ORGANIZATION

One of the most impressive aspects of the SET ski school operation is how they organize the public groups on the first day. Unlike in some other ski resorts, where beginners are just counted off into classes, here they separate out groups of 44 guests, with four instructors taking these big groups for an initial fun 'team teach' to observe each person's natural ability. Then, after an hour or so, these large groups are split into four separate classes best matched to each individual's aptitude, age and character, to go off with a now dedicated instructor. Therefore, everyone learns at an optimum pace. This procedure is repeated through all four ability standards offered (novice to advanced), giving 16 possible permutations of tuition levels.

Tourists usually see more of the ski school team than any other station personnel; the quality and professionalism of the operation is therefore paramount, uniquely affecting and influencing the quality of each visitor's holiday experience. The SET ski school can be relied upon to deliver to a high standard.

CONTACTS
ℹ️ Soldeu office +376 89 05 91
ℹ️ El Tarter office +376 89 06 41
ℹ️ Canillo office +376 89 06 91

CHILDCARE

Gentle Snow Gardens are fenced off and equipped with magic carpet conveyors and mini-button lifts and colourful obstacles; here, specialist ski school nursery monitors introduce children aged 3–6 years old to the world of snowsports. This service is bookable in 2-hour slots or for 15 hours spread over 5 days (3 hours per day) and is available next to the ski school offices at all three gondola lift upper stations. Equipment hire is not included.

A separate crèche service for infants aged 2–3 years is available; playrooms are bright, warm and welcoming. Some outdoor activities, such as igloo and snowman building, are arranged depending on how cold it is, but mostly the children remain indoors participating in games and activities. Staff speak English, Spanish, Catalan and French. The service is offered on a 2-hour; half-day; full-day; 5 consecutive full-day; and 5 x half-day basis: Snow Gardens and crèches are at the sides of the slopes, within sight and reach of the gondola top stations and service areas.

▲ *First steps in the wonderful world of snowsports*

SERVICES

Medical centres: there are well-equipped trauma and X-ray suites at the gondola lift base station buildings in Canillo and Soldeu and at the foot of the lower slopes at El Tarter base station. Special stretcher cabins are mounted on the gondolas to bring patients from the pistes; the Soldeu and El Tarter centres are also accessible by rescue sleds directly from the pistes. They are close to roads and helipads for emergency transport to hospital.

The medical staff will contact your insurance company, but you will have to pay any initial costs excluded by any excess clauses on site. Ensure your insurance policy covers heli-rescue, on-piste rescue and ambulance transport as well as medical and hospital expenses. Andorra is not in the EU and has no public health service; hospitals are very modern, but all are private.

🛈 Always carry some form of ID and your insurance details. Carry a small first-aid kit for dealing with minor cuts and bruises (see Health & Safety, pages 53–8).

WCs: located at the base station gondola buildings and close to the upper station arrival points, as well as at all major mountain bars and restaurants. There are some high-altitude no-flush 'eco toilets' at some of the highest link areas. All are free of charge.

ATMs: the nearest cash machines are located on Soldeu's main street and in Canillo village centre.

Telephones: there are phonecard-operated public telephones at all gondola base stations and at all major mid-level on-mountain services buildings. Phonecards are available from most shops and supermarkets. GSM mobile phone coverage is almost 100 per cent.

Shops: there are no station-managed shops within the ski area itself, but there are plenty of snowsports retail outlets based in or around the gondola lift base stations in all sectors, selling equipment and last-minute accessories such as film, disposable cameras, sunblock, fleeces, ski hats, gloves, backpacks, sunglasses, goggles, etc. The Soldeu town gondola lift station is the most convenient base for access to nearby food shops.

Mountain restaurants: you're never far away from food and drink anywhere on the mountains; there are eight different sites and around 20 venues throughout the ski area, ranging from simple snack kiosks up to full-service à la carte restaurants; most are self-service canteen types. There are some private enterprises located at Soldeu and El Tarter base stations, but all the on-mountain bars and restaurants are managed by the ski station and are branded according to size and type of fare on offer: **Espress'Oh!** cafes; **Xiris** (pronounced 'cheeries') snack kiosks; and **Fun Food** fast-food restaurants. Additionally, there are a number of large self-service restaurants and two more formal restaurants. See pages 268–72 for specific reviews. Prices are consistent and are slightly cheaper than in similar venues in the Alps.

Picnic areas: there are indoor picnic rooms at Soldeu and El Tarter main mid-level services areas close to the ski school offices and gondola lift upper stations. However, it has to be said that they are very uninspiring. There is a sheltered, secluded wooded area ideal for a picnic beside a reindeer corral at the base of Canillo's **El Forn** area slopes, otherwise anywhere safe on the mountain is fine. Take all your rubbish plus any that you find to a bin and note that it is forbidden to picnic on any of the restaurant terraces.

SNOWFALL HISTORY & ANALYSIS

Although precipitation is unpredictable at very long range, patterns do emerge that are observable over a number of seasons. Using this data, you can tell if your preferred period of travel has historically seen good snow cover. The magic figure is 100 cm (39 in) – once snow depth exceeds this mark, conditions are generally good throughout the ski area and will remain so for a more extended period.

As with all the Andorran stations, quantity of snowfall is not a problem. The station is also adept at maintaining what they get and all principal home runs to both base stations are protected by snowmaking cannons every 200 m (220 yd) or so. As long as there are sufficiently sound snowfalls and cold temperatures in the pre-season to preserve the piste base layer, then the core pisted ski area can be kept open for most of the high season. The volume of snow has regularly been over the 100 cm mark.

The chart below details combined averages recorded over three seasons immediately prior to the publication of this guide. Visit **www.ski-ride.com** for live snow reports.

Soldeu-El Tarter: weekly averages over most recent 3 ski seasons (2002/03 - 2004/05)

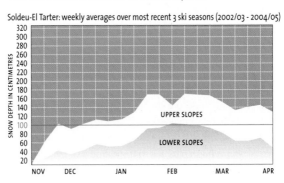

PREVIOUS SEASONS' SNOWFALL BREAKDOWN BY YEAR

The following charts detail the snowfall history for the three most recent seasons. Data from these charts was used to compile the combined averages chart on the preceding page.

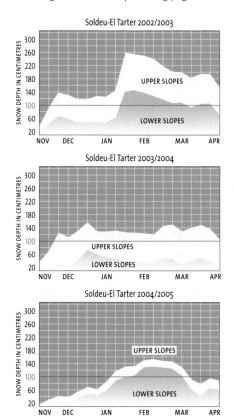

CANILLO SKI SECTOR

As the parochial capital, Canillo has long been the major share-holder in the SET stations, but only since the year 2000 has it been lift and piste linked with them. A gondola lift whisks passengers up to the sheltered, family-orientated El Forn area slopes above the village, offering an integrally complete beginners' area in its own right and providing onward lift links and return pistes extending into the upper El Tarter sector. The skiable zone begins at the top of the gondola, with no 'home-run' pistes back to the village; it does, however, have a testing blue and a fast black piste returning from the El Tarter sector link point.

CANILLO TELECABINA (GONDOLA)

  6 mins

- 500 m (1640 ft) vertical rise
- 1730 m (5676 ft) long
- 1500 passengers/hour

The base station building houses a multi-storey car park, equipment hire shops, exhibition gallery, medical centre, Fun Food restaurant and Espress'Oh! café, lockers, information desk and ski pass kiosks, as well as the Grandvalira commercial office. The gondola lift departs from the uppermost floor; all levels are accessible by elevator or escalators. On arrival, walk straight out on to the start of the pistes: all services and facilities in this sector are on this level, housed in the buildings sweeping round from immediately on your left to ahead right.

A chair-lift arrival point is just to your right, with the first pistes running parallel down each side of it to its get-on point beside the onward link chair towards the El Tarter sector.

◀ *Sheltered and compact, Canillo's El Forn area*

EL FORN AREA

All services and facilities in this sector are within a few metres' walk, with the pistes starting to your right as you exit the lift station. There is an absolute beginners' piste and a tubing piste to the immediate right on exiting the gondola, both sharing a short magic carpet conveyor; at the bottom of these are three waymarked snowshoe circuits. On your immediate left, there is an information kiosk and equipment lockers building; just past these is the ski school, plus the crèche and WCs; the children's Snow Garden is situated at the far side of the crèche. The main catering facilities are just 40 m (44 yd) ahead right on this same level, with a huge terrace overlooking the pistes and peaks beyond.

A chair lift rises up from the slopes below, making the connection back up to the gondola for return to Canillo.

All the lower pistes are gentle beginners' slopes served by easy-to-use lifts. There is a tranquil ambiance to the area, enhanced by its seclusion from the main ski sectors, which may appeal to nervous first-timers and those with small children.

FORN I & II

These are the two gentle main pistes which run parallel either side of the short TS4 Junior non-declutchable chair lift (2 minutes' journey time; closes 17.00 hours) back up to the start at the main services and gondola level again. Forn I is nearest to the restaurant building and is served by a magic carpet back up to the start level. Both pistes share the same slope and merge together to flow down to the chair lift get-on points. These slopes are mellow blue in profile, serving as the sole access route down to the get-on point for the TSD4 Portella chair lift to link into the El Tarter sector.

TSD4 PORTELLA CHAIR LIFT

5 mins

- 1225 m (4019 ft) long
- 1800 passengers/hour
- Closes 16.45 hours

The sole link chair to leave the Canillo sector, towards El Tarter, but also providing uplift to the start of this sector's own two high-level pistes – the Rossinyol blue and Gaig black. If approaching this chair from the Canillo gondola and services area, it's best to descend on the Forn I green piste on the far left. Approaching from the finish of the Rossinyol and Gaig pistes means you are already on the best side. On the journey up, the Gaig piste is directly below you. On arrival at the top, and to remain in the Canillo sector, U-turn to the right to start the Rossinyol blue and to access the Gaig black; or go straight ahead to start the gentle schuss on the Daina blue to link towards the upper El Tarter sector. A piste map is located over by the fence to the right and the lift operator's hut to the left is equipped as a first-aid post.

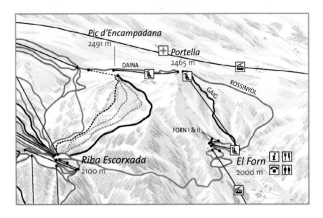

ROSSINYOL

A good mid-length blue which will return you to the El Forn lifts base, via some stunning scenery visible from this high ridge. The valley to the left is the Cortals d'Encamp, where the Funicamp cable car travels up from Encamp town; over to the right you are looking over the Canillo Valley towards the Coll d'Ordino Pass and as far as Pal–Arinsal ski stations in the far distance.

The whole upper section here is very gentle and sometimes needs a bit of a skate; around 100 m (328 ft) from the start the Gaig black piste begins by dropping off steeply to the right. Keep straight on to stay on the Rossinyol blue, which now begins to pick up gradient. The route then turns right and flows off the ridge as a motorway-wide blue with a couple of variations around copses of trees and some short mellow red sections towards the finish – check your speed approaching the lifts ahead. The Portella chair is the nearest, with the Junior chair up to the El Forn service area and the Canillo gondola just behind that.

GAIG

The only other true piste in the Canillo sector, and what a great one it is. It is more of a good red than a black, but no less worth a visit, giving a fast (1.4-km/1-mile) workout on a wide but often ungroomed motorway.

The entrance is via the Rossinyol blue. The drop in is quite steep and often mildly mogulled, before the run mellows out into a good wide red, with lots of opportunity to fly off mid- and side-of-piste bumps. Nearing the finish, check your speed since you are merging with the Forn I green piste which joins in from parallel right. The Portella chair is the nearest on the right; the TS4 Junior is next to it.

DAINA

Purely a flat link piste between the Canillo and El Tarter sectors, requiring you to schuss for almost its entire 800 m (875 yd) length. There is a short steeper top section to get you going, but then it's a tuck all the way, with a bit of a skate in softer conditions. The TS4 Cap de Clots chair rises back up parallel to the left to return towards the Canillo sector, otherwise keep straight ahead left to make a poor but manageable link with the Llosada button lift for onward links towards Soldeu and Grau Roig/Pas de la Casa; or turn left around the Cap de Clots chair to join the Guineu blue or start the Tamarro red towards El Tarter's Riba Escorxada zone – there is a gentler escape route for nervous novices out to the left to bypass the steep start section. The weekend-only Ratrac tow to the highest point on Pic d'Encampadana, for the freeride zone, departs from the far side of the Cap de Clots chair get-on point at the end of this piste.

TS4 CAP DE CLOTS CHAIR LIFT

 5 mins

- 770 m (842 yd) long
- Closes 16.45 hours

The sole lift connection between the El Tarter and Canillo sectors, along this flat and often exposed mountainside.

On arrival, turn to the left and then veer ahead right to start the Rossinyol blue and to access the Gaig black into the Canillo sector. The chair arriving from the opposite direction to this same point is the Portella chair from Canillo's El Forn area below. There is a piste map over by the fence to the left. The lift operator's hut is equipped as a first-aid post.

EL TARTER SKI SECTOR

Before the expansion of the SET ski area into the Cubil Valley at Grau Roig, the El Tarter 'Bowl' area was the station's largest sector. It is still a magnet for serious riders and has kept improving its facilities and pistes, with something for absolutely all abilities.

There are three methods of accessing the sector:
1. Directly from the El Tarter base station
2. On-piste link from the Canillo sector
3. On-piste link from the Soldeu sector

BASE STATION

As well as being the primary access point, El Tarter's base station area is, at 1710 m (5610 ft), the lowest altitude reachable by piste. Three routes make the home run to this level: the Esquirol and Gall de Bosc blues and the Aliga black, ensuring that virtually all visitors should be able to ski the mountain from top to bottom. The base station area has seen major remodelling, with the construction of a fast gondola lift to the mid-level services area at Riba Escorxada and an increase in the number of open-air parking spaces just off the main CG2 through-road; the ski bus stops are at the side of the main road. The base station is not attractive, but it is functional, providing all the facilities you need to start the day.

As well as the gondola lift station and station administration offices, there is a medical centre, a couple of major equipment rental shops, bars and restaurants, a 4-star hotel, information office, equipment lockers, ski pass sales points and WCs. There is a chair lift right at the foot of the pistes.

◀ *Llosada chair lift, El Tarter snowbowl*

TC10 TARTER GONDOLA

| 5 mins | ▲ ▼ | • 390 m (1280 ft) vertical rise
• 2000 passengers/hour
• 09.00–17.30 hours |

SET's most recent major lift investment has been the construction of this much-needed fast gondola link to the main beginners' zone and services base up at the Riba Escorxada area.

On arrival, simply walk out of the upper station on to the pisted area just above the services buildings; the onward lifts are all clustered ahead across this flat, wide and bustling area; the ski school and beginners' zone are immediately down to the right, as are all the other services.

TSD4 TARTER CHAIR LIFT

| 6 mins | • 1150 m (1258 yd) long
• 2400 passengers/hour
• 09.00–16.45 hours |

A handy alternative access chair to help beat the queues at the gondola. This was previously the fastest lift to the ski area and was rerouted slightly to provide uplift from the base of the home-run pistes back up to the Riba Escorxada area. One further advantage of this lift is that is delivers you on-piste at a point higher above the onward lifts, allowing you to glide away from the arrival point to make the best links – including a direct piste link with the Soldeu sector.

On arrival, you have two choices: turn sharp left to join the Gall de Bosc blue towards Soldeu and to access the Aliga black back to El Tarter; or leave straight ahead and veer down to the right for all other options. The children-only Mickey Snow Club fun-piste entrance is easily accessible just 100 m (328 ft) down on the right.

RIBA ESCORXADA AREA

This is the main focal point for services and lift links in El Tarter's snowbowl. Below the gondola lift upper station is a large chalet-style building housing information desks, lockers and a photo service; the ski school's English-speaking classes check-in desks and meeting points are also here, with the good-sized Riba beginners' zone flowing gently down behind these. Immediately next to this building is the entrance to the safely fenced-off children's Snow Garden, monitored by the ski school and crèche, which are in the adjacent chalet.

The third and largest building houses all other services, including the main catering operations in this area, with upper- and lower-level terraces all facing the sun and with great views up over the whole bowl. There are lots of simple gear racks, as well as a few lockable ones (€1 coin required), right next to the terraces. The lowest level terrace has plenty of simple tables and chairs and is served by a small café and snack cabin, which has a few interior tables and chairs too, plus access in to the lower ground floor of the services building. The main mid-level terrace has plenty of bench tables and seating plus a fair number of sunloungers, again with its own drinks/snacks kiosk at the sheltered far side of the terrace; the main entrance leads into an Espress'Oh! café and Fun Food fast-food canteen, a stairwell leading down to the lower ground floor and WCs, and up to the first floor Riba Escorxada self-service restaurant.

Above the gondola station is the Pi de Migdia restaurants' building, planned to house a café and various restaurants. All onward lifts depart from the area in front of the main services buildings, although there is a slight uphill gradient towards them. All major pistes also flow back to this area.

RIBA BEGINNERS' ZONE

Novice skiers have a fair-sized dedicated debutants' zone, which flows gently from the rear of the ski school and lockers buildings. The beginners' area is served by the slow-moving, easy-to-use TS2 Riba chair lift and by a magic carpet conveyor belt, running up the wide snowfield.

The slow-moving TS4 Pi de Migdia chair lift also departs from the base of these beginners' pistes, providing progressing novices with a readily available exit lift for their first forays out on the main pistes. This chair is also useful for exiting the Riba Escorxada area to access the gentle Gall de Bosc blue link piste towards Soldeu. The Pardal blue piste runs from the top of the Pi de Migdia chair back down to the service buildings, gondola station and beginners' area; you can also use this piste to connect more easily with the other lifts, use it to access the Mickey Snow Club chil-

dren's piste or flow with it past the beginners' area and then continue down to join the lower Esquirol blue piste for the long home run back to El Tarter base station. Otherwise, you can simply take the gondola back down. The Riba area is within reach of all facilities in the vibrant Riba Escorxada area, so you won't have to stray too far in your first few days.

MICKEY SNOW CLUB

This fantastic themed adventure trail has been specially designed for the station's younger visitors (children under the age of 12), and is accessed from the top of the TS4 Pi de Migdia and TSD4 Tarter chair lifts. Only 100 m (328 ft) from the arrival points of these lifts, the entrance is clearly visible and marked with flags and a kiddie-sized entrance arch. Entrance is free for all ski pass holders under 12 years of age.

The course is a winding piste through the woods, set out with colourful obstacles and cartoon characters. There is a little slalom just after the start, then some gently banked bends, followed by an exciting series of rolling bumps under low-hanging banners; next is a series of hoops forming a tunnel and finally a 'speed' straight with flashing lights and sirens exiting on to the Pardal blue piste towards the beginners' zone or, most probably, to the chair lift to go back up and do it all again!

The area is not suitable for complete beginners; children will need to be at least comfortable on skis to get the most out of this piste. The ski school frequently brings children's classes to this zone once they've mastered the basics. The area is patrolled by the station's entertainment staff, but no one will mind if you accompany your children on this piste if they don't want to go in on their own.

⬥ The Mickey Snow Club fun piste, a great kiddies' adventure trail

ESQUIROL

Strictly speaking, this long (4.5 km/2¾ mile) route begins at the top of the Tosa dels Espiolets area. However, most people usually encounter this piste as the main 'home run' to El Tarter base from the Riba Escorxada area.

The actual start from the top of the Tosa dels Espiolets is quite challenging for beginners, with some sections parallel to red-graded pistes. The run begins to the right after arriving on the Tosa Espiolets chair but, contrary to the piste map, this piste is not the first on the right (that's the Esparver red) and is in fact the second piste past the fence. The upper section is fairly gentle, before steepening to a mild red profile past the entrance to the Stadibump bumps zone, becoming a narrower track to pass the Freestyle tricks park entrance. The piste then widens out into a good blue motorway, curving down to the right to merge with pistes that join from the left. At the junction ahead stay on the upper track to schuss towards the Riba Escorxada area.

To continue on to the lower section of the Esquirol, go to the left of the services building and ride out wide to the left. From here you are beginning the long, mostly gentle, home run to El Tarter base station, via long straight sections and tight zig-zagging turns, manageable by confident beginners. If it's not too busy, more advanced skiers can tackle the route in full tuck all the way – give way to slow-moving piste traffic.

The finish section is quite steep, being joined by the Aliga black from above right and with a short variation black pitch dropping off to the right. Otherwise simply follow the wide main blue piste down to the lifts' access area below: go right for the TSD4 Tarter chair lift and for the snack-food restaurant and WCs; go left for the gondola and car parks.

TSD6 LLOSADA CHAIR LIFT

| 7 mins | • 460 m (1509 ft) vertical rise
• 2000 m (2188 yd) long
• 2400 passengers/hour |

The only lift serving the main section of the El Tarter snowbowl, rising up to the Tossal de la Llosada mountain looming straight above this sector, and allowing onward links towards the Canillo sector, the Soldeu sector and the Grau Roig sector for Pas de la Casa. The chair departs from a flat basin in front of the Riba Escorxada area; it is a fast declutchable chair, with the additional advantage of a magic carpet belt at the get-on point to ease mounting the lift and allowing it to run as quickly as possible. The views on the journey up are over the entire bowl stretched out before and below you, with a tantalizing view of some seriously steep couloirs and cliff jumps just to the right at the top section.

On arrival, go right for the Oreneta, Teixó and Guineu blues, as well as to head towards the link with the Canillo sector; or go ahead left, round the far side of the other arriving chair lift, for the Cortalets (linking with Grau Roig) and Solana blues; or U-turn left for the Gall de Bosc blue and Llop and Miguel reds, and to make a slightly easier start to the Teixó and Guineu blues – this way also allows advanced freeriders to traverse out towards the radio mast to drop off from the cliffs and couloirs above the Llop piste.

TOSSAL DE LA LLOSADA AREA

This is the highest point in the SET ski area, commanding 360-degree views over the ski area, plus the neighbouring Grau Roig sector, as well as most of Andorra and the surrounding peaks – there's a large panoramic image displaying the names of the major summits. There are WCs here and a handy little café cabin.

LLOSADA CLIFFS & COULOIRS – EXPERTS ONLY!

You can spy these seriously steep chutes as you ride up on the Llosada chair lift. To access this great extreme freeride, take the top section of the Guineu blue piste from the Tossal de la Llosada area, leaving the piste by the fence to the right to ride out towards the radio mast. Keep to the left of the mast when approaching to stay clear of the cliffs (unless you're up for them!) and continue on for about 70 m (77 yd) to access the most rideable couloirs dropping away to your right on to the Llop red piste below.

ORENETA & TEIXÓ

These two challenging blues are definitely the best to head to first thing in the morning, to escape the crowds and for warm-up runs, as well as offering the best late-afternoon snow conditions. As a bonus, the views ahead left towards central Andorra and the Spanish border are great. These routes are also the quickest way to reach the pick-up point for the weekend-only Ratrac freeride zone.

The Oreneta is the furthest left when descending, the Teixó is to the right of the dividing fence. Both are really twin-profile wide blues to begin with, then both steepen into mild-to-fair reds for the lower three-quarters of their 1.2 km (¾ mile) run. Both pistes link well with, and are served by, the TK Llosada II button lift; additionally, both also continue over to the Cap de Clots chair linking with the Canillo sector. The Teixó also allows you to keep right at the finish and merge with the Guineu blue to continue on down into the El Tarter bowl via that route or by the Tamarro red piste.

GUINEU

This good blue mirrors the Oreneta and Teixó pistes for its top section, and continues into the main El Tarter bowl all the way to the Riba Escorxada area. It also gives access in to the extreme freeride Llosada cliffs and couloirs, over the fence to the right at the uppermost section – for experts only!

Approaching the base level of the Llosada II button lift, running parallel to the left, either swing left for the lift, or keep straight down the fall-line, veering right to continue into the bowl. This section steepens considerably into a good red equivalent gradient; stick far right for the steepest line. Keeping highest to the left leads to the enjoyable Tamarro red piste.

The Guineu continues into the upper El Tarter bowl, via a fast schuss section running out over a flat crest, steepening again into a huge motorway good blue with dips and bumps. The run finishes with a long gentle schuss towards the Riba Escorxada area. An alternative is to keep on going all the way to the El Tarter base station for a top to bottom experience lasting 5 km (3 miles).

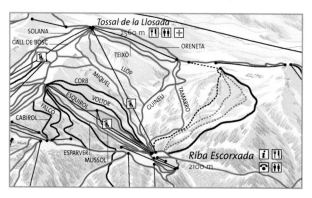

TAMARRO

A really enjoyable fast red starting from the area below the Llosada button lift, and just as you begin to descend into the El Tarter sector if travelling from the Canillo sector. The descent begins immediately as a fast schuss, leaving the left-hand side of this confluence area: after the initial 200 m (219 yd) blast, the piste rises over some high ground ahead – so keep your speed up to maintain sufficient momentum. Once over the crest, the piste steepens into a really nice red with good varied terrain.

More advanced riders can leave to the right just over this crest, through some deeper snow and young trees, before suddenly dropping into a deep and narrow gully for some great freeride lines, exiting again below, hopefully in one piece, to rejoin the main piste. The final portion of the Tamarro runs flat and straight towards the Riba Escorxada base.

TK LLOSADA BUTTON LIFT

   5 mins • 761 m (833 yd) long
• 700 passengers/hour

Not a difficult button lift but watch out for the kick at the start! Serves the Oreneta, Teixó and upper Guineu blues, which run parallel to each side of this lift, and provides the link towards the Soldeu and Grau Roig sectors. At the top, it's best to U-turn left for the Oreneta as well as the Teixó and Guineu blue; or veer ahead left for the Llop and Miguel reds; or go straight ahead under the line of the nearest arriving chair lift to begin the Gall de Bosc blue; or, ahead right above the chair-lift arrival points to enter the Solana blue and the Cortalets blue link track towards Grau Roig sector.

RATRAC FREERIDE ZONE

Open only at weekends and subject to avalanche risk approval from the snow patrol. This is a service unique to the Pyrenees, and well worth a go: an included-in-your-ski-pass tow behind a piste-basher (known locally as a Ratrac), giving access to the almost limitless freeride lines on this non-lift-served mountainside. Difficulty rating begins at good intermediate standard.

There are four tried and tested routes corresponding to the dotted lines marked on the piste map, but you're free to make your own tracks down this exciting and varied terrain. The area is left ungroomed and the slopes are almost all lightly wooded and rocky. There are also some great boulder drop-offs and natural kickers. The Ratrac providing the tow departs from just beside the

● *Freeride – free your mind and the ride will follow*

get-on point for the Cap de Clots chair lift, an area best accessed via the Oreneta and Teixó blue pistes from the Tossal de la Llosada, or via the Daina blue link piste from the Canillo sector. The operation is simply some ropes behind the Ratrac machine dragging riders en masse up to the 2491 m (8173 ft) summit of Pic d'Encampadana, where they then descend by any line down into the lower El Tarter bowl below. All routes lead out towards the Riba Escorxada services and lifts base.

LLOP

A good, fast and varied red beginning from the Tossal de la Llosada. There are two lines in: either go to the left of the panoramic display board to just where the Guineu blue piste veers off to the left, then drop in off the lip to the right for the steepest and most mogulled start; or, go to the right of the display board and head towards the Llop's first right-hand side piste marker to begin a less severe descent. Both variations converge after around 300 m (328 yd), on a motorway-wide red cruise beneath the Llosada cliffs and the chair-lift lines, running out through a gentler mid-section and flowing down into the lower bowl to merge with the Miguel red and Guineu blue towards the Riba Escorxada area. Keep highest to the right for some entertaining freerides through slightly steeper and deeper terrain to cross towards the Miguel red. The same applies on the left to traverse over to join the Guineu blue via some open ground with frequent large natural kickers.

MIQUEL

Almost a twin of the Llop red, but with three different entrances: one from the Tossal de la Llosada area and two from the Solana del Forn ridge from the Soldeu sector. The approach from the Tossal de la Llosada is shared with the Gall de Bosc blue, with the Miguel red peeling off to the left to drop with a good 35-degree slope angle. The two other entrances begin as narrow access tracks traversing the upper mountainside from the ridge to join the main piste. There are freeride possibilities to the left to play between this piste and the parallel Llop red, to the point where the pistes converge to continue as the lower Guineu blue.

FONT ROIGES BUTTON LIFT

| 4½ mins | • 700 m (766 yd) long
• 3 mins to mid-level |

Departs from just to the left of the six-seater Tosa Espiolets chair lift, and offers an alternative method of reaching the Freestyle tricks park. There are two dismount options on the journey: either get off at the mid-level exit (after 3 minutes) for the quickest access to the Freestyle tricks park, or stay on to the top to give higher access on to neighbouring pistes or to access the tricks park via an access piste and short freeride section.

On arrival at the mid-point, leave quickly to the right and swiftly clear the dismount zone to join the side of the Esquirol blue piste for 100 m (109 yd) down to the clearly marked entrance to the park. Otherwise, stay on to the top; on arrival, either leave to the left to start the Mussol red piste, or to link over with the Esparver red or Aliga black pistes; or leave to the right to join the Esquirol blue, which passes just above the Freestyle park after around 300 m (328 yd). Another option using the Esquirol route is to ride off to the left of the piste track to play in the deeper snow and light woods above the park.

MUSSOL

Short motorway piste, often used for slalom competitions and ideal as a first red, running down parallel to the Font Roiges button. The top section is shared with the Esparver red; from here it's just manageable to go with the contour line towards the trees at the far right and drop off on to the Aliga black. Otherwise, simply blast down the Mussol towards Riba Escorxada.

FREESTYLE TRICKS PARK

The SET Freestyle area is one of three dedicated tricks' parks spread throughout the Grandvalira domain; it is not only the biggest in this area, but also one of the best in the Pyrenees too. The park is situated just to the side of (and served by) the line of the six-seater Tosa Espiolets chair lift, just above the Riba Escorxada area. A secondary button lift, the Font Roiges, also serves the park. If you are riding over from the Soldeu sector, the park can be reached quickly via the Tosa dels Espiolets ridge by following the Espiolets blue piste.

Much thought and effort has gone into the layout of the park. Although geared up to offer advanced riders a serious terrain park, the SET team are aware that the majority of visitors are beginners and early intermediates; therefore this area has been designed to offer something for everyone – skier or boarder.

There is a novices' section just to the left after entering the park, set out with low rails, a low box and a series of gentle first-air jumps. If you're up for the full-on ride, then head straight into the main park – but do it well; everyone on the chair lift is watching!

🔺 *Halfpipe at El Tarter's Freestyle area tricks park, viewed from Llosada chair lift*

◆ *El Tarter's Freestyle area attracts major competitions*

FEATURES

Beginners' zone:
- Flat box
- Flat rail
- Flat-down rail
- 2, 3 and 4.5 m
  (6½, 10 and 14¾ ft) jumps

Main park:
- Halfpipe (120 m/394 yd long
  x 3.5 m/11½ ft high; difficulty
  rating 'mid-level')
- Wall ride
- 3 big in-line kickers
- Spine (8–10 m/26–33 ft high;
  mid-to-high level difficulty)
- Flat-down box
- Down-flat-down rail
- Rainbow (2.5 m/8 ft high,
  6 m/20 ft long)
- San Francisco rail
  (3 m/10 ft up, 2 m/6½ ft flat,
  3 m/10 ft down)

TSD6 TOSA ESPIOLETS CHAIR LIFT

6

10¹/₂ mins

- 367 m (1204 ft) vertical rise
- 1470 m (1608 yd) long
- Closes 16.45 hours

A major link chair between the El Tarter and Soldeu sectors, giving access to the specialist Stadibumps mogul zone (via the Voltor black) and the Freestyle tricks park (via the Esquirol blue), as well as serving a handful of fast blacks and reds off this high summit. There is a magic carpet conveyor to make things easier at the get-on; plus there is a single-rider fast-track queue at the left, so that all empty spaces can be filled up to keep queues to a minimum.

On arrival you have a huge choice: either go ahead right to make the flattish link into Soldeu and towards the Grau Roig sector; or go left for the Llebre red and Cabirol black, Mufló and Falcó blacks; or turn right for the Aliga black, Esparver red, Esquirol blue, Voltor and Corb blacks.

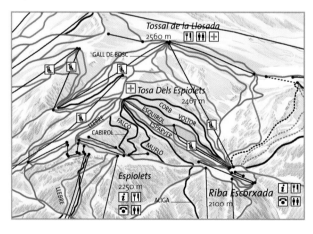

VOLTOR & CORB

Two reasonable blacks that descend into the El Tarter bowl from the Tosa dels Espiolets, each offering a slight variation but more or less running parallel down these steep upper slopes; the Corb runs widest into the bowl, furthest away from the line of the Tosa Espiolets chair lift, to give the longest and most varied route.

Both pistes' top sections are fair black in character, with steep bumpy pitches and plenty of side-of-piste kickers as you descend; the Corb definitely has the edge on steeper terrain and features a slightly narrower gully section just after the start. The lower sections of both pistes are really just fair reds, flowing together to merge with the Esquirol blue and swinging wide right towards a schuss finishing straight towards the Riba Escorxada lifts links and services base.

The Voltor can also be used to access the Stadibumps prepared mogul zone, easily identified by the banners and timer's hut at the entrance after the Voltor's mid-section. Otherwise, veer left to continue the wide fast main descent.

STADIBUMPS

This is the FIS-approved 'hotdog' bumps course, constructed and maintained by specialist piste-basher operators, on the slopes above the Freestyle park, accessed via the Voltor black and Esquirol blue from the Tosa dels Espiolets. The 'stadium' covers an area of 8000 sq m (86,114 sq ft), with a series of rolling offset bumps to give a challenging and continuous knee-bashing. The finish runs out to rejoin the Esquirol blue, allowing you to continue into the Freestyle park – if you have the stamina!

➔ *For a full appraisal of the Esquirol blue, see page 228.*

ESPARVER

This fast red is the FIS-endorsed competition course. The piste map shows it descending to the right of the Tosa Espiolets chair; in fact it starts as second to the left when looking down the chair-line.

After a gentle top section, the Esparver then swings to the right of the chair-line, corresponding better with the piste map and picking up speed as a fast motorway red. At the mid-point, there is a wide convergence area for almost all the pistes on this mountainside, permitting various permutations of onward routes. The Esparver goes to the right of the arriving button liftline, sharing the hill with the Mussol red before splitting off to the right to zoom straight down towards Riba Escorxada.

ALIGA

At 3.8 km (2½ miles), this is SET's longest black, giving a full summit-to-base run down to El Tarter. It really averages out as a good red cruise but is well worth a blast. The top section gently clears the junctions, then picks up to a fast red towards the wide convergence area above the Font Roiges button lift arrival point. You can mix-and-match any routes ahead, but the Aliga swings hard over to the right to plunge steeply off into a wooded side valley. The route runs out from here to merge with the flat Gall de Bosc blue, turning left to join the flow of traffic to reach the junction to the right just 200 m (219 yd) ahead. Exercise extreme caution ahead as the Gall de Bosc blue has U-turned round and now cuts across the line of the Aliga. Once safely past this hazard, the run begins its steepest section on a well-sheltered north-facing slope, although it can be patchy at this lower altitude. At the finish veer left to the gondola and chair lift.

MUFLÓ & FALCÓ

Basically two variations of the Aliga upper section, taking similar routes wide to the right of the Aliga. As with the Aliga, these two runs also drop out to join the gentle Gall de Bosc blue to return towards the El Tarter sector, the Falcó in particular exiting on to a very flat section close to the main Soldeu beginners' area, with a horizontal rope tow (the Telecorda) provided to aid onward progress. Although these blacks terminate here, you can of course link into the lower Aliga off the Gall de Bosc to up the pace again right down to El Tarter base station.

CABIROL

Entered by taking the flat ridge traverse shared by the start of the Llebre red from the top of the Tosa dels Espiolets. In many ways this is a very similar route to the Mufló and Falcó pistes; however, this variation has the added advantage of linking into the Soldeu sector by dipping down to the main Espiolets beginners' zone. This whole mid-level station at Soldeu is visible below right as you descend on this short mild black. Running out towards the Espiolets Plateau, you pass the get-on point for the Escola beginners' button lift – useful to gain height for accessing the services area – and can choose either to swing left towards El Tarter via the Gall de Bosc blue, or (best) carefully scoot through this debutants' zone towards the Bosc button lift arrival point dead ahead. Although very flat, it is just possible to glide across to link with the Isard and Perdiu reds falling away to the right of the arriving liftline. Taking these good fast reds makes the route worthwhile and delivers you into the lower slopes towards Soldeu base station and village.

LLEBRE

An incredibly varied route from the top of Tosa dels Espiolets, combining with the lower Soldeu sector blacks to create an almost 4 km (2½ mile) home run. Strictly speaking, this is a Soldeu sector piste, but the best access is still afforded by El Tarter's Tosa Espiolets chair.

The top section is very easy, simply traversing along the flat ridge to leave the Tosa dels Espiolets summit. It is possible to drop from here into the inviting deeper snow to the right to dip down to the pistes below. Otherwise, remain on the ridge; in poor visibility you should hug the line of the fence to the left. The Llebre truly commences when the ground plunges sharply with a short black-equivalent pitch dropping out on to a piste junction point below, where you turn 90 degrees left to schuss down to, and carefully through, the huge beginners' zone below. The traverse through the Espiolets area is an unavoidable hiccup in the flow of this route, but worth it to achieve the full summit-to-base descent. Aim for the left of the building furthest ahead on the far side of this wide plateau, staying alert at all times for erratic and nervous piste traffic throughout this debutants' zone. Once safely across this area, the Llebre gets going again with a short sharp drop to the right, inviting a schuss towards and under the line of the Soldeu gondola to continue as a mild but fast red motorway. The route then curves to the left, towards the final fast straight, finishing at the mid-point of the old Espiolets two-seater chair, under the line of the gondola.

This whole lower sector of Soldeu permits various alternatives to be constructed by combining the pistes at a number of crossover points; all deliver you to Soldeu base, for access to the gondola and the village.

GALL DE BOSC

SET's longest route, all 8.2 km (5 miles) of it accessible even by end-of-first-week beginners, touring through almost all sectors of these twinned stations. Beginning at the highest point in the El Tarter sector (the Tossal de la Llosada at 2560 m/8399 ft), accessed by El Tarter's TSD6 Llosada chair and Llosada button lift, as well as Soldeu's TS4 Assaladors chair (or the TSD6 Solana del Forn chair for a slightly lower starting point), it offers novices an almost unique opportunity to experience a true summit-to-base descent, and can be combined with pistes crossed en route to keep delivering a new route every time.

From the Tossal de la Llosada, commence the descent as a wide gentle schuss along the long ridge, eventually funnelling to the right with the Duc and Ós blues. After the next wide and undulating motorway section, the Gall de Bosc then makes a sharp turn to the left into a steeper, narrower track towards Soldeu's Espiolets beginners' zone, through which it flows, veering left to exit the area with the gentle gradient towards the rope tow (Telecorda) provided to alleviate the need to skate on this really horizontal section. This long excursion now brings you closer to El Tarter's Riba Escorxada area, but you are not finished yet! The route U-turns on a hairpin bend to the right, crossing the entrance to the lower Aliga black, and disappears into the forest as a narrow but very gentle and sheltered mountain track almost all the way to Soldeu base to merge with the almost equally long Ós blue again. Approaching Soldeu, the Gall de Bosc then peels off to the left to leave the Ós, making yet another long gentle traverse through the lowest wooded slopes, to finish across the meadows at El Tarter base station, which is 850 m below your starting point (that's almost 3000 ft). A truly epic trail!

SOLDEU SKI SECTOR

As the prime station and core sector in the SET ski area, Soldeu is most visitors' first point of contact with the region. The extent of terrain available is wide and varied, with easy links into the El Tarter and Grau Roig sectors opening up the whole Grandvalira domain. Soldeu's signature run has got to be the fall-line Avet black plunging back to the resort under the line of the gondola to finish via a pisted metal bridge high above a ravine below the village. Despite the severity of this initial aspect, the Soldeu sector is predominantly characterized by wide cruising blues above the tree line and focused around a huge beginners' zone spread out on an expansive sunny plateau. Soldeu also caters for good intermediates with some lovely fast reds on the forest-lined steeps immediately above the resort.

RESORT BASE STATION

The massive arched entranceway at the base station leads into a covered 'village square' space, with the Villager pub on one corner and a sports shop and equipment lockers on the opposite side. Straight ahead is a wide ramp down to the gondola station; there are also lifts and stairs to all other floors, serving the multistorey car parks and services housed within this same building: each lift holds up to 16 people and is accessible directly from the pistes, which run to the foot of the building. All main public areas are surfaced with rubber matting to ease walking and minimize noise levels.

The gondola access level also houses a large rental shop, WCs, information desk, ski pass kiosks, medical trauma centre, public telephone booths and some seating.

◀ *Almost there: top of the Soldeu gondola*

SOLDEU TELECABINA (GONDOLA)

6½ mins

- 450 m (1476 ft) vertical rise
- 1430 m (1564 yd) long
- 2000 passengers/hour

The principal shuttle between Soldeu village and the ski area above. All visitors, including beginners, need to travel to the mid-level services area at this gondola's upper station to access this sector and for all onward links; as a result, the queues in the mornings can be horrendous. Skis and boards should be placed in the outside holders (assistance given); poles should be taken inside.

Once you arrive at the upper station, simply walk out on to the big Espiolets Plateau: the ski-school office is to your right and the ski-school meeting points and main debutants' snowfields are straight ahead; it is also possible to put skis and boards on now and gently flow out of this area to either left or right to begin the day and access the pistes and onward lift links.

FIRST DAY & FIRST ACCESS

If you're with a tour operator, then Monday morning will usually be your first day on the slopes. You will be taken for your equipment fitting early in the morning, either in the village or at the large hire operation based within the gondola lift station itself, before ski school starts at 10.00 hours. There are lockers available at the base station for leaving your shoes and for storing equipment overnight. For the ski school, and for all other onward links, you need to take the gondola lift up to the Espiolets area immediately in front of the upper station.

TS2 ESPIOLETS CHAIR LIFT

9½ mins

- 465 m (1526 ft) vertical rise
- 1300 m (1422 yd) long
- 900 passengers/hour

- 6 mins from mid-point

This old chair was the principal access lift at Soldeu prior to the construction of the gondola. Although slow, it is handy as a queue-buster first thing in the morning: if the waiting time for the gondola looks long, take a peek out of the windows to the rear of the station to check that this chair is running; if so, then take a lift down to the lowest ground floor and simply walk across the pisted bridge to get to the chair lift get-on point. There is a 'get-on only' point serving the mid-level pistes, but the chair eventually delivers you to the same arrival point as the gondola, with the added bonus of being able to slide directly away on arrival.

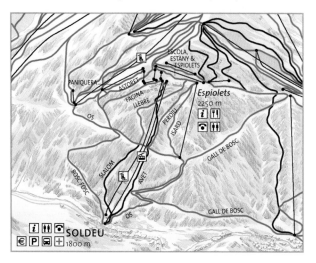

ESPIOLETS 2250 M AREA

The bustling hub of the Soldeu sector, home to one of the world's best ski schools and all the mid-level services. Arriving from the gondola or chair lift from Soldeu, the plateau is spread out in front of you. The ski-school classes meeting points are here too, with the office and crèche located in the first building on the right. Just next to these there are WCs, café and fast-food restaurant; plus a more refined à la carte restaurant on the roof terrace level.

● *Espiolets restaurant terrace, Soldeu*

To the left on arrival is the Espiolets services building, housing an information kiosk, lockers, WCs, café, self-service restaurant and indoor picnic space. Both buildings have large sunny terraces, overlooking the beginners' area and within strolling distance of the debutants' lifts.

To leave the area and move out to the main pistes and onward lifts, go past the ski-school office and services building to access the Llebre, Perdiu and Isard reds dropping off to the right, or join the very gentle Gall de Bosc blue to head into the El Tarter sector; or U-turn round to the rear of the gondola station to start the Avet black; or glide down in front of the Espiolets services building terrace to take the Astoret blue piste towards all other routes and lift links.

ESCOLA, ESTANY & ESPIOLETS

These are the names of the individual debutants' pistes on the Espiolets Plateau; however, in practical terms this whole zone is a huge shared snowfield, allowing freedom of movement across the area. There are easy-to-use rope tows and button lifts providing uplift to the top of the gentle and well-groomed slopes. There is no danger of you sticking out as a complete novice because there will be dozens of beginners just like you in classes all around you.

Children have their own dedicated Snow Garden, safely fenced off from the main pistes, with a magic carpet conveyor belt lift and colourful obstacles adding fun to the tuition process.

Once you're confident and competent enough to make your first forays out on the main pistes, you should be able to tackle the long Ós blue all the way back to Soldeu base.

ASTORET & PANIQUERA

Motorway pistes which flow out of the Espiolets Plateau, heading towards the first major chair lift and joining with the Ós blue to make the home run to Soldeu base.

The two routes run parallel but the Paniquera is at a higher altitude, accessed by the easy Bassots button lift, and has the edge on slope angle. The Espiolets I button lift serves the Paniquera, returning you to just above the Espiolets Plateau, but as with the Astorets, which merges at the lower section, it also provides all users with an exit route towards the TSD6 Solana del Forn chair lift for the upper sector and links with El Tarter and Grau Roig (there are great views of the Grau Roig area and the Envalira Pass in the distance).

ÓS & BOSC FOSC

Soldeu's home runs, down the foot of the base station and gondola via the skiable high metal bridge over the Valira River.

The Ós actually begins from the top of the Solana del Forn up near the Tosa dels Espiolets, but most people first encounter the lower section of the route as the long gentle traverse continuing down towards Soldeu from the end of the Astoret and Paniquera pistes. The piste is wide and quite easy, cutting diagonally across the wooded lower Soldeu slopes towards and past the mid-level get-on point for the old two-seater Espiolets chair (going back up to the Espiolets services and beginners' area) and maintaining a very steady flow all the way down to the base station (past a junction for the Gall de Bosc towards El Tarter base).

The Bosc Fosc is a variation final section, which leaves to the right well before you reach the line of the gondola passing overhead; as with the Ós, the finish is the flat schuss or skate across the bridge to the elevator lifts to the gondola and resort street level.

FAGINA

The name means Beech saplings, and is apt for the tree-lined route of this short wide red. It begins just to the left past the base of the rope tow which runs up parallel to the Espiolets restaurant terrace; use the left-hand side of the upper Astoret piste to reach it. Once clear of the ski-school classes using the button lift, start the run by dropping off to the left; the piste is wide and has plenty of deeper stuff to play in at the sides by the woods.

The run finishes by joining the route of the Ós blue to the Espiolets chair mid-point or to continue to Soldeu base. An ideal first red for early intermediates.

PERDIU & ISARD

Two great reds on the north-facing forested slopes above Soldeu village, accessible directly from the Espiolets area at the top of the gondola lift and served by a dedicated button lift. Both start from the area behind the ski-school office, near the piste-basher garages, sharing the same entrance area just beside the arrival point for the Bosc button lift; the Perdiu peels off to the right, while the Isard immediately takes a direct fall-line descent and is definitely Soldeu's best red. It also makes a good link with the usually less busy Bosc button lift to take you to the top again.

The Perdiu is also a good fast motorway red, but it takes a less direct line down the mountain to ride out into the wide junction area at the Espiolets two-seater chair mid-point; either get on here to get back to the top, or continue on any of the onward pistes – the Ós blue passes the Bosc button lift if you prefer to use that.

BOSC BUTTON LIFT

  13³/₄ mins
- Difficult lift. No beginners
- 1300 m (1422 yd) long
- 900 passengers/hour

A steep button with a vicious kick to start, usually without queues and ideally placed for playing on the Perdiu and Isard reds. The angle of ascent is steep, but the clearing for the lift-line is wide so if you fall off you can carefully ski back down to try again; there is also a sharp turn to the left as you approach the top. On arrival, turn left for the Isard and the Perdiu reds, or go right for the very gentle Gall de Bosc blue towards El Tarter's Riba Escorxada area. To reach the Espiolets services, ride straight off the lift and link over to the Escola U button lift to save a hike.

AVET ●

Soldeu's signature run, a straight fall-line descent right down the line of the gondola pylons to the foot of the base station. The run begins at the back of the gondola upper station, dropping immediately away into a decent black profile down the face of the mountain. This uppermost section is usually ungroomed and frequently mogulled, with boulders at the sides crying out to be used as launch pads. There are three distinct sections to the piste: the uppermost steepest, the challenging mid-section down the lift pylons and the lowest steep blast towards the finish; linking these steepest pitches are a couple of flat crossing points across the line of the Llebre red and then the Ós blue, so keep an eye out for traffic. The lower crossing point is the area around the Espiolets chair mid-point get-on, but it would be a shame to miss out on the 600 m (656 yd) long great finish section: do it well though – everyone on the lift and at the base station can see you! The Espiolets chair lift base is to the right at the bottom; otherwise end by skiing across the bridge to take an elevator to the gondola or street level.

SLALOM ●

Another good black on the lowest slopes of the mountain facing Soldeu, beginning from close to the mid-point of the Espiolets chair lift and descending all the way to the base station.

The run is 800 m (875 yd) long and is pretty consistent all the way, frequently mogulled and sometimes left ungroomed. At the bottom it swings to the left towards the bridge but also makes a fair link to the Espiolets chair lift.

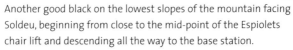
▶ *The Avet black run to Soldeu base*

TSD6 SOLANA DEL FORN

8½ mins

- 1833 m (2005 yd) long
- 2700 passengers/hour
- Closes 16.45 hours

The principal lift in the Soldeu mid-sector, giving access to the open Solana del Forn slopes between Soldeu and the Grau Roig sector. This chair also lets you run over to the fast reds and blacks in the El Tarter bowl, and towards the Freestyle tricks park.

The lift arrives on a flattish ridge between this valley and the El Tarter bowl, directly on to the side of the passing Gall de Bosc blue piste. Ride across the flat and frequently exposed ridge towards El Tarter. To stay in the Soldeu sector or link with Grau Roig, join the Gall de Bosc to flow down to the right into the Solana del Forn slopes (for the Ós, Duc and Fora blues), or take the steep Cucut red to the sharp right below. An alternative is to U-turn to the left around the lift operator's hut on arrival, to enter the steep Trenca L'Ós black and head towards the Grau Roig link.

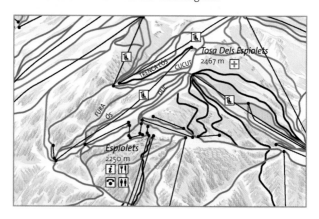

TRENCA L'ÓS

The name means Bone-Crusher, but relax; it's a familiar term for a rare Pyrenean bird: the Bearded Vulture, in fact, which has earned this soubriquet by dropping animal bones from a great height in order to break them open to get at the marrow inside.

The entrance is just to the side of the lift hut at the top of the Solana del Forn chair lift, and gives a good adrenaline rush as you plunge off the lipped start. It is short though, mellowing quickly into a fair red heading towards the Assaladors and Solanelles link lifts. This whole upper valley usually has great snow conditions, being at a sufficiently high altitude and well placed to catch any drifts blown off the exposed ridge, frequently reinforcing the pronounced lip at the entrance of this worthwhile short run.

CUCUT

A slightly milder twin of the Trenca L'Ós black, piste map marked as red but piste signed on-site as black! As with its tougher neighbour, you start immediately on a good steep pitch, before rapidly running out into a cruising red towards the finish at the Assaladors and Solanelles lifts bases.

NATURAL HALFPIPE

A great finish from the Trenca L'Ós and Cucut pistes is to stay high above the Assaladors and Solanelles lifts to traverse into the trees ahead, off the now merged Fura blue. There's a narrow gully in here which gives great freeriding off the lip and sides. Exit via the Fura blue or stroll up to the nearby lifts.

DUC & FURA

Flowing into the Solana del Forn area off the Tosa dels Espiolets ridge, you share the hill with a number of motorway-wide blues: the Gall de Bosc, the Ós, the Duc and the Fura. They all merge together to run through this slightly narrower, steepish funnel before fanning out to take their respective routes through this wide open upper valley: the Gall de Bosc and the Duc following the same line straight ahead, until the Gall de Bosc turns sharp left into a narrow, steep link track over towards the Espiolets beginners' zone and services base (see page 243). The Duc continues straight on, down what used to be the route of the old Solana del Forn button lift, now dismantled, to emerge parallel with the Paniquera blue to link with the Espiolets I button lift to the left, and continuing to a good link with the Solana del Forn chair.

Meanwhile, the Fura leaves the upper confluence area and cruises out to the right over the undulating terrain of the wide upper valley, merging with the finish sections of the Trenca L'Ós and Cucut pistes to link with the Assaladors and Solanelles chair lifts. Although the Fura makes good links with both these chairs, the route actually bypasses the area and swings down to the left bank of the small stream below, continuing on a pretty tree-lined track all the way round to the get-on point for the Solana del Forn chair lift (the route doing the same on the opposite bank is the Obaga blue). Another great option for more experienced riders is to leave the Fura piste while still above the chair lifts get-on area and ride into the trees ahead: there's a challenging natural half-pipe in here, which drops out to join the Fura again below.

There is plenty of opportunity to ride between all the upper sections of these pistes to increase the permutations of descent, all more or less blue in profile.

TS4 ASSALADORS CHAIR LIFT

| 10 mins | • 1400 m (1532 yd) long |
| | • 2000 passengers/hour |

A slowish but useful chair linking to the highest point in the sector, the Tossal de la Llosada at 2560 m (8400 ft). The Tossal summit is shared with the El Tarter sector and therefore allows full access to this linked sector's pistes, as well as permitting onward access towards the Canillo sector (see page 230).

On the journey up on the Assaladors, the pistes directly below are, from left to right, the Obaga, the Solana and the Marmotes blues; at the mid-point of the journey, you can see a great natural halfpipe down to the left, which is accessed off the upper Obaga.

On arrival, immediately to the left is a WCs cabin; U-turn left around this to start the Cortalets blue link track towards the Grau Roig sector, as well as to access the Solana blue and, via that, the Obaga and Marmotes blue variations too. The other chair arriving a short distance ahead is El Tarter's Llosada lift; head towards this point (slight incline) to access all options from here (see page 229). Otherwise, turn right to start the Gall de Bosc blue – SET's longest route covering a distance of 8.2 km (5 miles) all the way down to El Tarter base station, passing through and giving access to virtually all sectors en route (see page 243).

CORTALETS

This is simply a link track, which has a short sharp start and follows a contour line over to a short button lift (the Cortals) in the Grau Roig sector, for a more direct crossover point from the Tossal de la Llosada.

SOLANA, OBAGA & MARMOTES

Basically all variations of the prime Solana route. Follow the line of the fence parallel to the line of the arriving Assaladors chair lift, to the entrance for the route(s) dipping off the right-hand side of the ridge. The upper section is really a track which winds down through these rocky uplands. There is a junction point in the wider, more gentle slopes below: veer right for the Obaga blue; veer left for the Marmotes blue; or keep central to remain on the Solana. There is no real difference in the routes, but the Obaga does have a lovely natural halfpipe off to the left of the piste.

All three pistes merge to make a good link with both the Assaladors and the Solanelles chair lifts, the Solana and Marmotes ending there; the Obaga bypasses the lifts and continues descending on an attractive track merging with the finish of the Serrat de la Posa red piste, from where a rope tow makes the connection with the Solana del Forn lift and links with the Ós blue.

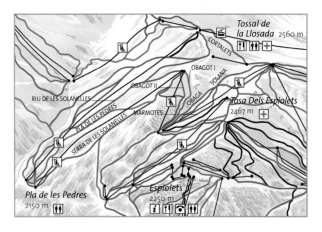

TS4 SOLANELLES CHAIR LIFT

| 8 mins | • 872 m (954 yd) long |
| | • 2000 passengers/hour |

The principal link lift from the Soldeu sector to the Grau Roig sector, also giving access to a couple of sweet reds and the opportunity to put first tracks in the deeper off-piste on the flanks of the Collada de les Solanelles, to the left of the chair-line, which you trace out on the trip up. The track-like piste traversing back down these slopes is the blue Obac Solana. On arrival, U-turn right to enter the Obagot I steep red; or turn left for all other routes; U-turning to the left off the ridge starts the Obagot II red, a slightly less severe variation of its twin to the left.

The view over the Solana del Forn area is expansive, likewise the view over the other side of the ridge gives a good route-planning vista towards the Grau Roig sector ahead: the cable car arriving on the neighbouring summit is the 'Funicamp' from Encamp town; the chair lift arriving up on this same ridge further ahead is the Pla de les Pedres Soldeu; head for this for all onward routes. There is a WCs cabin just down the ridge on the left.

OBAGOT I & II

Two short but challenging reds, which drop off back into the Soldeu sector under the upper section of the Solanelles chair-line. The Obagot I is the furthest out to the right (looking up) and is the steepest and longest. After its initial steep pitch, the Obagot II joins the blue Obac Solana to take a less direct route down to merge with the Obagot I to run to the base of the Assaladors and Solanelles lifts.

SERRA DE LES SOLANELLES

From the top of the Solanelles lift, run down towards the nearby arrival point of the Pla de les Pedres Soldeu chair lift and go to the left of the arrival pylons to continue along the flattish ridge. There are great views from this high borderline between Grandvalira's now-twinned Soldeu and Grau Roig sectors.

After passing the lift-arrival point, the piste runs under the line of the lift and continues parallel to it all the way along the ridge, with the Pla de les Pedres red piste dropping off to the right and the Obac Solana blue exiting to the left after around 300 m (328 yd). There is also plenty of opportunity to jump the fence to the right to freeride through the lovely flanks of deeper snow into the valley below. Continuing along the ridge brings you to a steeper, faster section, which would qualify as a mild red, before the piste peels off to the right as a still enjoyable blue all the way to the base of both Pla de les Pedres chairs. However, it is also possible just to keep on going straight ahead on the ridge to begin the Serrat de la Posa red, gliding on for another 100 m (109 yd) or so before curving to the left to take on a fair red pitch, running out to grab a rope tow in the valley below to make the connection with the Solana del Forn chair lift.

PLA DE LES PEDRES

A faster and more technical variation of the Serra de les Solanelles blue, which runs parallel above this decent fast red. Motorway-like dimensions offer a fast racetrack with opportunities to ride off to the sides (right best) into deeper, undulating freeride slopes. Links well with both sectors' Pla de les Pedres chair lifts: highest right is the Grau Roig lift, lowest left is Soldeu sector lift.

TSD6 PLA DE LES PEDRES SOLDEU CHAIR LIFT

10 mins

- 308 m (1010 ft) vertical rise
- 1930 m (2111 yd) long
- 2400 passengers/hour

Right on the south-eastern edge of the Soldeu sector, on the borderline with Grau Roig's Cubil sector. A declutchable, but nevertheless slow, chair that can be quite exposed in rough weather.

On arrival, U-turn round the arrival pylons for the Serra de les Solanelles and Obac Solana blues, and Pla de les Pedres and Serrat de la Posa reds; otherwise, turn ahead right for the Obagot II steep red into the Soldeu sector; or turn left for the short steep blue link piste to join the Riu de les Solanelles blue in the Grau Roig sector.

RIU DE LES SOLANELLES

From the high Collada de les Solanelles at 2458 m (8064 ft), this enjoyable blue begins as a short steep link dropping into the Cubil Valley area shared between the Soldeu and Grau Roig areas of the Grandvalira domain. Almost immediately after making the link there is a wide junction point ahead, offering the choice of keeping left on the Riu de les Solanelles blue, or go right for the Solanella, Ayelem and Riu del Cubil blues, with the possibility of riding over furthest right to make a link with the Llac de Cubil lifts base for onward links into the rest of the Grau Roig and Pas de la Casa sectors (see page 338). Staying on these immediate routes provides good links down to both Pla de les Pedres chair lifts serving this area. If you miss the last lift back to the Soldeu sector, don't panic – you can ride out from the base of the Pla de les Pedres Soldeu chair via a track to access the Ós blue back to Soldeu base and village.

POINT-TO-POINT ROUTES: COMPETENT NOVICES

SOLDEU BASE » EL TARTER BASE

Telecabina (Gondola) → Gall de Bosc → Pardal → Esquirol

EL TARTER BASE » SOLDEU BASE

TSD4 Tarter chair lift → Gall de Bosc → Ós

ESPIOLETS 2250 M (SOLDEU) » EL FORN 2000 M (CANILLO)

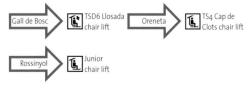

Gall de Bosc → TSD6 Llosada chair lift → Oreneta → TS4 Cap de Clots chair lift

Rossinyol → Junior chair lift

EL FORN 2000 M (CANILLO) » ESPIOLETS 2250 M (SOLDEU)

Forn → TSD4 Portella chair lift → Daina → Guineu

TSD6 Tosa Espiolets chair lift → Gall de Bosc

ESPIOLETS 2250 M » PLA DE LES PEDRES 2150 M (GRAU ROIG LINK)

Astoret → TSD6 Solana del Forn chair lift → Gall de Bosc → Fura

TS4 Solanelles chair lift → Riu de les Solanelles

PLA DE LES PEDRES 2150 M » ESPIOLETS 2250 M

TSD6 Pla de les Pedres Soldeu chair lift → Obac Solana → TS4 Assaladors chair lift → Gall de Bosc

🔻 *Early morning 'First Snow' on the Esquirol blue*

POINT-TO-POINT ROUTES: GOOD INTERMEDIATES AND ABOVE

SOLDEU BASE » EL TARTER BASE

Telecabina (Gondola) → Astoret → TSD6 Solana del Forn chair lift → Gall de Bosc → Àliga

EL TARTER BASE » SOLDEU BASE

TC10 Tarter gondola → TSD6 Tosa Espiolets chair lift → Llebre → Slalom

ESPIOLETS 2250 M (SOLDEU) » EL FORN 2000 M (CANILLO)

Astoret → TSD6 Solana del Forn chair lift → Miquel → TSD6 Llosada chair lift → Oreneta

TS4 Cap de Clots chair lift → Gaig → Junior chair lift

EL FORN 2000 M (CANILLO) » ESPIOLETS 2250 M (SOLDEU)

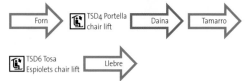

Forn → TSD4 Portella chair lift → Daina → Tamarro

TSD6 Tosa Espiolets chair lift → Llebre

ESPIOLETS 2250 M » PLA DE LES PEDRES 2150 M (GRAU ROIG LINK)

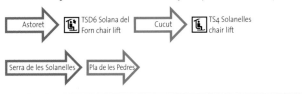

Astoret → TSD6 Solana del Forn chair lift → Cucut → TS4 Solanelles chair lift

Serra de les Solanelles → Pla de les Pedres

PLA DE LES PEDRES 2150 M » ESPIOLETS 2250 M (SOLDEU)

TSD6 Pla de les Pedres Soldeu chair lift → Obagot II → TS4 Assaladors chair lift → Gall de Bosc

---

ESPIOLETS 2250 M » SNOW PARK

Astoret → TSD6 Solana del Forn chair lift → Gall de Bosc → Esquirol

---

SNOWPARK » ESPIOLETS 2250 M

TSD6 Tosa Espiolets chair lift → Llebre

MOUNTAIN BARS & RESTAURANTS

Despite the expansive nature of the ski area, you're never far away from a piste-accessible food and drink service. Most are located in the three major mid-level hubs serving each respective SET sector – Canillo, El Tarter and Soldeu – with further easily accessible options over in Grau Roig and Pas de la Casa (see page 349).

◗ *El Forn terrace, Canillo*

Most of the venues are geared up as fast-food or self-service operations, but there are a couple of good-quality à la carte restaurants offering more refined gastronomic fare and ambiance.

All of the on-mountain bars and restaurants are operated by the ski station itself, which has branded each of the venues according to the type of service on offer. Prices are consistent throughout the ski area and are generally fair. All have free WCs. ⏱ All offer an all day bar and snack service; lunch is served between 12.30–15.30 hours. Off-mountain venues likewise.

Restaurants Charmants ('Restaurants with Charm'): haute cuisine and quality décor, offering à la carte and daily specials fixed menu; full bar service. Reservations are usually required during high season and at weekends; weekdays are normally quieter.
Restaurants: self-service canteens with a fair range of salads, vegetables, pasta, grilled meats and fish dishes, all with a choice of vegetable side dishes; basic desserts; plus bottled/canned drinks and lager on tap.
Fun Food: bright and buzzing fast-food canteens, offering pizza slices, hamburgers, paninis, etc.; plus bottled/canned drinks and lager on tap.
Espress'Oh!: cafés offering a range of hot and cold drinks, sweets and some snacks.
Xiris: (pronounced 'Cheeries'): Snack kiosks offering hot and cold drinks and snacks. Other than for a couple of piste-side cabins, all are sited on the Fun Food and Restaurant terraces.

Another option, of course, is to come off the mountain and return to the base station or your resort village for lunch. The enhanced choice and quality of venue can be worth the extra effort.

CANILLO SECTOR

There is an **Espress'Oh!** and a **Fun Food** restaurant in the Canillo base station but the main catering operations are based at the **El Forn** services area at the top of the gondola. The largest building ahead right on arrival houses all the venues and has a huge open terrace overlooking the pistes, with lovely mountain views. There are plenty of tables and seating, plus deckchairs.

Espress'Oh! Immediately in off the large El Forn terrace, at the entrance to the self-service restaurant, this bright and airy café has plenty of natural daylight and high coffee shop-style tables.

Restaurant El Forn Same entrance as Espress'Oh! café and with the same access to the terrace, this self-service cafeteria is the main catering venue in this sector. The interior dining area is plain but bright, with large picture windows looking out to the terrace and the views beyond. Microwave available for reheating food that is cooling too quickly on the terrace.

Roc de les Bruixes Gastronomic Restaurant The best-quality restaurant in the SET ski area, boasting a wide range of refined à la carte dishes and a daily specials fixed menu, with full bar service and a fair wine list. Separate terrace area and a bright, roomy interior dining saloon decorated in a chalet style, with a cosy open fireplace, sofas and a little cocktail bar. Housed in a separate section of the main El Forn services building, furthest away from the gondola-lift arrival point.

The Roc de les Bruixes is also open on weekend evenings and every night from Christmas through to Epiphany (6 January); you travel up using the gondola from Canillo, which runs specially for these evenings, the pathway to the restaurant being lit with flaming torches. Reservations recommended. ☎ +376 890 696

EL TARTER SECTOR

The Riba Escorxada area at 2100 m (6890 ft), at the Tarter gondola lift upper station, is virtually the sole focus for on-mountain food and drink in this sector. All the principal venues are housed in the main services buildings near the ski school and the main lifts. There are two huge sunny terraces facing into the El Tarter snowbowl ski area, with plenty of tables and chairs outside and in, plus a good number of deckchairs. As well as being the exterior seating areas for the interior restaurants, the terraces also have their own small snack/drinks kiosks.

Espress'Oh! Situated in the busy foyer area of the lower restaurants building, directly in off the upper terrace. Café-bar service and some simple snacks.

Fun Food Fast-food canteen on the same level and directly beside the Espress'Oh! café. It has a plain interior, but with reasonable levels of natural daylight and access to the large terrace outside.

Restaurant Riba Escorxada Self-service canteen on the uppermost floor, with its own small roof terrace. Bright and attractive, with exposed wood beams and carpeted to help minimize noise.

XiriGrill Snack and cold drinks kiosk located on the far side of the main upper terrace, offering pizza slices, crêpes and confectionery. This side of the terrace has windbreaks and feels a little more secluded than the busy area immediately in front of the building.

Xiri El Planell A larger snack bar cabin down on the lower terrace, with some interior coffee shop-style tables. Hot and cold drinks and snacks; similar to the other Xiris.

Pi de Migdia The latest addition to El Tarter's facilities; located just above the upper gondola station and planned to house a café, self-service and gourmet restaurant.

Xiri El Refugi: the only other on-mountain option in the El Tarter sector is a cute one; this simple but cosy little cabin is situated right on the summit of Tossal de la Llosada at 2560 m (8399 ft). Tiny interior with a bar along one side and a couple of coffee shop-style tables, offering hot drinks and confectionery. There is a tool point on the veranda.

Another option is to descend, by piste or gondola, to El Tarter base station, where there are a few privately owned restaurants and snack bars offering something a bit different from the station's branded venues. Reservations are not required.

El Clos Directly at the foot of the pistes nearest the Tarter chair lift. No terrace, but a reasonably nice interior bar and restaurant serving pasta, grills and salads. Place your order and pay at the counter first.

Llop Gris Part of the 4-star Llop Gris Hotel, accessible via a pisted track from the foot of the slopes nearest the Tarter chair lift. Quality grilled meats and fish dishes, full bar service and attractive Alpine-style décor; no terrace. Welcoming features include heated boot racks, with clogs on loan to wear while your boots are drying/warming.

La Gençana Located off the roadside by the lower car park entrance, about 5 minutes' walk from the pistes and lifts. Attractive, quaint interior bar and restaurant offering pasta, grills and salads, with a good-value *menu del dia*. Full bar service and a good spot for an après-ski snifter.

L'Abarset Another good après-ski choice in a similar position to La Gençana, but by the upper entrance into the base-station area. Attractive restaurant and bar with a relaxed ambiance. Full bar service and menu offering pasta, grills and salads.

SOLDEU SECTOR

All major catering services are based at the mid-level base at the top of the gondola lift. This Espiolets area at 2250 m (7382 ft) is a wide, sunny plateau and all the restaurants have large terraces overlooking the pistes, with plenty of bench-style tables/seating plus some deckchairs. Two restaurant buildings serve this plateau, one on either side of the gondola arrival area: the Espiolets building is to the left on arrival; the Gall de Bosc building is the one on the right. Free WCs are available at both buildings.

Espress'Oh! cafés There are two café-bars, one in each restaurant lobby, offering hot and cold drinks, snacks and confectionery.

Fun Food: A bright, airy fast-food canteen with direct access to a large sheltered terrace overlooking the children's Snow Garden and lower area beginners' slopes.

Espiolets 'Historic' Restaurant The main self-service restaurant at Espiolets, located on the upper floor of the building of the same name, nearest to the gondola. Quite plain interior, decorated with old black and white photo-posters of Soldeu's ski pioneers and the original pre-resort hamlet, but it does have a balconied terrace with good views over the whole beginners' zone. A second, little-known snow-terrace area is occasionally open at the rear of the building, affording views down towards Soldeu village. There are microwaves available for food that is cooling too quickly outside.

Gall de Bosc Restaurant Charmant 'Charming' restaurant on the top floor of the Gall de Bosc services building. Quality à la carte and daily specials set menu, full bar and table service and a fairly good wine list. Bright and attractive, with lots of exposed timbers used in construction, plus a separate roof terrace overlooking the children's Snow Garden and lower debutants' pistes.

● *XiriPizza kiosk on the Asoret piste at Soldeu*

XiriCrêpes Snack kiosk based on the terrace outside the Fun Food canteen, selling crêpes, paninis and bottled/canned drinks.

XiriGrill Snack booth on the big terrace at the Espiolets restaurant building, offering paninis, chips, hamburgers, and bottled/canned drinks.

XiriPizza Soldeu's only on-piste snack bar, located at the left-hand side of the Astoret blue piste about 750 m (821 yd) away from the main Espiolets area. Small snow terrace with some bench seating/tables at exterior only; no WCs.

Sol i Neu Although not actually within the ski area, this attractive large restaurant has traditionally been one of the most popular lunch venues in the Soldeu sector. It is perched on the side of the ravine overlooking Soldeu's home-run pistes, just below the village's main street next to the gondola building; its two huge tiered terraces face the sun all day. Accessible via a steep track from the foot of the slopes next to the piste-side elevators, and directly from the resort's main open-air car park. Fare on offer includes soups, salads, pasta, omelettes, grilled meats and fondue. A full bar service and lighter bites such as chips and paninis are available too. Part of the professional Ski Calbo company and one of the best alternatives to the 'official' mountain restaurants.

● *Vall d' Incles towards El Tarter*

ALTERNATIVE ACTIVITIES

As part of one of Europe's largest skiing domains, the SET resorts also offer a range of activities to keep all their visitors amused, whether on or off the pistes, skier or non-skier. All on-mountain activities are available subject to prevailing meteorological conditions and can be booked via the main information offices located at the base stations. See also page 357 for further information on activities available in the other Grandvalira resorts.

ⓘ Activities may not be covered by travel insurance (see page 58).

DISCOVERY GAME

This is a free DIY activity for all skiers/boarders, available at all SET sectors: the station provides a special map and orientation aids for players to get to know the ski area by visiting a series of checkpoints.

SKI SAFARI

A free service offered by the SET welcome team, who are on hand to guide you around the best pistes and snow stashes on a specified day in the middle of the week and at weekends; a choice of two meeting times is available, either mid-morning or around lunchtime.

ⓘ Only available at the Riba Escorxada area at El Tarter.

FIRST SNOW

A great opportunity for the keenest early birds. Every Sunday at 08.00 hours the SET welcome team will accompany competent skiers/boarders to catch a special early chair lift from El Tarter base station to make the first tracks on the pistes. A small charge is payable, and hot chocolate and doughnuts are included.

🔺 *Snowmobiling in the woods near El Tartar*

SNOWSHOES

There are three specially waymarked trails departing from the
El Forn area at the top of the gondola in the Canillo sector. Access
to the circuits is free, but you will need to hire snowshoes (or
bring your own). The snowshoe routes are graded similarly to the
ski pistes: there is a short green circuit for absolute beginners, a
longer blue circuit for progressing on to, and a more serious red
trail, which cuts through the forest to the Riba Escorxada area at
El Tarter (you can also begin here and do this route in reverse).
An instructor/guide service is available for a fee. Permanent
circuits, open to all visitors.

MUSHING

A wonderful activity for all visitors, accessible by piste or on foot at the Riba Escorxada area in front of the El Tarter gondola upper station. Teams of huskies pull Arctic sleds around a circuit on the edge of the El Tarter snowbowl; you can ask to steer yourself, or a guide will accompany you. Available every day and charged on a per passenger basis.

◐ *A taste of the Arctic: mushing at El Tarter*

SNOWMOBILES

Probably the most frequently requested alternative snowsport, open to everyone and available every day from the El Tarter base station area. Each machine holds two people; you can drive yourself or hang on tight as a passenger. Charged per machine and according to duration.

REINDEER SLEIGHS

Rudolph really does exist! Visit the reindeer corral and Sami teepee, then steer your own reindeer-pulled sleigh around a set circuit (children will be accompanied by a guide). An unusual, gentle activity open to all; set in the woods at the base of the Forn slopes at the top of the Canillo gondola. Charged per passenger.

HELICOPTER FLIGHTS

Take a panoramic sightseeing helicopter trip to see the stunning scenery of the High Pyrenees. The HeliAnd operation visits Soldeu's Espiolets Plateau a couple of times per week, offering pre-booked trips over the ski area and surrounding peaks. Prices depend on duration of flight booked and are charged on a per person basis.

PARAGLIDING

For this truly breathtaking experience, you are strapped into a steerable paragliding canopy in tandem with a professional pilot. You will glide high above the pistes and forests, with skiers far below your feet, finally landing on the meadows at El Tarter base for a real Bond-style buzz. Flights launch from the summit of Tosa dels Espiolets, so this activity is only available to those with a full ski pass.

APRÈS-SKI

Once the lifts close, the emphasis shifts to the social side of the snowsports experience and the reason for Andorra's reputation as the Party Principality becomes clear. The excesses of the 1980s and 90s have mellowed considerably, but Andorra still caters well for those for whom the clink in the glass is just as important as the swish on the snow.

Canillo and El Tarter have their own mellow vibe, but Soldeu is still one of Europe's most lively ski resorts and for such a small village it really rocks. Just remember, you'll never nail that 1080 if you're too hungover to hit the hill, and you'll waste almost 20 per cent of your ski pass if you miss a day!

SHOPPING

Other than the sports shops and supermarkets, there isn't any 'proper' shopping to be done in any of the villages, although duty-free cigarettes and booze are available just about everywhere.

Soldeu has a few sports shops selling equipment, clothing and accessories, a couple of small supermarkets and souvenir shops, a post office, a bank, a hairdresser's and a pharmacy. El Tarter only has a couple of sports shops and a small supermarket. Canillo has the widest range of shops, but even here it's very limited, with just a couple of small souvenir shops, three supermarkets, a butcher and fishmonger, a post office, three banks and a pharmacy.

If it's more serious retail therapy you crave, then the commercial attractions of the cosmopolitan capital Andorra la Vella are just 40 minutes away down the valley, easily accessible by either bus or taxi.

And the evening begins... Soldeu village

CASH MACHINES

Both Soldeu and Canillo have centrally located ATMs, as does Andorra la Vella. English language instructions are quick to find and operation will usually be as familiar as at your own bank.

➲ See Soldeu town plan on page 201 for ATM location.

PAMPERING

The Hermitage Wellness Spa at Soldeu is a recent and important addition to the resort's attractions. It features a hydromassage pool, whirlpool, saunas, hammam steam room plus a range of beauty and massage treatments and is perfect for winding down and limbering up. Located opposite the Sport Hotel.

ICE SKATING

The Palau de Gel d'Andorra sports complex in central Canillo is home to the country's only full-sized indoor ice rink, frequently hosting important international ice-hockey matches. The rink is open every day; skate hire and footwear lockers available.

☎ +376 800 840 🌐 www. palaudegelandorra.com

SWIMMING POOLS

The only public swimming pool in the area is at least a proper full Olympic-sized one, based at the Palau de Gel d'Andorra sports centre in central Canillo. This centre also has a children's pool, large gym, sauna and an artificial climbing wall. A few of the larger hotels also have their own indoor swimming pools and fitness facilities, which are often accessible to non-residents.

CAFÉS & RESTAURANTS

Virtually every bar in Andorra doubles as a café and many offer at least a basic snack menu. Most of the larger and better quality hotels offer a café service in their lounge bars and are often the best choice for a more refined après-ski experience. The following are some of the most popular café-bars and recommended restaurants in each of the resorts.

➔ *For further authentic Andorran venues, see pages 24–6.*

SOLDEU

The lounge bars at the Sport Hotel, Sport Hotel Village, Hotel Piolets and Hotel Naudi are all good recommendations for a quiet coffee or relaxing G&T, and all welcome non-residents.

Slim Jims €+ A bright US-style diner with Internet points and a decent snack menu: jacket potatoes and all-day English breakfasts. Located just off Soldeu main street, behind the church.

Drac Vermell (Red Dragon) €€ Chinese restaurant with a fair range of reasonably authentic dishes. Tucked down the steep side street towards the main open-air car park.

Sol i Neu €€ Huge, popular lunchtime and early evening venue, with massive terraces cantilevered out over the ravine and overlooking Soldeu's lower slopes. Attractive venue, offering a full bar service and a choice of snacks or full meals; fondues available by reservation. Situated at the lower edge of the main open-air car park, down the steep side street at the junction near the church. Reservations can be made in person earlier in the day.

🔺 Carns a la brasa *(grilled meats): staples of the Andorran diet*

Fontanella €€ Italian pizza and pasta restaurant which is part of the Hotel Piolets, on the main street in the centre of the village. ☏ +376 871 787

Colorado Tex Mex €€ Fajitas, chimichangas, burittos, chilli con carne, nachos and more, washed down with margaritas. Excellent range and special deals for groups. Upstairs at the Aspen Bar on the main street. Reservations can be made at the bar.

Cort de Popaire €€ Cosy, atmospheric old Borda barn conversion, with low ceiling, exposed beams and stonework. Specializes in grilled meats, cooked on the open fire. Definitely the best restaurant in town. Located under the Pussycat Pub on the side street above the village centre. ☏ +376 851 211

L'Esquirol €€ Indian restaurant offering a fair range of popular classics. Located in the lower village, right on the main road.

EL TARTER

El Mosquit €€ El Tarter's only real restaurant away from the base station. Attractive venue offering Tex Mex, pizzas, fondue, raclette and grills. Located on the main street of the upper residential area.

➔ *See page 270 for descriptions of L'Abarset, La Gençana and Llop Gris restaurants at the base station.*

CANILLO

La Roda €€ Small bar with restaurant service and good-value set menus. Located in the cellar of an original village house, up a side street (Carrer Perdut) at the upper end of the village centre.

Delices del Jimmy €+ A proper little coffee shop and patisserie with enticing cakes and chocolates, located on the main street in the village centre.

Cal Lulu €€ Popular and well-established restaurant with a cosy ambiance and quality menu; featuring French specialities (including frogs' legs) and great pizzas cooked in a wood-fire oven. On the main street at the lower end of the village centre. There are a couple more standard pizza restaurants in town, but none truly competes with Cal Lulu. ☎ +376 851 427.

Montarto €€+ Adventurous gastronomic restaurant with an attractive décor and open fire, specializing in unusual meat dishes – calf's head and hoof anyone? Located near the gondola base station, in the apartments of the same name ☎ +376 853 008.

BARS & CLUBS

Most resort hotels have their own in-house bars, plenty of which can be fairly animated, depending on how sociable and lively each week's clientele turns out to be. Canillo and El Tarter aren't really on the map as far as nightlife is concerned, but Soldeu still reigns as one of snowsport's après-ski capitals. Most bars stay open until 03.00. The following are some of the best.

SOLDEU

Piccadilly Pub The in-house bar at the Sport Hotel, open to non-residents and once one of the liveliest bars in town; now more mellow, but with a proper pub feel and frequent live music.

Villager Pub Big, buzzy, traditional pub with an Irish theme; music/extreme sports videos, frequent live music and a small dance floor. Located at the main street entrance to the gondola station and thus very popular as an après-ski first base.

Iceberg Small but popular bar attached to the Hotel Piolets on the main street; pool table, darts and Karaoke nights.

Avalanche Small and plain, yet seems to hit the spot for many visitors; basically just a small local music bar, also offering late-night snacks. On the main street, facing the Hotel Piolets.

Fat Alberts One of the village's most popular music bars, housed in an atmospheric converted barn: DJs, live music and good varied programme of themes/events. On the side street towards the 'old town', behind the church.

T-Bar Although just a small local bar, the T-Bar has recently been taken under the wing of a couple of snowboard instructors from the Soldeu ski school and has had a bit of TLC and a new image: chilled boarder-friendly hangout with a cool, unpretentious vibe. On the main street, facing the Hotel Piolets.

Capitol Big games arcade and sports pub in the basement under the Hotel Piolets: big-screen sports and lots of arcade machines and Internet stations. Under 16s permitted until 22.30.

Aspen Classic ski resort après-ski bar and one of Soldeu's key venues, situated on the main street in the village centre: daily videos of current week's visitors on the slopes, live bands, DJ, major sports events on big screen and pool table/arcade machines upstairs. Also home to the Colorado Tex Mex restaurant.

Pussycat The original, and still the best, late-night venue in town: DJs, live bands and a good, varied theme-nights programme; dancing encouraged! Located on the upper floor of an old village house, above the lovely Cort de Popaire restaurant on the street above the village centre.

Esqui The in-house bar at the Piolets Parc Hotel located at the lower end of the village: standard pub atmosphere with occasional live entertainment.

The Roc Tiny, chilled in-house bar at the cosy Roc St Miquel hotel, tucked away on the bend of the main road out of town, at the lowest end of Soldeu village: well-established and popular with *saisonnaires*; occasional live acoustic nights and a welcoming vibe.

EL TARTER

Arthurs Nice venue with aspirations to be a disco pub: mostly DJs and occasional live music. Situated at the top end of the residential area in El Tarter village.

Peanuts Best pub in El Tarter, situated on the main street in the village's upper residential area: big-screen sports, karaoke, pool table/games room.

CANILLO

This is pretty much just a quiet, traditional mountain village, with nightlife revolving around a meal out. Try **La Roda** bar/restaurant at the upper end of the village centre (see page 283); or the **Moli** bar off the main road out of town towards Soldeu: Danish beers, local crowd. Otherwise, anyone got a deck of cards?

PAS DE LA CASA–
GRAU ROIG
Grandvalira

INTRODUCTION

  If you are entering Andorra via the French border, then Pas de la Casa will be your first impression of the Principality. Unfortunately, although the surrounding mountains are as beautiful as in the rest of the Pyrenees, the same cannot be said of the view of the town.

Like many border towns around the world, Pas de la Casa has developed as a sprawling frontier townscape of hastily erected, austere buildings and is crammed with duty-free supermarkets, electronic goods retailers and cheap jewellery shops. Of course this might be exactly what you're looking for and the town does have more of a welcoming feel when viewed from the pistes, even a certain charm in the cluster of restaurants and patisseries whose terraces face up to the main slopes from the main street, Avinguda d'Encamp.

Pas de la Casa, usually simply referred to as Pas, was Andorra's pioneer ski station; founded in 1957, it was the first to install mechanical ski lifts and automatic snowmaking equipment. The town is Andorra's largest resort and continues to be one of the most popular in the Pyrenees. Following the link with old rivals Soldeu–El Tarter, the now-twinned ski stations form the impressive Grandvalira ski domain, putting them firmly in Europe's top 20 for sheer scale and variety of pistes and facilities.

PRONUNCIATION

Grau Roig	Grau Roash	**Encamp**	On~camp

◀ *Pas de la Casa and towards France*

Pas de la Casa is part of the Andorran parish of Encamp, but bizarrely Encamp town itself sits exactly at the geographical centre of Andorra, quite a way from border-hugging Pas de la Casa; the only road between them has to pass through the neighbouring parish of Canillo, via Soldeu. To save skiers coming all the way from Encamp to reach these ski stations, a cable car link was built stretching for over 6 km (3¾ miles) from Encamp to the pistes at Grau Roig – the resulting area covered by the full Grandvalira ski domain now extends to almost one-tenth of the surface area of the whole country!

There are two distinct sectors to the local ski area: the Pas sector immediately above the town, and the Grau Roig sector on the other side of the dividing Envalira ridge. Both stations are characterized by motorway-wide, snow-sure pistes mostly above the tree line, offering big mileage cruising and wide ranging vistas.

PAS DE LA CASA RESORT

Pas de la Casa town is integrally complete as a ski station and resort, offering direct access to a huge ski domain and a wealth of facilities and off-slope attractions. On top of this, it is consistently one of snowsports' most lively destinations, with a wide-selection of music bars and clubs pandering to the predominantly young English-speaking tourist market, but overall with a more Gallic ambiance than any of Andorra's other resorts. Although brash, the resort also has a number of upmarket boutiques and quality restaurants, plus a modern sports centre with swimming pool.

Andorra's duty-free status helps make this possibly Europe's best resort for purchasing snowsports equipment and clothing. There is a huge selection of rental businesses and retail outlets vying for trade, keeping prices as low as possible.

SOMETHING FOR EVERYONE

Absolute beginners and rusty novices will find that the wide, flowing pistes aid confidence building and flatter their style. The high numbers of other first-timers and second-weekers help dispel the normally elitist attitude common in some Alpine resorts, helping debutants relax and enjoy the learning experience. The standard of tuition provided is high, for all ability levels, and the Andorran authorities have developed one of the highest quality snowsports teaching systems in the world (see page 209).

Intermediates can make the most out of the mileage and variety offered by the full Grandvalira domain, and since all ski passes of more than two days' duration are automatically full area passes there is no need to upgrade or pay a supplement to range out over the linked sectors. There are also a couple of well-maintained tricks parks, one directly above town, giving budding freestylers an opportunity to hone their skills.

Advanced ability visitors will find the variety of terrain available a little tame, but there is more than enough ground to cover here to keep a week's holiday interesting and, since it all depends on the prevailing snow conditions on the day, Andorra's excellent snowfall record helps keep the chance of powder days high. Nordic skiing enthusiasts have just the one traditional and skating-style circuit available at the Grau Roig station. More experienced Langlauf enthusiasts should investigate Andorra's dedicated cross-country station of La Rabassa on the Spanish border to the south (see page 62 for more details).

All in all, Pas de la Casa offers one of snowsports' best-value resorts, with something for everyone in a lively and fun environment. Pack a box of Resolve and leave room in your luggage for the duty free.

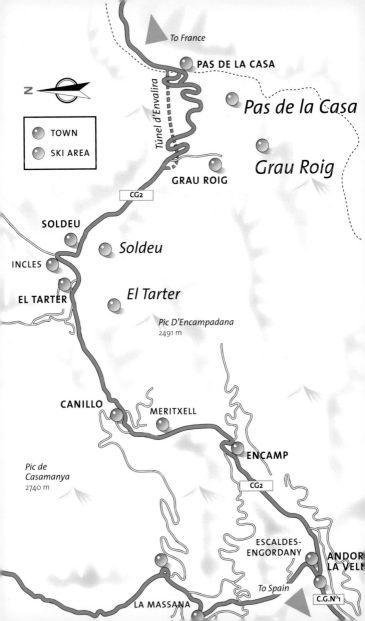

COMING & GOING

Being so isolated from the rest of Andorra, there are only two options for accessing the resort by road:

1. Directly from France;

2. Driving the whole way across Andorra from Spain.

From France: after passing through the customs station, which straddles the RN20 approach road from France, go straight on at the roundabout to cross the border straight into Pas de la Casa.

Grau Roig is on the far side of the mountains, reached either via the Envalira toll tunnel, or by continuing above Pas de la Casa on the long route over the Envalira Pass (Port d'Envalira) which, at 2408 m (7900 ft), is the highest road pass in the Pyrenees and can be cut off by heavy snows (snowchains obligatory).

From Spain: see page 198 for details of how to reach Soldeu. Passing through Soldeu village, continue climbing towards the Envalira Pass; Grau Roig is just to the right at the roundabout approaching the Envalira Tunnel.

Either take the Envalira toll tunnel or the Port d'Envalira road to reach Pas de la Casa.

DISTANCES
- Toulouse to Pas de la Casa — 160 km (99 miles)
- Barcelona to Pas de la Casa — 174 km (108 miles)
- Pas de la Casa to Grau Roig:
  - via Envalira Tunnel — 5.5 km (3½ miles)
  - via Envalira Pass — 10.5 km (6½ miles)
- Grau Roig to Andorra la Vella — 25.5 km (16 miles)

PAS DE LA CASA TOWN PLAN

KEY

i	Information point	🚡	Ski-pass kiosk
✝	Church	🎿	Equipment hire shop
🚌	Bus stop	P	Parking
€	ATM cash machine	🛒	Supermarket
✚	Medical Centre	✚	Pharmacy
✉	Post box		

HOTELS & APARTMENTS

1. Hotel Llac Negre
2. Hotel Parma
3. Hotel Panda
4. Hotel Els Isards
5. Hotel Bellroc
6. Sandy IV Apartments
7. Hotel Reial Pirineus
8. Hotel Cims
9. Hotel Font Argent
10. Hotel Catalunya
11. Hotel Catsby
12. Hotel Kandahar
13. Hotel Himalaia Pas
14. Frontera Blanca Apartments
15. Paradis Blanc Apartments

CAFÉS & RESTAURANTS (see page 364)

1. Croissant Express
2. Auteuil Brasserie/Pizzeria
3. Marisqueria Campistrano
4. La Raclette
5. Marquet
6. Xadoc
7. El Garantua

BARS & CLUBS (see pages 365–8)

1. Carrer del Maia Zone
2. Carrer de Bearn Zone
3. Plaça dels Vaquers Zone
4. Carrer de la Solana Zone
5. El Pandero Nightclub
6. Provinçal City Pub

SKI AREA DATA

- Opening time   09.00 hours
- Last lift up   17.00 hours
- Skiable area   1776 hectares (4389 acres)
- Altitude   1710–2640 m (5609–8660 ft)
- Vertical drop   930 m (3051 ft)
- Access points   6
- Ski schools   2 (450 instructors at 7 different centres)

- Ski lifts   63

Cable cars	1	*Gondolas*	3
Chair lifts	28	*Button lifts*	17
Rope tows	9	*Conveyor belts*	5

- Capacity   94,500 passengers/hour

- Pistes   108 (= 193 km/120 miles)

Green	18	*Freeride*	4
Red	37	*Mogul stadiums*	2
Blue	32	*Children's*	6
Black	21	*Halfpipes*	1
Nordic	1	*FIS*	3
Tricks parks	3		

- Hands-free ski pass   Yes
- Snowmaking   914 cannons
  64.3 km (40 miles) = 33.3 per cent of ski area
- Medical centres   5
- Mountain bars/restaurants   17 sites

Figures given are for the full Grandvalira domain.

- Visitor information   www.grandvalira.com

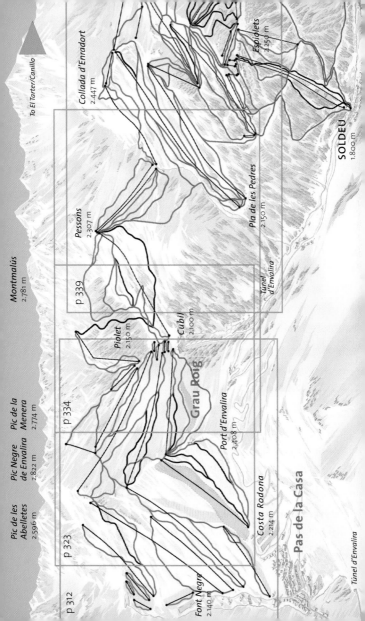

SKI PASSES

Local passes for the Pas–Grau sectors are available as day passes only; all other options over two days' duration are full Grandvalira area passes covering Pas de la Casa–Grau Roig and Soldeu–El Tarter (including Canillo). A small supplement applies if travelling via cable car from Encamp.

All ski passes are hands free; a deposit is payable for the pass-card, which can be kept to be recharged in the future or returned to a ski-pass kiosk for deposit refund. The passcard should be secured in a left-hand pocket and operates the lift turnstiles by remote control.

High season = every weekend; week leading up to Christmas until week after New Year; all February and Easter.

Low Season = all other dates (only three per cent cheaper than high season).

All passes are available for adults (12–64 years) and children (6–11 years): half-day (09.00–13.00 hours or 13.00–last lift); full-day and multiples thereof: the longer the duration, the cheaper the equivalent daily rate. Ski passes are free of charge for all children under 6; for those aged 6–11, prices are approximately 20 per cent cheaper than those of adults. To encourage the wearing of helmets, a small discount is also given on children's day passes if the child wears a helmet. Ski passes for guests aged 65–70 are available at a much reduced daily rate; passes are free for the over 70s.

ⓘ Proof of age is required for all child and senior ski passes.

SKI ANDORRA SKI PASS

See also page 76 for full details of the Ski Andorra ski pass, which permits access to all of Andorra's ski areas.

SKI PASS SALES POINTS

You can purchase any of the passes available at any of the sales kiosks dotted around the resort.

The main sales points are:

1. In the centre of Pas de la Casa, on Avinguda d'Encamp at the foot of the slopes;

2. At the Font Negre car park, beside the beginners' zone at the top of Avinguda d'Encamp;

3. At the Costa Rodona area, by the roadside on the Envalira Pass;

4. At Grau Roig – at both the Grau Roig and Cubil parking area services buildings;

5. At the Funicamp cable car base station in Encamp.

Grandvalira ski passes can also be purchased at any of the Soldeu–El Tarter gondola lift base stations (see pages 223 and 245). The hands-free passcards can be returned to any of the sales points for deposit refund.

ⓘ Accident insurance is not included in ski pass prices. Make sure you are adequately covered (see page 58) or purchase the insurance supplement offered when you buy your ski pass.

SKI BUS

Since nowhere in Pas de la Casa is more than a few minutes' stroll from the pistes, there is no real need for a resort ski-bus service. The Andorran local bus services operate around a dozen times daily to the capital Andorra la Vella and back; these can be used by pedestrians to reach Soldeu, El Tarter, Canillo and Encamp, as well as Andorra la Vella itself. Timetables are available at ski-pass kiosks and at tourist board offices.

NON-SKIERS

Pas de la Casa is the only Andorran ski resort to have pistes which run directly into town. This means that non-skiers can share in the snowsports experience and feel part of the day's activity. However, if you're not actually participating in skiing or snowboarding, but still wish to travel up into the high mountain areas and access the on-mountain restaurants, then unfortunately there aren't any options by ski lift direct from Pas de la Casa.

The Funicamp cable car from Encamp is an excellent option for non-skiing pedestrians, because it arrives at the high-altitude Collada d'Enradort area at 2447 m (8028 ft), affording stunning vistas over the upper ski area and surrounding peaks from an excellent restaurant and services station (see page 354). You can purchase a 'pedestrian pass' permitting one return journey, but would need to travel to and from Encamp by road to access the cable car. The only other options would be to travel by road to the base station at Grau Roig or to one of the Soldeu–El Tarter gondola stations. Grau Roig is simply a base station and parking area, but it does have full facilities and pistes passing directly through, as well as providing various alternative activities such as a snowshoe circuit, dog sleighs and snowmobile rides (see pages 357–8). The Soldeu, El Tarter and Canillo gondolas each offer a pedestrian pass to access the mid-level stations at those resorts.

PRICES

For current prices for all ski passes, tuition, childcare and other resort services, please go to our website:
www.ski-ride.com

EQUIPMENT

Hiring snowsports equipment in Andorran resorts is very easy and very affordable; there is a sports shop on every street and 99 per cent of them have a rental service, the sheer volume of competitive businesses helping to keep prices as keen as possible. As well as boot hire, all offer traditional Alpine skis, carvers, snowboards and snowshoe hire. All also provide equipment servicing and repair, waxing and edges/base preparation for your own gear, as well as technical clothing and accessories.

Most visitors travelling with a tour operator tend to leave the organization of equipment hire to their reps, usually being taken for fitting en masse early on their first morning on the slopes (normally Monday).

With so much similar-looking rental equipment on the mountain it is very easy to confuse your gear with someone else's and vice versa; while it's unlikely that anyone will steal identifiable rental gear, it is common for people to take the wrong gear by mistake. All hire equipment is marked with a serial number of some sort; make a note of this and carefully observe what your gear looks like before leaving it near similar models. Other than using a lockable rack, a good alternative tip is to mix-and-match each ski with one of your mates' if you need to leave them unattended; snowboarders should carry a light chain and padlock to secure their gear.

STORAGE

All of the larger rental operations provide storage facilities. There are also lockers available at Grau Roig services complex and at the Solanelles restaurant and services building on the Collada d'Entradort at 2447 m (8028 ft).

TUITION

The central ski-school office is housed at the base station building underneath the main ski lifts in the middle of Pas de la Casa; the main entrance is on Avinguda d'Encamp, just next to the ski-pass sales kiosks. This large well-established operation has a team of over 200 multilingual instructors, many of whom are of British or Commonwealth nationality, offering a complete range of instruction for all ability levels, for Alpine skiing, snowboarding, competition-level skiing and Monoskiing.

Grau Roig base station has two ski-school centres: one is based in the principal Grau Roig services building, just beside the main ski-pass sales kiosks; the other is housed in the Cubil services building, in the lower parking area nearest to the beginners' zone. In addition to the services offered by their colleagues at Pas de la Casa, they also offer instruction in Nordic skiing – with a fair-sized cross-country circuit close by.

Public group classes are grouped by language, ability level, age, ski and snowboard. Children 3–6 years old have their own separate Snow Garden; from 6 years old they can join the regular classes out on the pistes. All public group lessons are for 15 hours, 3 hours per day spread over 5 days, Monday to Friday. Reduced rate prices apply for children aged 6–11 years old. Private lessons are also available.

CONTACTS
🛈 Pas de la Casa office +376 871 900
🛈 Grau Roig office +376 872 900
🖃 info@grandvalira.com

CHILDCARE

Gentle Snow Gardens are fenced off and equipped with easy-to-use rope-tow ski lifts, colourful obstacles and cartoon statues; there specialist ski school nursery monitors introduce children aged 3–6 years old to the world of snowsports. This service is available at both Pas de la Casa and Grau Roig and is bookable either for 2 hours, half-day, full-day or for 15 hours spread over 5 days (3 hours per day). Equipment hire is not included.

A separate crèche service for infants aged 1–3 years old is also available. Some outdoor activities are arranged depending on how cold it is, but mostly the children remain safely indoors, either participating in games and activities or watching cartoons. Staff there speak English, French, Spanish and Catalan. The crèche service is offered on a 2-hour; half-day; full-day; 5 x half-day or 5 consecutive full-day basis.

The Snow Gardens and crèches are tucked safely away to the sides of the slopes; in an attractive purpose-built chalet at the top of Avinguda d'Encamp, by the beginners' zone, in Pas de la Casa; and beside the beginners' zone, within easy sight and reach of the main service complex, located at Grau Roig.

◆ *Beginning the adventure in safe hands*

SERVICES

Medical centres: well-equipped trauma and X-ray suites are located at both Pas de la Casa and Grau Roig. The Pas de la Casa centre is situated in the centre of town (see town plan on page 295) and is accessible by ambulance from the base of the main town slopes; the Grau Roig centre is located in the principal base station services building and is accessible by rescue sleds directly from the pistes. Both centres are close to roads and helipads should emergency transport to hospital be required.

The medical staff will contact your insurance company, but you will have to pay any initial costs, excluded by any excess clauses, on site. Make sure your insurance policy covers heli-rescue, on-piste rescue and ambulance transport as well as medical and hospital expenses. Andorra in not in the EU and has no public health service; hospitals are very modern, but all are private.

ⓘ Always carry some form of ID and your insurance details. It is also advisable to carry a small first-aid kit (see Health & Safety, pages 53–8).

WCs: located at all base station buildings, as well as at the upper Avinguda d'Encamp in Pas de la Casa. All mountain bars and restaurants also have public access WCs and there are no-flush 'eco toilets' in a cabin by the base of the Pla de les Pedres Grau Roig chair lift. All are free of charge.

ATMs: cash machines are distributed throughout Pas de la Casa (see town plan on page 295); the closest to the slopes are located at the Pas de la Casa base station building on Avinguda d'Encamp, and at the Costa Rodona restaurant at the base of the FIS competition course by the roadside on the Envalira Pass.

Telephones: phonecard-operated public telephone booths are sited at all base stations. Phonecards are available from most convenience shops and supermarkets. GSM mobile phone coverage is virtually 100 per cent.

Shops: although there is only one small station-branded souvenir shop in Pas de la Casa, there is a plethora of retail outlets immediately below the main town slopes in the resort. At Grau Roig there are a couple of rental shops selling equipment, technical clothing and last-minute accessories. Pas de la Casa is the most convenient base for access to nearby food shops.

Mountain restaurants: you are never too far away from access to food and drink anywhere in the ski area. There are nine sites at convenient intervals around the mountains, ranging from simple hot drinks' and snack kiosks up to full-service à la carte restaurants, although the majority are of the self-service type, mostly in a canteen style. Other than a couple of private enterprises at Grau Roig, all of the on-mountain bars and restaurants are managed by the ski station. Prices are consistent and are slightly cheaper than in similar standard venues in the Alps.

➔ *See pages 349–54 for specific reviews.*

Picnic areas: the only official facility is a designated saloon on the lower ground floor of the Grau Roig services complex; it is very plain, but roomy and bright with plenty of natural daylight in the interior and access to a small exterior terrace overlooking the beginners' zone. Otherwise, anywhere safe on the mountain is fine. It is forbidden to picnic on any of the restaurant terraces. Take all your rubbish plus any that you find to a bin.

SNOWFALL HISTORY & ANALYSIS

Although precipitation is unpredictable at very long range, patterns do emerge that are observable over a number of seasons. Using this data, you can tell if your preferred period of travel has historically seen good snow cover. The magic figure is 100 cm (39 in) – once snow depth exceeds this mark, conditions are generally good throughout the ski area and will remain so for a more extended period.

Pas de la Casa is the highest of all the Andorran ski stations and has a slightly more Atlantic orientation and influence. Therefore the snow conditions are usually fairly stable and do not experience wide fluctuations. This higher altitude doesn't really guarantee more precipitation, but it does ensure that what does fall does not do so as rain in warmer periods. The condition of snow on the ground is better maintained, however, by the resulting colder temperatures.

The chart below details combined averages recorded over three seasons immediately prior to the publication of this guide. Visit **www.ski-ride.com** for live snow reports.

Pas de la Casa-Grau Roig: weekly averages over most recent 3 ski seasons (2002/03 - 2004/05)

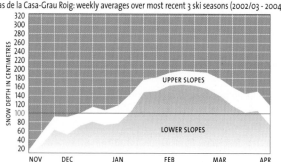

PREVIOUS SEASONS' SNOWFALL BREAKDOWN BY YEAR

The following charts detail the snowfall history for the three most recent seasons. Data from these charts was used to compile the combined averages chart on the preceding page.

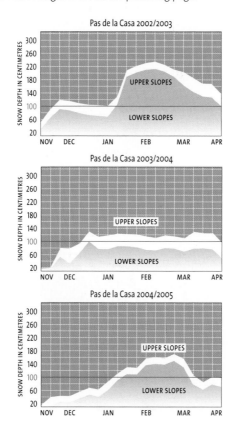

PAS DE LA CASA SKI SECTOR

Characterized by huge motorway-wide cruising pistes and high snow-sure terrain, Pas de la Casa feels much more like a traditional French Alpine ski area than any of Andorra's other ski stations do. A major advantage is that it facilitates skiing right down into the town. As the town sits bang on the international border at the eastern edge of Andorra, all lifts and pistes leading away from the resort head west towards Grau Roig and beyond, adding to the sense of big mileage offered by the area.

BASE STATION

The town of Pas de la Casa acts as the resort base station itself, fanning out in a welcoming horseshoe shape at the base of the main pistes, with a wealth of restaurants, bars and shops accessible either at the sides of the slopes or just a few steps from them. The ski station's central services building is tucked underneath the ski-lifts' base at the foot of the lowest slopes, right in the middle of town on Avinguda d'Encamp: it has ski-pass kiosks at roadside level, a hole-in-the-wall cash machine, central ski-school office, information desk, WCs and public telephones.

As you descend on-piste towards town, keep high to the left to access the Costa Rodona service area, by the roadside on the Envalira Pass, or continue into town. There are a number of snack bars and basic restaurants on the edge of the Tubs blue piste, on the left above the get-on points for the TS4 Solana and TSD4 Pas de la Casa chair lifts. Otherwise, from the foot of the pistes, simply walk down to the main streets – Carrer de Bearn to the left, or Avinguda d'Encamp to your right (see town plan on page 295).

◀ *Costa Rodona terrace*

FIRST DAY & FIRST ACCESS
If you are travelling with a tour operator, then Monday
morning will usually be your first day on the slopes; you
will be taken for your equipment fitting early on Monday.

If you're in ski school, then you will be advised where to
meet, or be accompanied to the beginners' rendezvous area
for around 10.00 hours. Otherwise, simply take one of the
major chair lifts out of town and head for the hills.

ABELLETES

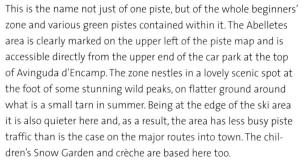

This is the name not just of one piste, but of the whole beginners'
zone and various green pistes contained within it. The Abelletes
area is clearly marked on the upper left of the piste map and is
accessible directly from the upper end of the car park at the top
of Avinguda d'Encamp. The zone nestles in a lovely scenic spot at
the foot of some stunning wild peaks, on flatter ground around
what is a small tarn in summer. Being at the edge of the ski area
it is also quieter here and, as a result, the area has less busy piste
traffic than is the case on the major routes into town. The children's Snow Garden and crèche are based here too.

There are four easy-to-use rope tows serving these snowfields:
three clustered at the upper end of the zone and one running
parallel to the road, with easy on-piste access to snack food and
drinks at the small Font Negre services point just below. Returning
to town is easy once you have mastered the basics: simply glide
down towards the foot of the town slopes by taking the final
gentle portion of the Fletxa blue piste.

TS COLL DELS ISARDS CHAIR LIFT

| 13½ mins | • 316 m (1037 ft) vertical rise • 6½ mins to mid-point
• 1605 m (1756 yd) long
• 1000 passengers/hour |

Solely serving the long blue Isards cruise, used to take novices out on their first forays into the ski area. The journey up is at a pedestrian rate, but gives you time to take in the beautiful surroundings of this peaceful side valley. The stream to the left marks the international border; everything beyond is in France.

There's a mid-journey get-off point on this chair, so nervous novices can work their way up to the full descent. Dismount here to join the lower Isards blue or stay on for the full Isards run. On arrival at the top, turn left to begin the Isards blue.

ISARDS

Motorway blue all the way, but fast if you want it to be. A perfect first true blue for progressing beginners, with the possibility of riding off to the sides for some more interesting terrain for the more experienced: there is a tricky little river gully providing a narrow natural halfpipe off the piste to the right at the point where it crosses under the line of the chair lift. Exit out to the left of the gully if riding in here to avoid dropping out into the Abelletes beginners' zone. Beginners will find that this wide, gentle, well-groomed blue flatters their progress and provides a good long run back towards, and past, the Abelletes beginners' zone. The entire upper section of the piste is usually quiet as it has no adjacent pistes, further enhancing this run's suitability as a proving ground. Unlike the piste map would seem to suggest, this piste converges with the Fletxa blue to run all the way to town.

TS COLL BLANC

8¼ mins

- 197 m (646 ft) vertical rise
- 980 m (1072 yd) long
- 1200 passengers/hour

One of the four chair lifts leaving Pas de la Casa town base, on the left side of the pistes right next to Avinguda d'Encamp. The chair is aimed at novices, providing uplift from the base area to mid-way up the principal town pistes and specifically serving the Fletxa blue run. On arrival, U-turn left for the Fletxa, or turn right to join the Directa 1, which, although piste-marked as red, is really a wide motorway blue for the whole lower section from here. The Fletxa traverses on a contour line across the mountainside to join with the wide gentle pisted slopes running beside the lower Abelletes debutants' zone to give access to the lifts' base and lower town slopes.

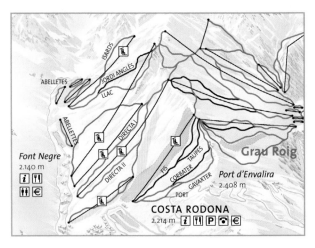

TSD6 FONT NEGRE

| 7½ mins | • 482 m (1581 ft) vertical rise
• 1708 m (1869 yd) long
• 3000 passengers/hour |

Swift modern lift departing from just above the road on Avinguda d'Encamp, opposite the Frontera Blanca apartments. Rises to a higher altitude than any other lift out of Pas, making a good fast link towards the Grau Roig sector and its Freestyle Park.

There are great views on the way up, with the spectacular cirque above the Abelletes area to your left and the whole lower sector of Pas to your right. On the upper section you pass over the Llac red and beside the Jordi Anglès black; approaching the top, you also get a good close-up look at the Gasex avalanche-protection blast pipes to your right. On arrival, you are immediately on the side of the upper Llac red piste, although the whole ridge here is pisted. U-turn sharp right to access the Jordi Anglès black piste, or go straight on over the ridge for Grau Roig.

JORDI ANGLÈS

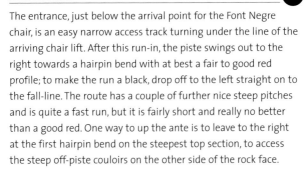

The entrance, just below the arrival point for the Font Negre chair, is an easy narrow access track turning under the line of the arriving chair lift. After this run-in, the piste swings out to the right towards a hairpin bend with at best a fair to good red profile; to make the run a black, drop off to the left straight on to the fall-line. The route has a couple of further nice steep pitches and is quite a fast run, but it is fairly short and really no better than a good red. One way to up the ante is to leave to the right at the first hairpin bend on the steepest top section, to access the steep off-piste couloirs on the other side of the rock face.

LLAC

Good red starting from the Pic Blanc ridge, accessed by the Font Negre and Pic Blanc chair lifts. Keep right when riding along the ridge to drop to the right below the big circular Coll Blanc restaurant; the piste is at its steepest at this point and is frequently very bumpy, almost black. Once through this funnel into the Pas sector, keep turning to take the high contour line track out to the right; this whole side of the mountain is all pisted and it's possible to merge straight in with the sector's other principal reds to keep varying the routes. The most challenging and fun way to do this is to launch off the edge of the upper Llac track to bounce through the steeper and deeper freeride slopes above the twin Directa pistes. The Llac traverse goes on to squeeze through a narrow cutting through the rock pinnacles ahead, spitting you out via a fairly steep chute pitching to the left on to the ever-widening piste, eventually converging with the Isards blue.

TSD4 PAS DE LA CASA CHAIR LIFT

7 mins	• 425 m (1394 ft) vertical rise • 1860 m (2035 yd) long • 2800 passengers/hour

The major chair lift from the town base area, providing a fast ride to the Coll Blanc for the link to the Grau Roig sector and all principal red routes back to Pas, with a great bird's eye view over the lower town and Costa Rodona slopes on the journey up. At the top, clear the arrival area quickly as it's quite narrow and traffic often backs up. Ride out to the wider col down to your left; from here you can go back into the Pas sector on the motorway reds or go over the watershed and into the Grau Roig sector ahead.

DIRECTA I & II

These two pistes are in effect simply the left and right sides of the motorway-wide superpistes from the Coll Blanc heading straight towards Pas de la Casa. Only the very top section is truly red, the rest of the descent being undulating fast cruising, with some opportunity to drop into a little steeper and deeper inter-piste stuff to the left. The whole mountainside is pisted, expanding the permutations of the route well beyond the two named pistes drawn on the piste map. The busy, narrower top section is the principal crossing point back into Pas from Grau Roig, so it is a real bottleneck and tricky for novices, but the rest of these runs should not present any problems.

High to the left after the uppermost section is a junction point and entrance to the BoarderCross/SkierCross course, as well as a parallel blue-graded traverse towards the Costa Rodona services area.

BOARDERCROSS / SKIERCROSS COURSE

Entered from the left side of the upper Direct II red coming from the Coll Blanc. Good signage at the entrance junction and well fenced off from the main pistes, with a start gate to push off. The course is about 600 m (656 yd) long, featuring three or four humps and about nine banked turns. There is quite a straight between the first few bends, so you'll have to go for it on the top section to get a good fast ride up the banking curves, but the lower section is much better and faster, with tighter banks and more frequent turns. Exit into the wide shared finish area for the FIS course – look out for fast traffic joining from parallel left. Veer left to link with the TS4 Costa Rodona chair lift or to reach the bar and restaurant; or right to descend towards the Freestyle Park.

TS4 SOLANA CHAIR LIFT

8 mins

- 190 m (623 ft) vertical rise
- 1080 m (1182 yd) long
- 1500 passengers/hour

One of the main Pas base lifts accessible from the side of Carrer de Bearn, near the Marseilles Bar. Like the Coll Blanc lift, this chair only provides uplift to midway up the lower Pas slopes; however, its function is to connect with the higher satellite Costa Rodona area and it works well as the dedicated lift for the Freestyle Park. From the arrival point go either to the right or left, both giving you adequate height to ride over to the Costa Rodona area or to start the Tubs blue piste, which accesses the Freestyle Park below.

PAS DE LA CASA FREESTYLE PARK

One of two parks in the Pas–Grau area, offering a series of decent modules and so close to town that it mitigates a late start after a heavy night. Enter using the Tubs blue piste running directly below the line of the Solana chair lift. The start of the park is well signed and clearly fenced off from the standard piste, which runs parallel to the right. The netted enclosure above the park is a paintball battle cage (see page 358).

The park's modules include: flat rail, flat box, double-kink rail, two C-rails (left and right), a bin and a spine. There is usually also at least one big-air cheese wedge, putting the town beneath your feet as you launch off. A chillout zone and DJ hut are situated at the bottom of the park, from where you can easily ride over to any of the principal base lifts and to return to town. The nearest food and drinks are available below left on the edge of the Tubs piste.

▶ *Strolling up for another go on the rails*

TS4 COSTA RODONA CHAIR LIFT

7½ mins

- 320 m (1050 ft) vertical rise
- 950 m (1039 yd) long
- 2000 passengers/hour

Departs from the Costa Rodona satellite services area, by the roadside on the Envalira Pass, and serves the FIS-approved competition course. The lift also makes the link to the Grau Roig sector and accesses the Pas sector blacks and reds furthest out to the high right on the crest of the Envalira Pass, near the huge transmitter mast and control tower.

On arrival, the competition course is immediately to the left, although this is a closed course normally only accessible to official events' competitors. U-turn to the right around the lift hut for the steepest immediate entrance for the FIS black; or simply glide along the gentle ridge to access all other routes. There is good signage and a piste map positioned on the ridge for route finding.

FIS / TAUPES

Two fair blacks, albeit short, off the Port d'Envalira above the Costa Rodona area. The most challenging start for the FIS is right beside the Costa Rodona lift hut; after this initial adrenaline rush the piste widens more like an excellent red to flow fast towards the services area and lift base below. If you are fazed by the severity of the first entrance, there is a chicken run in from slightly further along the ridge; cutting in to join the run clear of the steepest top section, yet still delivering you at a high enough point to make the most of this good run. The Taupes black also starts from close to this second entrance and is almost a twin of the FIS, descending on the far side of the rocky outcrop separating these pistes.

CORBATER

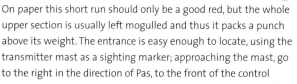

On paper this short run should only be a good red, but the whole upper section is usually left mogulled and thus it packs a punch above its weight. The entrance is easy enough to locate, using the transmitter mast as a sighting marker; approaching the mast, go to the right in the direction of Pas, to the front of the control tower complex. The piste steepens off the ridge straight into the mogul field, with a right-to-left camber further increasing the fun. Just when your knees start to burn, you slide into a much mellower section to flow in to the right-hand side of the Gavatxa red for the onward descent.

GAVATXA / PORT

These are the pistes nearest to the high Port d'Envalira road pass. Although designated as red there is not too much here to frighten early intermediates; indeed, these routes are much less busy than the central Directa pistes they make an ideal alternative for returning to Pas from Grau Roig (via the Antenes chair lift).

To find, ride along the ridge past the Ràdio de les Valls transmitter, keeping to the left of it and, although it seems strange to do so, veering down to the left on the Grau Roig side of the ridge. The junction ahead allows you to go ahead left for the Pastora blue towards Grau Roig, but the Gavatxa turns sharp right to run along the back of the ridge almost as far as the Port d'Envalira road, before flowing over into the Pas sector as a wide, mild red. At the mid-section below, there is a less direct variation even wider to the left; this is the Port red and it shares the same wide hillside to rejoin the Gavatxa towards the finish at the busy confluence area just above the Costa Rodona services area and chair-lift base.

GRAU ROIG SKI SECTOR

This is most extensive sector in the Pas–Grau shared domain, with a lot more variety than in Pas but again characterized principally by long wide cruising motorways and parallel routes sharing the same mountainsides. However, there is only one hotel at the base station and no other 'resort' to speak of; in fact Grau Roig exists as a ski station simply because it saves visitors from the south having to drive over the long Envalira Pass or pay the toll for the tunnel to reach Pas de la Casa. As a result, the area has a more noticeable Spanish ambiance than Pas.

BASE STATION

Although the surrounding scenery is breathtaking, Grau Roig station itself is nothing more than a couple of huge car parks, with two day-lodge service buildings: one at the main upper car park and the other at the slightly lower Cubil parking area. The more central Grau Roig lodge is the busiest of the two and is the one most readily accessible by piste when travelling from Pas.

A good-sized beginners' zone fills the slopes down to the flat valley floor below the lodges and can be used as a gentle warm-up by all visitors to access the two principal lifts: the Pic Blanc and Cubil chair lifts. These serve the major pistes and, depending on which one you take, access the Pas sector or the link with Soldeu–El Tarter. There are two other chair lifts departing from close to the main lodge, both making links with the Pas sector.

The only other facility at Grau Roig is the lovely Hotel Grau Roig. This is an excellent-quality 4-star hotel, with good facilities and the nicest bar and restaurant in the base area.

◀ *Approaching Grau Roig*

GRAU ROIG BASE LODGES

Although slightly old-fashioned and plain, the central Grau Roig day lodge is nevertheless the buzzing focal point of the station and handy both for visitors by car and by piste. The facilities are good and the approach to and departure from the building on-piste is easy.

Approaching from the Pas sector, all of the pistes can be used to reach the lodge, but the best are the Pista Llarga red and the pistes accessed via the Costa Rodona chair lift. Approaching from the Cubil side, either from the Soldeu sector or from the Funicamp, then you will need to skate over to the Pessons beginners' zone on the valley floor in order to take one of its short lifts up to the lodge level. For this reason, the station has begun upgrading the facilities at the secondary Cubil 2100 m lodge, which is more readily accessible from this side of the mountain, via the pisted track off to the left of the Lower Moretó black and Mirador red pistes. This less extensive site currently houses a café, self-service restaurant, large sunny terrace, information desk and ski-pass sales point, WCs, lockers and a first-aid post.

ⓘ Please note that there are no cash machine facilities at the Grau Roig area; the nearest machines are in Pas de la Casa town.

MAIN GRAU ROIG LODGE

First floor: Pizza Hut.

Ground floor: ski-pass kiosks and information desk, ski-school office, public telephones, equipment rental shop, Tito's fast food and bar, patisserie, La Tornada cafeteria and restaurant.

Lower ground floor: WCs, lockers, picnic saloon, medical centre. There are also equipment lockers available in the cabin in front of the lodge.

PESSONS

The beginners' area at Grau Roig is wide and has long green pistes served by button lifts and a chair lift. It flows down from the central day lodge and upper car park area to the flat valley floor below.

There is a Slope School at the bottom of the zone with a dummy chair-lift seat and button-lift pole for absolute beginners to practise on before they even have to use a real ski lift, as well as a full display of piste markers and signs to aid familiarization with route finding and piste safety. This initiative is in place at all of Andorra's ski stations and is part of the drive to keep Andorra's world-class tuition quality standards as high as possible.

The Pessons slopes are a useful traverse to the major Pic Blanc and Cubil chair lifts for onward links. Likewise the zone's lifts are useful for gaining height from the base of the Cubil area pistes if you want to reach the main lodge and upper car park.

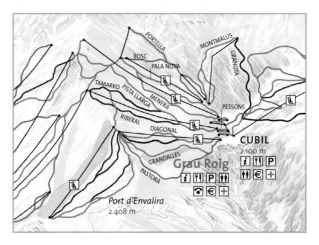

ONWARD LINKS

The Grau Roig sector has three distinct zones:

1. The Cubil mountain slopes served by the Cubil chair lift, which links towards the Funicamp and Soldeu–El Tarter;

2. The quiet, wooded Montmalús area served by a single button lift high into the impressive Circ del Colells;

3. The principal motorway-wide pistes flowing down to the base station and served by the Pic Blanc, Riberal and Antenes chair lifts, all linking with the Pas de la Casa sector.

TSD6 PIC BLANC CHAIR LIFT

10½ mins	• 520 m (1706 ft) vertical rise • 2230 m (2439 yd) long • 3000 passengers/hour

Key lift in the Pas–Grau ski area, rising to the highest point in the whole Grandvalira domain: 2640 m (8662 ft) above sea level. Covers a lot of ground, over 2 km (1¼ miles), making an excellent link between the Grau Roig and Pas sectors and, naturally, enabling the highest and longest descents on all routes from here. As the journey up takes over 10 minutes, take the time to sit back and absorb the great views over the whole sector and plan the next descent.

On arrival, turn left on to the Pista Llarga red to begin all onward descents. U-turning left gives the steepest start to the Pista Llarga red. Novices will find the steep slopes away from the arrival area challenging, but can stick to the ridge to make a manageable move into either sector from the Coll Blanc area to the left of the circular Coll Blanc restaurant below.

PISTA LLARGA / MENERA / PALA NOVA

Pista Llarga means 'long piste' and indeed this is the arterial route from the Coll Blanc all the way down to Grau Roig base, and the first impression of this sector for skiers coming over from Pas. The entire mountainside at the Coll Blanc is open, fully pisted and all signed as the Pista Llarga red. The steepest lines are to each of the sides, with frequent mogul fields and a fair red pitch to begin, eventually running out for a very flat schuss below. Peeling off to the right to run under the line of the chair lift (TS Riberal) is the true line of the Pista Llarga; keeping to the left to schuss straight on takes you towards the Menera and Pala Nova reds, linking with the Coma Blanca III button lift visible below left to reach the Freestyle Park. Nervous novices can ride out to the middle of the Coll Blanc and pick their way down the least steep parts of the top section to move down into the easier sections below.

After the initial steep start, all of these routes become flat schusses often demanding a skate to maintain momentum. Once the ground begins steepening again it does so as motorway-wide superpistes filling the whole mountainside between the Pic Blanc chair lift to your left and the Antenes chair lift to your right. Grau Roig base station buildings and car parks are then visible directly below and are easily reached by keeping over to the right. To make the onward link towards the Cubil area and links with Soldeu–El Tarter, keep wide to the left and descend to the valley floor.

Another variation of these routes is to peel off to the left immediately past the queue for the Coma Blanca III button lift to enter the Bosc blue piste. Although designated a lesser grading, it's really the same profile overall and has the advantage of making a connection with the Montmalús button lift to access the Montmalús red and Granota black pistes.

COMA BLANCA III

2½ mins	• 100 m (328 ft) vertical rise • 505 m (552 yd) long • 800 passengers/hour

A relatively short button lift departing from the left of the Pala Nova / Menera pistes a short way in front of the Coma III snack bar. It provides uplift towards the Portella blue piste and Grau Roig Freestyle Park and helps you escape from the traffic on the main trunk pistes.

🛈 Immediately on take-off as there is a strange camber to the ground which can catch you unawares when the drag kicks in.

At the top, leave to the right and quickly clear the limited arrival area, U-turning right to enter the Freestyle Park, or running down the steep little ramp away from the lift to follow the meandering route of the pleasant Portella blue.

GRAU ROIG FREESTYLE PARK

Not a big park, but a fun one nevertheless. Because it is tucked away at the extreme edge (no pun intended) of the ski area, and requires you to take two lifts to reach it, this park has the advantage of usually being a lot quieter than the much more accessible Pas de la Casa zone.

The wild scenery in this more peaceful side valley also adds to this secret-stash feel. There is plenty of room for you to chill out at the sides of the zone, to watch the action or simply take in the wonderful views.

Modules include:
S-rail, square rail, flat down rail, flat rail and flat box.

PORTELLA / BOSC

Aside from accessing the Freestyle Park, the Portella piste is well worth a visit on its own merit, with gorgeously wild surroundings and a real away-from-it-all feel. The peaks up to the left of this peaceful meandering piste are the Pic Negre and Pic Blanc d'Envalira, the Pic de la Menera and the Bony d'Envalira, demarcating the international border with both France and Spain. Looking ahead to the north-west, you can see right over to the line of the Cubil chair lift rising towards the link with Soldeu, with the Mirador red and Moretó black descending below it.

As it flows down into the tree line, the piste swings down to the right for a final steeper (fair red) pitch to merge with the wider Bosc blue. However, if you stay high to the left you can ride on into the trees for some great off-piste – the trees are fairly tightly packed and there is a nice gully to keep you busy too.

From the standard finish you continue as the Bosc blue, with a slope angle comparable with those of the other Grau Roig trunk reds; indeed, this piste can quickly take on a fair red character once it gets chopped up in the late afternoon. There is a clear, well-signed junction ahead: go right to merge over with the Pala Nova red towards Grau Roig base and onward link lifts, or go left to remain on the Bosc and to join the short and easy Clot blue towards the pleasant Piolet restaurant and Montmalús button lift. The Bosc blue turns to the right, above the arrival pylon for the Clot button lift, to continue the descent towards the Coma Blanca 1, Pic Blanc and Cubil chair lifts (the Coma Blanca 1 chair remains in this sector, delivering you to the start of the Bosc blue again).

If heading for the Montmalús zone, keep momentum up to pass the Piolet restaurant and continue over the flat little bridge ahead to reach the button lift.

MONTMALÚS BUTTON LIFT

- 239 m (784 ft) vertical rise
- 926 m (1013 yd) long
- Closes 16.30

6½ mins

This gives access to a lovely peaceful side valley within the impressive scenery of the Circ dels Colells. To first approach this lift, take the short Clot blue spur off the Bosc blue, passing the Piolet restaurant to cross the little flat bridge to reach the lift. After the initial few metres, the lift-line inclines steeply into the tree line and goes on to cross the line of the descending red piste, before the line turns up to the right for the final steep section of the climb. On arrival, go right for the flat traverse to the start of the Granota black, or go left for the Montmalús red.

MONTMALÚS

An enjoyable fair red with a good variety of terrain and an attractive route winding through sheltered wooded slopes. There are some steeper and narrower sections, but nothing too serious, and with plenty of opportunity to play off the sides on natural windblown kickers in the edges of the woods. Take care at the mid-section as the route crosses the line of the button lift, after which you can speed up again for the final pitch towards the base of the button lift again. Coming out into the clearing at the finish, go sharp right for the lifts and for the restaurant. Unfortunately, the piste is on the 'wrong' side of the Montmalús lift queues, so you will have to carefully ride across the departing lift-line. If the lift is closed when you get here, you can exit this area using the Clot button lift or keep descending via the flat track ahead left to reach the base station.

GRANOTA

Despite the very flat, almost inclined hike/skate for 20–30 m
(66–98 ft) from the top of the Montmalús button lift to reach
this piste, it really is worth the effort to have a go and it delivers
an enjoyable descent. Although gradings are always subject to
prevailing conditions on the day, this is a good red overall and if
you can handle the Montmalús red, then this would make an
ideal first black. More advanced visitors can up the ante by leaving
to the sides for some serious off-piste in the forested slopes, or
simply take the piste on at full tilt for a really good workout.

The Granota kicks off with a steep pitch, sufficiently narrow to
force short turns and keep you working. There are another couple
of sections like this, but you do get a chance to catch your breath
on some milder intermediate stages separating them, before
running out easily to join the lower Tortuga blue and Mirador red
on the Cubil slopes towards good links for the major lifts below.

● *View towards Montmalús area and Cirque de Pessons*

TS RIBERAL CHAIR LIFT

2	13 mins	• 420 m (1378 ft) vertical rise • 1750 m (1915 yd) long • 6½ mins to mid-point	• 1200 passengers/ hour

One of Grau Roig's original slower chairs, departing from just in front of the central base lodge. It is worth taking for the best access to the Tamarro and Riberal blacks, which begin nearest to its arrival point on the ridge separating the two sectors. Early intermediates can also take this lift for the mid-journey get-off point on to the flattest middle section of the Pista Llarga run.

On the journey up, you have great views over the whole sector and can see the twin blacks dropping to each side of the arrival point above. On arrival, you can see the back of the top station of the Pas de la Casa chair lift; go towards this to access the Tamarro black, which drops off to the right after around 10 m (33 ft), or you can ride over to the Coll Blanc saddle area for all options from there. Turning left on arrival you take the very flat access track about 30 m (98 ft) towards the start of the Riberal black.

TAMARRO & RIBERAL

Twin short blacks plunging down into the Grau Roig sector off the Envalira ridge separating the Pas–Grau sectors. Both pistes are fair blacks/very good reds, lasting only for about 500 m (547 yd). The uppermost sections are the toughest; often mogulled and with plenty of opportunity to freeride between the runs. The pistes are quite wide and pose no extreme challenges, running out at the bottom to join the Pista Llarga towards Grau Roig base – unfortunately at its flattest section, so really dulling the rush from the steep blacks and presenting a bit of a slog for boarders.

TSD4 ANTENES CHAIR LIFT

7 mins	• 450 m (1476 ft) vertical rise • 1500 m (4921 ft) long • 2500 passengers/hour

A much overlooked chair lift, despite being the closest to the car parks and base lodge, which serves the whole left side of the Grau Roig area and makes a useful, less busy link with the Pas sector. Most visitors tend to head for the Pic Blanc and Cubil chair lifts to make onward links, thus usually bypassing this lift and keeping queues to a minimum (although now the secret's out!).

On arrival at the wide easy get-off area, you have a full choice of routes: U-turn to the right around the lift hut to start the Diagonal red; go straight on for the Taupes black into Pas; or go left along the ridge for all other options back into Grau Roig or towards the Pas sector, including the Gavatxa red, which is usually a lot quieter and easier than the Coll Blanc routes into Pas.

DIAGONAL

Begins descending to the left of the Antenes chair-lift arrival point. The top section swings to the right under the line of the arriving lift, traversing across the upper slopes to clear the avalanche-prone chutes below left. The piste proper begins by dropping parallel with the line of the Antenes lift above, developing a standard red gradient with a couple of variation routes splitting to the left and right at the junction ahead; the more direct right-hand route is the Antenes black, which is very similar but usually offers a wide manageable first mogul field for progressing intermediates. Both routes' lower sections flow into the same superpiste as the Pista Llarga towards Grau Roig.

GRANDALLES

Fair red which is accessed via a junction off the Diagonal red and Antenes black, below the ridge and not directly from it as the piste map would suggest. The top section of the run is a fast straight cutting across the mountainside, with far-reaching views directly down the Valira Valley towards Soldeu village. The sweeping curve to the left below takes you past the start gates for the Grau Roig competition course; however, this is a closed stadium and usually only accessible to events competitors. The Grandalles flows fast around the left-hand perimeter of the course before swinging to the right past the course exit to drop out on to the Pastora blue – check your speed and turn 90 degrees left to join it.

PASTORA

The best way for novices to move from the Pas sector into the Grau Roig sector. The run begins to the right of the arrival point of the Antenes chair on the Envalira ridge, sharing the upper entrance with the Antenes black, which drops off down to the left after some 350–400 m (383–438 yd); stay highest right to remain on the blue piste which continues to traverse out past the position of the radio mast above. The route down to Grau Roig is a lovely, open motorway-wide curving piste, with great views down the Valira Valley ahead and over to the rest of the Grau Roig sector to the left. There are also some snowfields to the sides of the piste, which make ideal first-powder playgrounds for progressing intermediates. The lowest section of the route finishes as a gentle, narrow track running behind the Grau Roig Hotel and out into the base station area: look out for piste traffic dropping in from the Grandalles red and competition course above left.

🔺 *Grandalles red looking towards Soldeu*

TSD4 CUBIL CHAIR LIFT

6 mins

- 352 m (1155 ft) vertical rise
- 1286 m (1407 yd) long
- 2400 passengers/hour

The sole lift to the Cubil ridge from Grau Roig, serving all pistes on this mountain and providing a link for the onward journey towards Soldeu–El Tarter and the Funicamp. The piste to the right is the Moretó black, the one parallel to the left is the Mirador red; the challenging gully in the middle is the short Tub de Bosc black.

On arrival, turn right on to the wide ridge, U-turning right to begin the Cami de Pessons and Mirador reds; or riding slightly further along the ridge to access the Moretó black. Alternatively, go over the far side of the ridge to access the Aigües Tortes red and l'Avi blue, or ride along the ridge to take the Serrat Pinos red towards the link with the Soldeu sector.

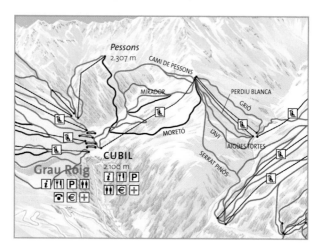

CAMI DE PESSONS

Although graded red, there is little after the initial choppy traverse to worry confident novices on this attractive winding mountain track, and it accesses probably the most authentic mountain restaurant in Grau Roig – the Refugi dels Llacs dels Pessons (see page 354).

The top section is shared with the start of the Mirador red; traverse across the hill heading for the flatter Cami road-route itself, which you can see running gently away to the far right. Once on the track, it's an easy, almost pedestrian route through a peaceful and relatively unspoilt upper side valley. The route picks up a better gradient as you near the lakeside restaurant, which is right next to the piste on a sweeping hairpin bend, before swinging away in the opposite direction through the woods to rejoin the Mirador red returning to the Grau Roig lifts.

MIRADOR

The prime piste on the Grau Roig side of the Cubil ridge, motoring directly down the mountainside; with a couple of interesting variations on the way. At the mid-section (after 800–900 m/ 875–985 yd) there is a junction point; keeping straight on is the best red line on the Mirador itself. To the right is an easier blue variation called the Tortuga, which simply takes the sting out of the Mirador by traversing it in sweeping S-bends to clear the steepest section. Going left at the junction takes you to a really steep and narrow gully called the Tub de Bosc black. It is a good black going in, but lasts only for around 300 m (328 yd) before rejoining the Mirador and Tortuga again. All the routes sweep down together towards the lifts, or you can keep higher to the left and access the Cubil restaurant and services lodge.

MORETÓ

Although designated a black grading, this wide undulating piste is really a twin of the Mirador red, descending parallel on the same mountainside over to the far side of the Cubil chair-line. One advantage of this route is that the black grading puts off many people – this means that the run is a lot clearer than the busy Mirador. The finish section joins with the Mirador towards the lifts base, or you can leave slightly higher to the left for the Cubil restaurant and services lodge.

SERRAT PINÒS

This is the prime link piste between Grau Roig and the neighbouring Grandvalira ski station Soldeu. Despite being graded red, this route harbours no nasty surprises for confident novices; it is wide and undulating, resulting in a blue equivalent overall. It runs straight along the Cubil ridge, giving expansive vistas over the Moretó Forest to the right towards Grau Roig and the Envalira Pass, and to the left over the wide snowbowl shared with the Soldeu ski area. Approaching the chair lifts at the end of the route, turn down to the right for the nearer Pla de les Pedres Grau Roig chair to head up to the Collada d'Enradort services complex and the Funicamp; or keep crossing to the lower Pla de les Pedres Soldeu chair to make the link with that station via the Collada de les Solanelles ridge. If you're returning to Soldeu in the afternoon and miss the last link lift here, don't panic; simply go past the lift base and continue on the flat easy track, which eventually joins the Ós blue route back to Soldeu village.

There is a WCs cabin just to the right before the base of the Pla de les Pedres Grau Roig lift.

L'AVI

Good wide blue starting from the same ridge line as the Serrat Pinòs red, but sweeping down towards the Llac de Cubil lifts base in the valley below. The piste swings out wide to the right of the Aigües Tortes red, then gently curves to the left to funnel into a narrow, but easy, access track towards the lifts. The Llac del Cubil button lift and chair lift are nearest to the left, the Enradort chair lift is ahead right; take the Enradort to reach the Funicamp and the Solanelles restaurant.

GRIÓ / PERDIU BLANCA / AIGÜES TORTES

A trio of good warm-up reds descending parallel to the liftlines down to the Llac de Cubil. The Grió is the one furthest out to the left and, although reachable by linking over from the central Perdiu Blanca piste, begins at the top of the Llac del Cubil chair lift. All these routes share the same profile and make good links with all three lifts below.

🔺 *From Cubil towards Solanelles*

TS4 LLAC DEL CUBIL CHAIR LIFT

5 mins

- 207 m (679 ft) vertical rise
- 718 m (785 yd) long
- 2400 passengers/hour

One of two lifts sharing this name and making the link towards Grau Roig via the Cubil ridge. The button lift arrives at the slightly lower altitude so you have a flat traverse to reach the watershed for the ridge. The button lift is the quickest option, but snowboarders are not permitted to use it! The chair runs at the maximum permitted speed for a non-declutchable chair lift (2.42 m/second) and there is a magic carpet at the get-on point.

On arrival, turn left only, U-turning to the left to start the Grió red or continuing down the ridge-line past the Cubil chair arrival point to access all other routes. If you're travelling towards Grau Roig, the view ahead is over the whole sector towards the Envalira Pass dividing Grau Roig from the Pas de la Casa sector beyond.

⬤ *Top of Cubil towards the Envalira Pass*

TS4 ENRADORT & TS4 COLIBRÍ CHAIR LIFTS

- 250 m (820 ft) vertical rise
- 1550 m (1696 yd) long in total
- 2400 passengers/hour

A series of two linking chair lifts making a slow journey up the high Collada d'Enradort. The Enradort chair departs from the Llac del Cubil area and rises to the lowest point on the Enradort ridge, where you dismount straight ahead to get on the second Colibrí lift for the final leg up to the summit.

On arrival at the top of the Colibrí chair, dismount straight ahead for the Funicamp station and the Solanelles restaurants. The blue piste parallel to the chair lift on the ridge accesses the Enradort and Colibrí red pistes back to the Llac del Cubil lifts base, while the Riu del Cubil and Riu de les Solanelles blues depart from the far side of the summit ahead, past the Funicamp station.

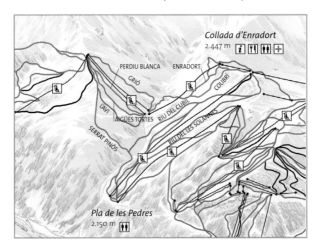

ENRADORT & COLIBRÍ

Twin reds from the Enradort ridge, which run down to the Llac del Cubil lifts for the onward/return trip towards Grau Roig. The Colibrí is the steepest; the Enradort hugs the ridge-line as a gentle blue before flowing off the ridge nearest to the chair-lift line. The entire ridge is pisted, inviting you to drop off at any point that appeals to make tracks through any fresher and deeper powder between the actual pistes. Less confident novices can follow the gentler ridge route to clear the steepest top section.

Both these pistes merge together as a wide gentle cruise to cross to the right of the Enradort lift-line for the final flat run to the lifts base. You need to keep up momentum to reach the lifts, but the link is fair.

RIU DEL CUBIL & RIU DE LES SOLANELLES

From the Collada d'Enradort, the principal routes into the wide snowbowl below are these two wide undulating freeways that branch into another set of twin variations after leaving the high ridge. Shortly after reaching the col below you veer to the right to flow into the valley, being joined by visitors from the El Tarter and Soldeu sectors via the button lift behind you and from the summit above to the left. At the wide junction ahead, go right for the Riu del Cubil and its two parallel variants (the Solanella and the Ayelem blues), or go left for the Riu de les Solanelles. It's possible to ride wide to the right off the Riu del Cubil piste to link over with the lower Enradort red; otherwise all these wide blues cruise down to make good links with both the Grau Roig and the Soldeu Pla de les Pedres chair lifts directly below. The Soldeu sector link lift is the one slightly lower on the left.

TSD6 PLA DE LES PEDRES GRAU ROIG CHAIR LIFT

 8 mins

- 350 m (1148 ft) vertical rise
- 2000 m (2188 yd) long
- 3000 passengers/hour

A good fast chair, travelling for 2 km (1¼ miles) up to the high Collada d'Enradort to the excellent Solanelles services complex and the Funicamp for Encamp town. This lift also effects the link into the Grau Roig sector for those visitors joining from Soldeu and El Tarter. The journey up affords great views over this wide open snowbowl; from the line of the Soldeu lift of the same name running parallel up on the ridge to the right, all the way over to the Llac del Cubil lifts far to the left, as well as over the four motorway blues which flow beneath and to the sides of this chair-line.

On arrival, leave straight ahead, veering left for the Funicamp, the Solanelles restaurant and to access the Colibrí and Enradort red pistes, or turning right to begin the Riu de les Solanelles and Riu del Cubil blues. There is also a little-known black variation entrance into the Riu del Cubil blue, which requires a double-take at the piste map to spot, accessed by turning sharp right after arriving on this chair to deliver a short, sharp pulse-booster off this high rocky summit.

◭ Panoramic terrace at the high-altitude Solanelles restaurant

SOLANELLES SERVICES COMPLEX

A spectacular spot, with commanding views over the ski area below and the high peaks and passes beyond. Fully accessible to pedestrians arriving on the Funicamp from Encamp town, making it an ideal destination for non-skiers to meet their skiing friends and family for lunch.

Terrace level: snack bar counter serving the huge sunny terrace (no table service), drinks vending machines, Espress'Oh! café, self-service restaurant.

Lower ground floor: WCs, public telephones, lockers.

Upper floor: à la carte restaurant, WCs.

FUNICAMP

15 mins ▲▼

- 1169 m (3835 ft) vertical rise
- 6137m (6714 yd) long
- 1765 passengers/hour

Gondola-style cable car link from the parish capital Encamp. The town sits at the geographical centre of Andorra and so the lift travels an astonishing 6 km (3¾ miles) plus to reach the high Collada d'Enradort summit via the long Cortals d'Encamp Valley. The base station in Encamp has a multi-storey car park, ski-pass sales points, information desk, cafeteria with terrace overlooking the town, WCs, lockers, souvenir shop and small pharmacy. The upper station is simply an arrival/departure building, with direct access out to the start of the pistes and a short stroll to the Solanelles restaurant and services complex. Funicamp is a contraction of the words Funicular and Encamp, and always raises a smile from English-speaking visitors.

⬤ *The twin cable Funicamp from Encamp to the Collada d'Enradort*

POINT-TO-POINT ROUTES: COMPETENT NOVICES

PAS DE LA CASA » GRAU ROIG

TS4 Solana chair lift → Tubs → TS4 Costa Rodona chair lift → Pastora

GRAU ROIG » PAS DE LA CASA

TSD4 Antenes chair lift → Gavatxa → Tubs

GRAU ROIG » PLA DE LES PEDRES 2150 M (SOLDEU LINK)

Pessons → TSD4 Cubil chair lift → Serrat Pinós

PLA DE LES PEDRES 2150 M » GRAU ROIG

TSD6 Pla de les Pedres Grau Roig chair lift → Enradort → TS4 Llac del Cubil chair lift → Camí de Pessons → Tortuga

GRAU ROIG » FUNICAMP

Pessons → TSD4 Cubil chair lift → L'Avi → TS4 Enradort chair lift → TS4 Colibri chair lift

FUNICAMP » GRAU ROIG

Enradort → TS4 Llac del Cubil chair lift → Mirador → Tortuga

⬤ *The Coll Blanc, between Pas de la Casa and Grau Roig*

POINT-TO-POINT ROUTES: GOOD INTERMEDIATES AND ABOVE

PAS DE LA CASA » GRAU ROIG

TSD4 Pas de la Casa chair lift — Pista Llarga

GRAU ROIG » PAS DE LA CASA

TSD4 Antenes chair lift — Taupes — FIS — Tubs

GRAU ROIG » PLA DE LES PEDRES 2150 M (SOLDEU LINK)

Pessons — TSD4 Cubil chair lift — Serrat Pinós

PLA DE LES PEDRES 2150 M » GRAU ROIG

TSD6 Pla de les Pedres Grau Roig chair lift — Colibrí — Enradort

TS4 Llac del Cubil chair lift — Moretó

PAS DE LA CASA » PAS GRAU ROIG SNOWPARK

TSD6 Font Negra chair lift → Pista Llarga → Menera → Coma Blanca III button lift

GRAU ROIG SNOWPARK » PAS DE LA CASA

Bosc → Pala Nova → TSD6 Pic Blanc chair lift → Llac → Fletxa

GRAU ROIG » FUNICAMP

Pessons → TSD4 Cubil chair lift → Aigües Tortes → TS4 Enradort chair lift → TS4 Colibrii chair lift

FUNICAMP » GRAU ROIG

Colibrí → Enradort → TS4 Llac del Cubil chair lift → Mirador

MOUNTAIN BARS & RESTAURANTS

Despite the extent of the ski area, you're never very far away from on-piste access to food and drink, with nine different locations spread throughout the Pas–Grau region. Although most rely heavily on snack-food menus, there are also a couple of real gems which are worth featuring in your route planning. All offer a bar service and all except the smallest snack kiosks have free WCs.

PAS DE LA CASA SECTOR

As the main streets of the town are so accessible from the foot of the Pas sector's slopes, the whole base station area is a major focal point for lunch and snack breaks. The most easily accessible venues on the town slopes are the frontline terraces to the left of the Tubs blue piste, running down towards the Solana chair lift: all have piste-side patios and all offer snacks, lunch menus and full bar service. The Olimpiades, Xadoc, L'Husky, Tupi and Pic Blanc are the most popular. It is easy to ride away from the terraces and link with the lifts directly below; non-skiers can stroll up the sides of the piste to reach these venues, or can enter via the rear doors in Plaça dels Vaquers.

➔ *See also page 362 for recommended cafés and restaurants in the town (street plan on page 295).*

The ski station runs its own purpose-built catering sites on the mountain, including two venues on the lower Pas slopes just above town. All of the snack bars have standardized menus; prices are consistent and are cheaper than in comparable venues in the Alps.

🕒 Snack bars open 09.30–16.30 hours; restaurants offer full catering 12.30–15.30 hours; all offer all-day bar service.

◀ *Costa Rodona restaurant, Pas de la Casa*

Font Negre Small snack bar with a piste-side snow terrace, offering an exterior service only – pizza slices, sandwiches, paninis, chips, *caldo* (hot consommé) plus hot and cold drinks. Situated just below the Abelletes IV button lift in the lower beginners' zone, at the side of the Fletxa blue piste next to the upper Avinguda d'Encamp. There are steps down to the car park and street below at the rear of the bar, for easy access by non-skiers. The key Font Negre link chair lift is close by and it's a short way on-piste to the base of the town slopes.

Costa Rodona Large purpose-built restaurant and services complex, which serves as a satellite base station for the Pas sector, located at the FIS competition stadium and Costa Rodona lift at a bend on the Port d'Envalira road above town.

Lovely bar in the upper building with quality décor and a homely chalet feel, offering a reasonable selection of salads and grills, plus a full bar service and decent wine list.

The large terrace on this level is also served by an exterior snack kiosk for pizza slices, sandwiches, paninis, chips and drinks. The terrace has plenty of seating, including loungers, and faces directly into the sun looking up towards the upper pistes. There are WCs on this level, plus a cash machine on the roadside corner of the building.

On the lower ground floor there is a large interior self-service restaurant with the usual selection of ready made salads and daily specials hot dishes, but it also features fresh meat grills, which are a lot better than those in most canteens of this type. There are microwaves available for reheating food that is cooling quickly on the coldest days, and there are WCs on this level too. This lower venue is fairly bright and modern, but lacks any views.

Coll Blanc The distinctive, futuristic circular building cantilevered out on the edge of the ridge at the Coll Blanc, overlooking the principal pistes towards Pas de la Casa and Grau Roig. The restaurant is reachable via the Font Negre lift from the Pas sector and the Pic Blanc lift from the Grau Roig side.

There is a small snow terrace by the entrance door, but the bar and restaurant here are solely an interior service. A full bar service is available, plus the standard snack menu of pizza slices, paninis, sandwiches and chips. Additionally, there is a cordoned-off dining area with a slightly more elaborate lunch menu of basic grills and pasta dishes. The main attractions of this venue are the 180-degree views from the floor to ceiling windows, as well as the fact that it is a shelter from the elements on this exposed ridge in rough weather. WCs are on the lower ground floor.

🔺 *Panoramic views from the Coll Blanc restaurant*

GRAU ROIG SECTOR

From the Coll Blanc ridge, you are now crossing into the Grau Roig sector; the on-mountain food and drink choice continues at the Coma III snack bar just below.

Coma III A simple snack bar hut, but in a lovely location on a sunny, open plateau near the base of the Coma Blanca III button lift and handy for the Freestyle Park. Easy to reach from the Coll Blanc ridge immediately after dropping into the Grau Roig sector. Pizza slices, paninis, sandwiches, chips, hot and cold drinks. Piste-side snow patio with loungers, chairs and tables; WCs available.

Piolet Pleasant snack bar and restaurant tucked away in a peaceful wooded dell by the Clot and Montmalùs button lifts, first accessed via the Bosc and Clot blue pistes. Attractive, stone- and wood-built chalet with a good-sized terrace facing south-east and with great views up to the impressive Circ dels Colells.

Reasonably priced *menu del día*; plus a range of salads, pastas and grills, on top of the usual snack-food selection; full bar service. Order food at the cashier point along with your drinks; once your meal is ready it will be brought to your table. Public telephone and WCs available.

Grau Roig Hotel Situated at Grau Roig base station. The lovely public lounge bar/restaurant La Vaqeria has a windbreak-sheltered terrace, warmed by patio heaters and furnished with chunky natural log seating and tables, directly accessible from the pistes. The interior lounge is homely and welcoming, with quality décor and a more refined menu and wine list. In addition to the full lunch menu, filled baguettes and tapas are available.

Grau Roig Base Lodge The principal day-lodge at the base station houses a number of catering establishments, all usually buzzing with Spanish daytrippers and all offering a standard snack and fixed menu selection. Venues include:

Titos Good old-fashioned snack bar near the main ground floor entrance, offering a full bar and a flame-grill hot snack service, plus chips, omelettes and pre-packed salads. Order and pay at the cashier point first.

Patisserie Cream buns and cakes counter in the main lobby, with a fair display of pastries and confectionery plus hot chocolate and coffee.

La Tornada Self-service cafeteria at the far end of the lodge: canteen-style, but not unattractive, with a bar service, fast-food menu and a good range of filled baguettes. Rear terrace overlooking beginners' slopes towards Cubil mountain.

Pizza Hut Occupying the entire upper floor: does exactly what its name implies.

As well as these catering facilities, the lodge also houses a large, bright picnic saloon with its own terrace on the lower ground floor. WCs are also here on the lower ground floor.

Cubil Base Lodge Secondary day-lodge set in off the left side of the Moretò black and Mirador red pistes on the Cubil side of the Grau Roig base area, saving skiers on that side of the valley having to slog up to the primary lodge in the upper car parking zone. There is a large terrace with views over the Grau Roig area and up to the rugged cirques beyond; catering outlets include an Espress'Oh! café and a canteen-style self-service restaurant with standard snack food menu, plus daily specials hot dishes. Full bar service and WCs.

Refugi dels Llacs dels Pessons Although just a simple mountain refuge, with a basic interior bar, the Refugi also houses an authentic and atmospheric Andorran restaurant offering quality à la carte fare and a decent wine list. The restaurant has a cosy, convivial ambience, with exposed wood beams and a log fire. The venue has only a dozen tables and is very popular with local mountain guides and station personnel, so reservations are recommended: ☎ +376 759015

There is a lovely sunny terrace outside the bar, served by its own snack kiosk selling chips and paninis; the views over the frozen lake and Circ dels Pessons beyond are suberb.

The Refugi is reached via the Cami de Pessons red piste from the Cubil ridge, and sits next to the piste at 2307 m (7569 ft) altitude.

Solanelles The highest altitude full-service catering in the entire Grandvalira domain, perched above the Collada d'Enradort beside the upper Funicamp station at the boundary limit for the Grau Roig ski area. Huge curved construction facing the sun and occupying a commanding position overlooking the Soldeu/Grau Roig shared Solanelles and Cubil Valleys. Massive sun terrace on the main level, with a fast-food snack counter and bar service; interior Espress'Oh! café and self-service restaurant plus full bar service. The self-service venue is big and bright, offering half-a-dozen daily specials combination dishes and a hot-plate grill service; a fair buffet salad selection and an excellent-value *menu del día*.

On the uppermost level there is an excellent large à la carte restaurant, with a cosy chalet-style lounge bar, sofas, log fire and slippers to change into for a break from your ski boots.

▶ *Coma III snack bar, Grau Roig*

ALTERNATIVE ACTIVITIES

As all-round winter sports stations, Pas de la Casa and Grau Roig promote a number of other activities to appeal to all their visitors, whether skiers or not. Full details and bookings can be made at the dedicated Adventure Activities Centre at Grau Roig base station.
❶ Activities may not be covered by travel insurance (see page 58).

SNOWMOBILES

This thrilling motorsport is consistently the most requested alternative wintersports activity. The Pas–Grau area has a good-sized, closed circuit marked out at the Port d'Envalira at 2408 m (7900 ft), one of the highest-altitude driving circuits in Europe. The circuit is fast, with long straights, humps and twisting bends, and great views down the Valira Valley over Grau Roig and Soldeu. Each skidoo can carry two people; charged per machine.

DOG SLEIGHS

This is a wonderful activity for all visitors. Teams of husky dogs pull Arctic sleds round an attractive trail looping out in the Valira Valley; passengers can either steer themselves or be guided by an experienced musher. Available at Grau Roig base station.

IGLOO BUILDING

Learn the basics of snow-shelter design and construction and get to build a dome igloo. Accessible to all visitors, this unusual activity is available at both Pas de la Casa and Grau Roig base stations. Practical course and construction lasts around three hours.

◀ *Snowmobiling: big engine and deep snow equals great fun*

PAINTBALL

A classic fun activity to really release any leftover energy and, more importantly, shoot your mates. Both Pas de la Casa and Grau Roig have battle cages furnished with obstacles and crash-mats for cover, but there is nowhere to run to once you're locked in the cage... so go on the offensive or eat pigment. A minimum of eight players is required, charged per person.

SNOWSHOES

Definitely the best way for non-skiers to get out on the snow and into the snowfields. Modern snowshoes are made of lightweight materials and are very easy to learn to use. By spreading your weight over a greater surface area, they allow you to confidently grip on the hard-packed pistes and walk over deeper snow, using ski poles for balance. A waymarked itinerary has been marked out in the quiet upper Valira Valley, looping out below the access road into Grau Roig. This activity can also be arranged in Pas de la Casa,

● Snowshoes: access all areas

to follow the route of the Ariege River, which marks the French border beside Pas de la Casa town and the beginners' zone. Access to the circuits is free of charge, but you'll need to bring or hire your own equipment: most ski rental shops offer snowshoes too. Instruction from a professional guide can be arranged via the Adventure Activities Centre, for a fee.

ORIENTATION & AVALANCHE RESCUE

Thinking of moving up to riding off-piste and ski-touring? Obtain some basic mountain guidance and survival skills and learn to use ARVA® avalanche victim search equipment on this three-hour practical course at either Pas de la Casa or Grau Roig. The mountains may be fun, but they are also deadly: educate yourself to take them on in the safest possible manner.

LANGLAUF

Nordic skiing enthusiasts are not well catered for at any of Andorra's downhill stations, but at least Grau Roig does have a permanent circuit. The route is graded blue and is 12 km (7½ miles) long, the actual route traced out according to the condition of the snow. The course is prepared for both traditional technique and skating, and loops out alongside the snowshoe trail in the Valira Valley just

🔺 Langlauf, the most aerobic snowsport

below Grau Roig base station. Serious cross-country skiers should investigate Andorra's little-known but dedicated Nordic resort La Rabassa, situated on a scenic high-altitude plateau next to the Spanish border above the town of Sant Julià de Lòria, south of Andorra la Vella (see page 62 for more details).

APRÈS-SKI

Most visitors to Pas come for the nightlife as much as for the skiing. The town is Andorra's largest resort and is crammed with cafés, restaurants, music bars and small late-night clubs. Stepping off the slopes at the end of the day you are immediately in the thick of the action, with a wide range of après-ski venues and distractions to delay you on the way back for a shower.

⬤ *Sundown over Pas de la Casa*

Of course, there are other milder off-slope attractions, too:

FITNESS & WELLNESS

A few of the resort's larger, quality hotels have their own in-house spa facilities, but the town also has a modern, well-equipped sports and social-cultural centre (Centre esportiu i sociocultural del Pas de la Casa) boasting a large indoor swimming pool, hydromassage and Jacuzzis, sauna, fitness room, squash court, aerobics/dance studio, artificial climbing wall, paddle tennis court and multi-sports hall, as well as housing the town's public library and exhibition gallery. The centre is the huge, silver box-like edifice looming behind the police and customs offices near the border post. The centre also houses a large-capacity covered car park too – special rates are available for long-stay parking.
☎ +376 856 830 ⓦ www.centre.ad

PAMPERING

The only real facility is the small spa at the Hotel Font d'Argent on Carrer de Bearn. Sports and relaxing massages, facials, manicures and pedicures are available by prior arrangement for residents and non-residents. ☎ +376 739 739

ICE-DRIVING CIRCUIT

An international standard circuit which hosts the Andros Trophy Grand Prix as well as regional competitions. The circuit is floodlit for night events and is something a little bit different for visiting motorsports enthusiasts. Unfortunately, the course is for professional drivers only so this is a spectator-only activity. Located on the Port d'Envalira road high above town. Enquire at the tourist office regarding current events programme.

SHOPPING

Another thing that Pas doesn't lack is shops; as a duty-free frontier town it has always been a magnet for French bargain hunters who drive here to fill up with cheaper fuel, cheaper alcohol, cheaper cigarettes, cheaper electronic goods, cheaper music, cheaper DVDs, cheaper… you get the idea. Although the town is crammed with booze and tobacco duty-free superstores, it also has a fair selection of boutiques and department stores stocking sports and street fashions, sunglasses and jewellery, as well as a large number of music shops, electronic goods outlets and perfumeries. If you're serious about your snowsports and want your own kit, then Pas is probably the best resort in Europe for purchasing gear. The main shopping streets are Carrer Major, Avinguda d'Encamp, Carrer Sant Jordi and Carrer de Catalunya.

If your retail therapeutic requirements are even more serious, then a visit to Andorra's capital, Andorra la Vella, should feature in your plans. However, with so much choice on your doorstep right here in Pas, there is no real need to leave the town at all.

Remember, Andorra is not a member of the EU; please go to our website **www.ski-ride.com** for details of duty-free limits.

CASH MACHINES

There are ATMs dotted all around the centre of town (see town plan on page 295). English-language instructions are quick to find and operation will usually be as familiar as at your own bank.

CAFÉS & RESTAURANTS

Virtually all of the bars in Andorra also function as café-bars, offering at the very least proper espresso coffee and a basic snack/tapas selection, so there's always somewhere near to hand for a quick caffeine fix in a more chilled atmosphere away from the raucous music and sports bars. The resort also has quite a few attractive cafés and patisseries, especially on the narrow walkway behind the restaurant terraces on Avinguda d'Encamp.

As for restaurants, the town has a wide range, from McDonald's all the way up to haute cuisine: French, Spanish, Italian, Morrocan, Indian, Chinese, Tex-Mex, and even Andorran! Unlike in Andorra's other ski resorts, many of the restaurants in Pas have a pronounced French flavour, featuring Alpine specialities such as raclette and fondue Savoyarde, and with vin chaud as ubiquitous as sangria. The majority of establishments offer standard 'international' menus focused on pizzas and grilled meats.

Avinguda d'Encamp The entire street opposite the foot of the town pistes and lifts is lined with good restaurants and cafés. Most have front terraces and cosy interior dining rooms with rear window views overlooking the contrastingly undeveloped French mountains behind. Many also feature lovely front window displays of cakes and pastries and operate as coffee shops as well as full-on restaurants. Some of the nicest are Del Roma, La Brasa, La Gratinada, La Gralella and Café Portofino.

⏷ *Avinguda d'Encamp café*

Croissant Express €+ Proper coffee, warm croissants and fresh bread. A little oasis of calm amongst all the retail madness on Carrer de Catalunya.

Auteuil Brasserie and Pizzeria €€ Tucked away in an uninspiring back street, with an entranceway squeezed in between the shops on Carrer Sant Jordi. Pleasant venue with a fair range of pizzas and grills. ☎ +376 855 448

Xadoc €€ Attractive Moroccan restaurant with a cosy low-lit interior and tasty *tagines*. Accessible from the lower Tubs blue piste or down a flight of steps from Carrer de la Solana.

El Garantua €€ Pleasant restaurant at the entrance to the Paradis Blanc apartments on Avinguda d'Encamp. Extensive menu featuring French specialities, pizzas and grills.

La Raclette €€ Very good French restaurant, with a pleasing ambience and décor. Incongruously sited in the dingy Carrer del Maia back street off the Carrer de Catalunya.

Marquet €€+ Classy, tiny delicatessen and wine bar serving gourmet tapas. Located on Carrer de Bearn next to Burger King.

Marisqueria Campistrano €€ Good fish restaurant on Carrer de Bearn, also featuring decent steaks. ☎ +376 856 488

Panda Restaurant €€ At the hotel of the same name in Plaça dels Coprínceps. Excellent T-bone steaks and grilled meats, fondues and fish. ☎ +376 855 361

BARS & CLUBS

There is quite an overlap between what constitutes a café, pub, bar or a restaurant in Pas, with many venues functioning as a bit of everything. Most have happy hours from around 16.00–18.00, and many have live music or DJs to kick off the early evening après-ski.

Despite being known as an 'Ibiza in the snow', Pas doesn't actually have any superclubs and most of what it does have are basic disco-bars with theme nights; expect Euro Dance and House at most. That said, the town does rock, and with so many bars and venues vying for business there's always some event or promotion going on, mostly sponsored by the big drink and tobacco companies, offering free shots and free cigarettes on top of duty-free prices... welcome to Andorra.

Carrer del Maia, Plaça dels Vaquers, Plaça Sant Josep, Carrer de Bearn and Carrer de la Solana are where most of the liveliest venues are concentrated. But remember: altitude and alcohol form a dangerous combination – dehydration is a killer on the mountains. At the very least, if you've overdone it and are too wasted to hit the hills the next day, then that's a serious percentage of your skiing time and ski pass investment wasted, too.

Provinçal City Irish bar on Avinguda d'Encamp on the lower corner of the Frontera Blanca apartment complex. Lively après-ski, live music and late-night singalongs.

El Pandero Nightclub With regular lap dancing. Underground beneath the Frontera Blanca apartments.

Little Rock Café Last on the left at top end of Avinguda d'Encamp. Tex-Mex food and early après-ski live music.

CARRER DEL MAIA

A dingy back street off Carrer de Catalunya, housing the rear entrances for the hotels and restaurants on Carrer de Bearn above as well as a couple of late-night music bars and clubs, alongside one or two incongruously sited good-quality restaurants.

El Mexicana Disco-pub with Tex-Mex food and tequila slammers.

Surf.on.in Cyberpub Internet station and small pub.

Billboard One of Pas's longest-running clubs, with frequent promotional nights. Music policy is mostly Euro and House, although anything that gets the crowd going is fair game.

West End Another of Pas's original clubs, now promoting lap dancing as one of its 'features'. Plays Euro and House music.

CARRER DE BEARN

Marseilles Daytime pizzas, burgers, salads and pasta; après-ski and late-night music bar.

La Perla Negre Pirate-themed pub. Above the supermarket on the corner with Plaça de Sant Josep.

La Copa Large pub, with pool table, wood-fired pizzas and grills.

Milwalkee One of Pas's key pubs, always lively and with a good programme of themed events and big-screen sports.

PLAÇA DELS VAQUERS/PLAÇA DE SANT JOSEP

Two small cojoined squares, behind the Hotel Kandahar, located just off Carrer de Bearn, which are crammed with pubs and music bars. Many of these venues also have terraces at the front on the edge of the Tubs blue piste and operate as daytime snack bars.

Underground Music bar playing music 'from the swinging 60s through to the naughty 90s'.

KSB Reasonably cosy pub and late-night grill.

Vertigo Music bar with Internet stations.

KYU Disco-pub, music from the 60s to the 90s.

Pas 83 Often lively basement bar with pub food.

Tupi Mexican food, SKY Sports. Good buzzing après-ski pub (with daytime piste-side terrace too).

Zamakaze Surf Bar Buzzing après-ski bar with pool table and pub food (piste-side terrace).

Tropical Club Billed as a 'cocktail bar', although really this is just a standard bar featuring the usual list of amusingly named concoctions.

Mulligan's and **Club Havane** Two more unpretentious and lively pubs housed in these squares.

CARRER DE LA SOLANA

Continuation of the Carrer de Bearn, heading up the hill from the corner past the Milwalkee pub.

Pub Mambo Music bar with frequent theme nights. Underneath the Snowlake apartments.

Catsby In-house bar at the British-run hotel of the same name. Good traditional pub food, including curry nights and midweek 'Sunday roasts' (so that you don't miss out on your weekend transfer day). Pool table, SKY sports.

Club Orange Small club, but with a decent music policy – mostly House, Techno, R&B and Hip-Hop.

Most of Pas's hotels have their own in-house bars and many of these can be quite lively and fun, depending on the nature of each week's clientele. At the very least they're good for a reviving drink.

> **CAUTION**
> All of the town centre buildings in Pas de la Casa tower directly above the streets below; although all have roof- and gutter-edge guardrails, rooftop snow and icicles frequently fall. Be aware and stay under the arcaded walkways where they exist. Snow may be fluffy and light in small amounts, but once it compacts and freezes together in lumps it can cause serious injury if it falls on you from a height.

EXPLORING ANDORRA

Although this book is a specialist snowsports guide, and given that most readers will be visiting Andorra on a snowsports holiday, it would be a shame not to make a point of getting out of your resort for at least an afternoon to see more of this fascinating little country.

Getting around is not too difficult; nowhere is too far away and buses and taxis are readily available. Many tour operators also organize at least a shopping trip to Andorra la Vella once per week. Unless you have your own vehicle, one of the easiest modes of transport is by taxi; all Andorran taxis are officially licensed and all use standardized meters. Local buses are not too frequent, but are reliable and cheap. There are seven different lines operated by the national transport company:

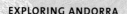

⊕ **Line 1** Sant Julià de Lòria **»** Andorra la Vella **»** Escaldes-Engordany

⊕ **Line 2** Andorra la Vella **»** Escaldes-Engordany **»** Encamp

⊕ **Line 3** Andorra la Vella **»** Escaldes-Engordany **»** Encamp **»** Canillo **»** Soldeu

- **→ Line 4** Andorra la Vella » Escaldes-Engordany » Encamp » Canillo » Soldeu » Pas de la Casa
- **→ Line 5** Andorra la Vella » Escaldes-Engordany » La Massana » Arinsal
- **→ Line 6** Andorra la Vella » Escaldes-Engordany » La Massana » Ordino
- **→ Line 7** Andorra la Vella » Escaldes-Engordany » La Massana » Ordino » El Serrat

Once you arrive at your outbound destination, the return bus stop is generally on the opposite side of the road at the same location. In Andorra la Vella there are various bus stops and routes through the capital, depending on the bus line. However, if you get lost, all seven lines depart from opposite the tourist office cabin on Avinguda Meritxell, near to the Pyrenees department store. Timetables are posted at all stops and are available from tourist information offices.

▼ *Andorra la Vella, capital of Andorra*

ANDORRA LA VELLA

The capital of Andorra is really just a large town, but it is buzzing and cosmopolitan nonetheless; filled with upmarket boutiques, glitzy department stores, cutting-edge consumer goods outlets, quality restaurants and enticing duty-free hypermarkets. Away from the bustle of the main thoroughfares, though, there are gentler, more tranquil corners where you can catch a glimpse of the history and culture of this unique micro-state.

Although there are now a number of traffic-calming bypasses around the capital, the country's original main arterial road still cuts directly through the middle of town, and is the focus for all the main retail activity. The principal shopping streets are Avinguda Carlemany and Avinguda Mertixell. From the north, coming from Pas and Soldeu or any of the other villages en route, you enter first into the suburb of Escaldes-Engordany on Avinguda Carlemany. The retail extravaganza begins almost immediately, with shops lining both sides of the street all the way down to the indistinguishable point where Escaldes-Engordany ends and Andorra la Vella officially begins. The thoroughfare now becomes Avinguda Meritxell, crossing the Gran Valira River at the intersection with the route from the La Massana/Ordino region of the country, before continuing up towards the Pyrenees department store and into the historic heart of the capital.

The Casa de la Vall is an interesting focal point here, tucked away off Avinguda Princep Benlloch at the top end of Avinguda Meritxell. The building was constructed around AD 1580 and is a fortified Catalan mansion house filled with history and still the state's seat of Government and Parliament. You can arrange a free guided tour of the building or just wander around the small quiet gardens surrounding it and take in the panoramic views.

CALDEA

Situated in Escaldes-Engordany, overlooking Andorra la Vella, Caldea is a spectacular thermal spa and leisure centre offering every possible combination and variety of hydrotherapy and relaxation facilities: indoor and outdoor lagoons and whirlpools, Indo-Roman baths, pressure showers, Sirocco air bath, saunas, Turkish bath, an 'Ice Patio' and negative ion light relaxation suite. The general entrance fee permits up to 3 hours' stay with use of all the above listed facilities.

🔻 *The main central lagoon at Caldea*

△ *Caldea spa*

Massages, facials, beauty treatments, UV-sessions and childcare facilities are available to pre-book at an additional cost. The centre also has an exclusive Club suite offering a range of spa and fitness programmes, and markets its own range of skincare products.

Caldea's natural thermal water source is one of the hottest in the Pyrenees, rich in sodium and sulphur (the latter mostly extracted for your olfactory comfort) and thermal plankton. The effects of the minerals and hydrotherapy are reported to be healing, decongestant and good for reducing allergic reactions. The water temperature in the various installations ranges between 14–36°C (57.2–96.8°F); maximum depth is 1.3 m (4¼ ft). Bathing caps are not obligatory.

The complex has off-street parking and houses a range of art galleries, shops, restaurants and a penthouse cocktail bar with panoramic views over the capital and its surrounding valley.
ⓐ Parc de la Mola, 10   ⓣ +376 800 995   ⓦ www.caldea.ad
ⓛ Open 09.30–23.00 daily.

NATIONAL AUTOMOBILE MUSEUM

The first car didn't appear in Andorra until 1939, because there wasn't any driveable road into the country before then, but the Andorran love affair with motor transport began and quickly spread to the bumper-to-bumper proportions we encounter today at rush hour in the capital.

Thanks to the country's favourable tax and customs status, new cars have always been less expensive here than in the rest of Europe – although there are strict rules about registration. This has meant that many of the earliest automobile enthusiasts imported a huge range of the most important marques and models spanning the glory years of motorsport. Many owners retained these vintage cars and an initiative by a group of private collectors, assisted by the Andorran Government, culminated in the establishment of a permanent collection housed in the Museu Nacional de l'Automóbil in Encamp. The museum is located on the main street in the middle of town and houses around a hundred vehicles, plus over fifty classic motorcycles and even a collection of bicycles. The earliest car on display is a steam-driven Pinette dating from 1898.

🕿 +376 832 266 🕒 Open Tues–Sat 09.30–13.30 and 15.00–18.00, Sun 10.00–14.00, Mon closed. Small admission charge.

MUSEU DE PIN

Billed as the only one in the world, this unusual little museum dedicated to pin badges is housed in the basement of the Hotel Sant Miquel in the hamlet of Ansalonga near Ordino. There are an incredible 61,000 pins on display, in over 100 different categories, yet the owner reckons he has over 100,000 in total, many yet to be classified and displayed. If you have a spare pin from your local club or association, why not take it along to add to the collection? The museum proudly holds a certificate of world-record status from the *Guinness Book of Records*. Entrance to the display is free, but it is courteous to buy a drink from the hotel's bar.

🕿 +376 800 625 🕒 Open Tues–Sun 10.00–13.00 and 16.00–19.00, Mon closed. Free admission.

CASA ARENY-PLANDOLIT

Other than tobacco cultiva-
tion and smuggling, one of
the only early industries to
have flourished in Andorra
was limited iron mining and
forging. Many of the first
forges were established by
Andorra's most historically
important families, and the
Areny-Plandolit family of
Ordino was among them.
Their ancestral home in the

△ *Casa Areny-Plandolit*

centre of the small parish capital dates from 1633 and has been
preserved and opened as a museum as part of the European Rural
Habitat Route. This important mansion gives the visitor an insight
into the life of an Andorran noble family.

✆ +376 836 908 🕒 Open Tues–Sat 09.00–13.30 and 15.00–18.30,
Sun 10.00–14.00, Mon closed. Small admission charge.

MERITXELL SHRINE

Nostra Senyora de Meritxell (Our Lady of Meritxell) is a symbol
of national and religious identity for Andorrans. The Andorran
Government commissioned the architect Ricard Bofill to redesign
and rebuild an enlarged sanctuary in a more modern and eclectic
style following a fire that destroyed the original in 1972. You can
visit this focal point of Andorran heritage just off the road
between Canillo and Encamp.

🕒 Open Wed–Mon 09.15–13.00 and 15.00–18.00, Tues closed.
Entrance free.

OUT & ABOUT IN THE SUMMER

In may never have occurred to you before to visit a ski resort in summer: after all, what is there to do after the snow has melted? Quite a lot, actually – the mountains are just as beautiful and even more accessible in summer. Andorra's ski lifts reopen in July, transporting mountaineers and mountain bikers to access the high ridges and peaks. The pistes may all be green in colour now that the snow has gone, but the routes of the red and black pistes still carry those gradings for downhill mountain-biking; pointing your wheels rather than your ski-tips or board down the fall-line takes just as much skill and guts. Horse riding and trekking, white-water kayaking, paragliding and rock climbing are just some of the other ways in which summer visitors get their kicks. Evenings in the resort bars and restaurants may be more mellow, but there are still rocking venues if you know where to look.

Before Mediterranean beach holidays became so popular, tourists flocked to Europe's most scenic and historic regions, steeped in culture and bathed in more bearably warm sunshine. Tranquil lakeside towns, invigorating spas and the peaceful mountain villages of Europe's Alpine regions were tourism's original resorts. Today, lakes and mountain holidays still enjoy a loyal following but have long been regarded as appealing mainly to an older, retired clientele. Now, however, the secret is out!

The massive popularity of snowsports has seen skiers and snowboarders develop an enthusiasm not only for their sports, but also for the environment in which they enjoy them. The explosion in high-adrenaline adventure sports has also contributed to a dramatic shift towards more outward-bound pursuits and holidays and the High Pyrenees provide the perfect setting in which to pursue them.

PAL–ARINSAL

The focus for all activities shifts to Pal, around La Caubella base station. But the cable car operates to take hikers and mountain bikers to the high Port Negre col; imagine the awesome ride on a mountain bike all the way down to Arinsal village from the cable car top station, non-stop! Another great activity at Pal is Devil-karting (go-karts with chunky tyres which you steer down the pistes at El Planell). Horse riding, quad biking, 4 x 4 off-road driving tours over the mountain tracks into Spain and aerial zip wires are also on offer.

SOLDEU–EL TARTER

The Camp Base adventure sports centre is SET's summer sports focal point, promoting a wide range of activities including mountain biking on the pistes, Via Ferrata (climbing extreme rock faces on fixed ropes and metal hand/footholds), horse riding, archery, paragliding and much more. White-water kayaking and rafting can also be arranged for day-trips out of the resort.

PAS DE LA CASA–GRAU ROIG

The town is just as busy in high summer, with tourists still attracted by the duty-free shopping and the buzzing nightlife. The Adventure Activities Centre organizes mountain biking, quad biking, archery, horse-riding and trekking tours, with the Pessons lakes tour above Grau Roig drawing visitors from all over Europe. The resort also often hosts important international downhill mountain bike events and the Tour de France has previously passed through on the special section over the high Envalira Pass.

◑ *Springtime in Vall d'Incles, near Soldeu*

GLOSSARY

Alpine skiing: the proper name for the sport of Downhill skiing, where participants use gravity to descend the slopes; as opposed to propelling themselves along.

Arête: a sharp ridge separating two glacial valleys or cirques.

Base station: the main access point and ski lifts departure point for a particular ski area; ideally the resort itself.

Base lodge: the main services building at the base station.

Bucket lift: a type of gondola lift where passengers stand in a basic open cabin, usually installed in hilly resort centres and lower slopes areas as public transport from one sector to another.

Button lift: a type of ski lift which consists of a pole hanging from the haul cable, fitted with a circular 'button' that is placed between your legs to pull you uphill.

Carver: a type of ski that is much wider at the tips (front) and tails (rear), allowing for wide, exaggerated turns on the piste.

Cirque: a semi-circular sweep of steep mountains surrounding a generally flat high-altitude valley; a product of glacial erosion.

Couloir: a steep and usually narrow gully sometimes called a chute.

Declutchable chair lift: the fastest type of chair lift, which disconnects from the fast haul cable at the passenger get-on and get-off points to allow for easier mount/dismount.

Drag lift: generic name for all ski lifts that pull passengers along whilst they are standing on the snow.

FIS: Fédération Internationale de Ski (International Ski Federation). The governing body of snowsports, which sets rules and regulations for piste safety and international competitions.

Freeride: a form of skiing away from the pistes where participants ride wherever and however the terrain (usually extreme) allows.

Funicular: a type of railway, usually steeply inclined.

Gondola lift: a type of ski lift where passengers ride inside a small cabin. Also called a Télécabine or Telecabina in Europe; smaller versions are also known as 'bubble lifts'.

Halfpipe: a specially prepared, semi-circular, pisted trough allowing users to ride up its high side walls to perform tricks.

Kickers: ramps of snow which provide a launch point for jumping high into the air.

Langlauf: the correct term for cross-country/Nordic-style skiing where skiers propel themselves in a walking or skating motion; Langlauf skis are much longer and narrower than Alpine skis.

Magic carpet: a conveyor belt.

Mogul (mogul field): bump (series of bumps) formed after heavy use of a ski slope has left the slope deeply rutted; advanced riders relish the challenge of riding through/over these bumps.

Monoskiing: a single large ski where binding attachments are side-by-side and close together.

Nordic skiing: see Langlauf

Nursery slope: a gentle slope designated as a beginners' area.

Off-piste: skiing/snowboarding away from the prepared ski slopes.

Piste: a way-marked slope/trail, where the snow has been groomed to make it easier to ski on. Pistes are graded by difficulty and colour coded to reflect this: green runs are the easiest; blue runs are slightly more challenging but still relatively easy; red runs are difficult slopes requiring technical ability from users; black pistes are the most difficult slopes reserved for expert users.

Piste basher: a tracked snowplough vehicle, fitted with a large rake with which to groom the pistes.

Rope tow: a basic ski lift consisting of a simple loop of rope, where users just grab on to be pulled along.

Schuss: the onomatopoeic term for skiing fast down a straight slope.

Ski-Doo: trade name for a snowmobile, a tracked vehicle fitted with steerable skis resembling a motorbike.

Ski school: the generic term for an organization which provides snowsports tuition.

Slalom: a form of skiing/snowboarding involving weaving in and out of a series of spaced poles/gates, normally against the clock.

Snow park: a specially designated area set out with ramps (kickers), halfpipes and high rails for sliding along for performing tricks.

Snowshoe: a specialized form of footwear which spreads the wearer's weight over a greater surface area, making it easier to walk over snow.

Telemark skiing: a old form of classic Alpine skiing where the skier's foot is secured to the ski binding only at the toe end, requiring the skier to flex their ankle and knee to effect turns.

Tool point: a collection of spanners and screwdrivers at a designated location on the mountain, provided to allow experienced skiers/snowboarders to adjust their own equipment.

INDEX